CROSSROADS

RICHARD DAVIES
GLEN KIRKLAND
JEFF SIAMON

Gage Editorial Team
Joe Banel
Patrice Peterkin
David Friend
Christine McClymont
Diane Robitaille

gage EDUCATIONAL PUBLISHING COMPANY
A DIVISION OF CANADA PUBLISHING CORPORATION
Vancouver · Calgary · Toronto · London · Halifax

Managing Editor: Darleen Rotozinski
Contributing Writer: Tricia Armstrong
Copy Editors: Sue Kanhai, Sheree Haughian
Permissions Editor: Elizabeth Long
Photo Researcher: Mary Rose MacLachlan
Bias Reviewer: Margaret Hoogeveen
Cover Illustration: PhotoDisc
**Design, Art Direction
& Electronic Assembly:** Wycliffe Smith Design

Canadian Cataloguing in Publication Data

Main entry under title:

Kirkland, Glen
    Crossroads [10]

Title on cover: Gage crossroads.
ISBN 0-7715-1332-1

1. Readers (Secondary). I. Davies, Richard.
II. Siamon, Jeff. III. Title. IV. Title: Gage crossroads ten. V. Title: Gage crossroads 10.

PE1121.K57 2000   428.6   C99-933087-X

We acknowledge the financial support of the Government of Canada through the Book Publishing Industry Development Program for our publishing activities.

ISBN 0-7715-**1332-1**
2 3 4 5 BP 04 03 02 01 00
Printed and bound in Canada.

Lines
for a
Bookmark
by Gael Turnbull

You who read...
May you seek
As you look;
May you keep
What you need;
May you care
What you choose;
And know here
In this book
Something strange,
Something sure,
That will change
You and be yours.

TABLE OF CONTENTS

ALTERNATE TABLE OF CONTENTS

ISSUES

WHAT MAKES A HERO?

Superman's Song

Song by Brad Roberts
(from the CD *The Ghosts That Haunt Me*)

Tarzan wasn't a ladies' man
He'd just come along and scoop 'em up under his arm
Like that, quick as a cat in the jungle
But Clark Kent, now there was a real gent
He would not be caught sittin' around in no
Junglescape, dumb as an ape doing nothing

Superman never made any money
For saving the world from Solomon Grundy
And sometimes I despair the world will never see
Another man like him

Hey Bob. Supe had a straight job
Even though he could have smashed through any bank
In the United States, he had the strength, but he would not
Folks said his family were all dead
Their planet crumbled but Superman, he forced himself
To carry on, forget Krypton, and keep going

Tarzan was king of the jungle and Lord over all the apes
But he could hardly string together four words: "I Tarzan. You Jane."

GOALS AT A GLANCE

- Respond personally and critically to a song.
- Present an oral reading of a song.

Sometimes when Supe was stopping crimes
I'll bet that he was tempted to just quit and turn his back
On man, join Tarzan in the forest
But he stayed in the city, and kept on changing clothes
In dirty old phonebooths till his work was through
And nothing to do but go on home.

---

1. RESPONDING TO THE SONG

a. Use words and phrases from the song lyrics to describe Tarzan and Superman. Which character, if any, do you think the songwriter, Brad Roberts, respects the most?

b. When you think of these two characters, what images come to mind? Do your images match those of the songwriter?

c. Why is Superman trying to save the "world from Solomon Grundy"?

d. Why would Superman be tempted to stop what he's doing and "join Tarzan in the jungle"?

e. Are Superman and Tarzan symbols for types of people? If so, what might they symbolize?

f. Which character, if any, would you rather be? Explain.

2. ORAL LANGUAGE PRESENTING A SONG

Listen to the recording of "Superman's Song" from the album, *The Ghosts That Haunt Me*. How does the music affect the way you interpret the words? Is the song's meaning clearer with or without the music?

Work with a partner or small group to plan a reading of another song.

- First choose the song. Think about how you will read it to the class so its meaning is clear.
- Practise reading the song, working together to read it effectively. Focus on the tone, volume, gestures, and emphasis to use as you read the lyrics. Discuss how reading a song is different from singing it.

GROUP ASSESSMENT: Tape your reading and discuss how your group worked together. What two elements of your presentation were most effective?

Action Hero

Essay by
Rulon Openshaw

A few years ago, I stopped at a neighbourhood market for some late-night ice cream. As I got out of my car, a young man hailed me from across the street. He was college-aged and dressed to the nines: expensive pullover, dress shirt and slacks so sharply creased they could have cut frozen fish. I thought he wanted directions; he had that urgent late-for-a-party look. When he reached me, he pulled up his sweater and smoothly drew a pistol from inside his waistband. "Get in the car," he ordered.

My brain went into hyperspeed. I remembered watching a personal-security expert on a talk show advise victims not to stare at an assailant's face. His reasoning was that if a robber thinks you cannot identify him, he's less likely to kill you. No one asked how much less likely. Given its importance to my future, I focussed instead on his weapon—a .38 Smith & Wesson revolver, blued steel, short barrel. I'd fired others like it at pistol ranges. This was no mouse gun. Nervously, I directed my gaze lower. His shoes were highly polished. Strange as it sounds, I admired his sense of style.

The click of the revolver's hammer being cocked snapped my head up eye-to-eye with his. So much for not looking at his face. Contrary to the belief that when death appears imminent, a person's entire life passes before him or her, I was completely focussed on the moment. Instinct told me that a car trip with this guy would turn out to be a one-way journey for me. I held out my keys. "Take my car," I said in a tone I prayed would inspire calmness and reason. "I'm not getting in."

GOALS AT A GLANCE

- ■ Analyse the theme, message, and tone of an opinion piece.
- ■ Identify active and passive voice.

He hesitated, then ignoring my proffered keys, thrust out a hand and yanked off my shoulder bag. In it were my wallet and a couple of rented videos. He took a step back, his gun still aimed at me. Neither of us spoke.

Laughter broke the silence, making us both turn. Several couples were leaving a Chinese restaurant on the opposite corner. The mugger gave them a fast scan, then lowered his revolver. Holding it against his thigh to conceal it, he began to stride quickly across the almost-trafficless street, my bag clutched under his arm.

Incredibly, I took off after him. "Hey," I shouted to the people in front of the restaurant. "This guy just robbed me." I was halfway across the street when I realized my would-be posse was not mounting up. The mugger, now aware of my proximity, pivoted in my direction. As I watched him raise his gun, everything went into slow motion. A tongue of flame flashed from the snub-nosed barrel, followed by a loud crack.

I lost my balance. I felt no pain, but when I looked down, I saw my left leg flopped out sideways at my shin. A half-dollar-size spot of blood stained my jeans. When I looked up, my assailant was sprinting down a dark side street.

Later that night at a nearby hospital, I was told that the bullet had fractured my tibia and fibula, the two bones connecting the knee and ankle. Doctors inserted a steel rod secured by four screws into my leg. They also gave me a "prosthesis alert" card to show security personnel if the rod set off a metal detector.

But a remarkable thing began to happen—my popularity soared. When friends introduced me as "the guy who got shot," women who a moment before had no interest in me suddenly got friendly. Men wanted to buy me drinks. They considered me "brave" for running after the mugger. I'm reminded of war movies in which the green recruits behave reverentially around the grizzled vets who have "seen action."

I found it difficult to forgive myself for what I considered an act of colossal folly. Sometimes I thought I had chased the kid out of anger at being victimized; other times I attributed my actions to an adrenaline rush that needed a physical outlet. Whatever the reason, I knew it had nothing to do with bravery.

Clearly, I was being given credit for something I didn't deserve, yet I was reluctant to give up my newly acquired status. After all, it wasn't as if I were taking an active part in any deception; I was merely allowing people to come to whatever conclusions they wished. I finally rationalized my decision to maintain the *status quo*: I considered any misperception to be my compensation for having gone through a horrible situation.

Things went well until the day I was approached by a panhandler. On a whim, I told him I had no money because I'd been unable to work since being shot in a robbery. His eyes grew large, and it was obvious that the information impressed him. "That's heavy," he said, then leaned closer, conspiratorially. "Did you get caught?"

---

1. RESPONDING TO THE ESSAY

a. Would you agree or disagree with the author's friends—that he was some kind of hero?

b. Why do you think his friends treated him so well after they heard what he had done?

c. What reasons does the author give for going after the robber? What would you have done in his place?

d. Do you think the way the robber was dressed affected the way the author reacted? Explain.

2. LITERATURE STUDIES ANALYSE OPINION PIECES

"Action Hero" isn't only an interesting anecdote about the author's life. It has a point of view and a message to deliver to the reader.

- What is the author's theme or message? Is it effectively delivered? Why or why not?
- Is it clearly stated or do you have to infer its meaning? Explain.
- What elements of fiction writing does the author use? How do they help make his point?
- How does the ending of "Action Hero" reflect the author's theme?
- Is the **tone** the author uses appropriate to what he is trying to say? Explain. If you were writing a piece with a similar message, what tone would you use and why?

> **Tone** is the mood of a piece of writing. It can also be an author's feeling toward a subject or a reader, for example, formal, intimate, serious, ironic, or sarcastic.

3. LANGUAGE CONVENTIONS ACTIVE AND PASSIVE VOICE

Writing that is clear and effective speaks directly to the reader. Sentences are to the point, don't use unnecessary words, and are usually in the active voice. For example:

Active Things went well until the day a panhandler *approached* me.

Passive Things went well until the day *I was approached by* a panhandler.

> In the **active voice** the subject of a verb does the action.
> In the **passive voice** the subject of the verb receives the action.

The first example is more direct and uses fewer words.

Reread "Action Hero" and note the type of active and passive sentences the author uses. Give an example of both. Are the majority of sentences in the active or passive voice? Why is the active voice better for describing action?

SELF-ASSESSMENT: Select a piece of writing from your portfolio and examine the sentences you use. Do you use the active or the passive voice or a combination of both? How could you revise your writing so that it's more clearly written?

The Michelle I Know

SHORT STORY BY ALISON LOHANS

Rob was late. And last night he'd gone to the after-game dance.
With Vanessa.

Michelle turned over. The hospital bed was hard and confining. The
entire back of her neck felt like one giant pillow crease. She rubbed it and
as always, her fingers crept upward to explore the terrifying bleak landscape
where her hair was supposed to be. She didn't have the energy to pound the
pillow good and hard. Even if she did, she'd probably knock the intravenous
needle out of place and then she'd have to lie there gritting her teeth while
nurses poked and jabbed to set another IV.

It wasn't fair. Sometimes she felt so tired and sick it was even hard to
lift the remote control for the TV.

Her clock radio said it was 7:27. Maybe Rob wasn't coming. She wasn't
much to come to. Not any more. Even after the other kids quit showing up,
he'd stuck it out. Once he'd even smuggled in his mom's poodle pup to
break the monotony. But now maybe he was having second thoughts.

All Michelle could see outside the fourth storey window was cottony
orange light dissolving into darkness. In the distance a siren screamed, drew
nearer, then passed beneath her window. If she got up, she'd see blood-red
lights flashing below and people hurrying into Emergency, all softened by
the winter fog. Sometimes the fog got so thick it looked like you could
walk right out the window and keep on going. Michelle's mouth quirked.
In reality, it would be more like plunging down—gown flapping about her,

---

GOALS AT A GLANCE

■ Analyse the plot of a short story.
■ Write a short story.

IV monitor and pole and bottles all set to smash on the sidewalk. How much would it hurt, before...? But that might be a quick escape.

The guitar started playing again. Michelle relaxed a bit and fidgeted with her earrings. One of the holes in her left ear was kind of sore. She sighed and took out the tiny purple triangle, feeling for a safe spot on the bedside table. If her earlobe got infected, Dr. Warkentin would give her major heck.

She closed her eyes and tried to let the music wash away her frustration. It was total boredom, being in hospital for almost two months. Probably she was turning into a turnip. Or some kind of squash. No wonder Rob wasn't here. Vegetables weren't the greatest company. At least the music made everything more bearable. This was the third day. Or was it only the second? Time got pretty blurry, cut off from her normal life.

The soft scuff of rubber soles on carpet, the faintest swish of clothing  told her that Brenda, the evening nurse, had come in. "Hi, kiddo," came the cheery voice. "Anything I can do for you?"

Eyes still shut, Michelle shook her head. She'd had it with hospitals. With routines. Needles in her arms. Chemotherapy that left her feeling like something a pulp mill spat out.

Brenda's voice prodded at her. "Your friend's late."

Michelle looked dully at the young nurse. "I don't think he's coming."

"Oh hush!" Briskly the older girl straightened the untouched pile of magazines left by the occupational therapist. "I bet—"

"Watch out for my earring." Michelle tensed, then heard the predictable *thkk* sound of a tiny object hitting the carpet.

"Sorry." Brenda stooped. "I'll put it in your top drawer, okay? Now. Your friend. I bet the fog's keeping him. When I went out at supper it was like walking through whipped cream."

Michelle smiled faintly and waited while Brenda took her pulse and temperature, then checked the drip from her IV bottle.

Brenda patted her hand. "Cheer up. Doctor says your blood counts are super. You're on your way to remission, kid, and you know what that means."

"Yeah," she said sourly. "I get to go home and wait six months before I have enough hair to do anything with." It would be heaven to go home, though. It seemed ages since she'd been *someone*, with thick dark hair that swished against her cheeks. Who had lots of friends, and clothes that fit right. Who felt like the world was hers.

Now it was safest not to hope.

Brenda tossed her straw-coloured braid over her shoulder, then placed her hands in her uniform pockets. "You'll feel lots better once you're home. But you may not want to leave us..." The nurse's voice lowered. "You've got an admirer right here in our midst and *he* thinks you're gorgeous."

"Yeah, right. Tell me another one." Michelle shifted and the IV pole rattled.

"Honest. It sure isn't me." Brenda indicated her comfortably padded waistline. "If I ever get a boyfriend I'll know I'm dreaming."

"At least you've got hair." What she really meant was that Brenda had a face that was...friendly. The kind that was sure to draw people to her—but it would sound pretty sucky to say it out loud.

"So have you," Brenda countered. "Where is it, stuffed in the drawer with your washbasin?"

To be exact, the wig was stuffed in the drawer *under* the washbasin. Mom bought it when her hair first started thinning. It was awful. The colour was right, but that was all. Any way you looked at it, it was fake hair—like what you'd see on a Barbie doll.

Michelle glared at her skinny arms, mottled with bruises and needle scars. "It's gross," she muttered. "It's too hot. And prickly. Who cares, anyhow, with a death sentence hanging over your head?"

Brenda swished across the room to get a handful of clean straws from the cabinet. "Cases like yours go into remission for years now, Michelle," she said firmly. The way she said it, it sounded like she knew exactly how it felt to lie there at 3:00 a.m., scared cold, and faking sleep as the night shift crept in with flashlights to check the IV and write on the chart. "We had the cutest little guy in here once—he never came back, so we all started thinking maybe he didn't make it. But Doctor says she sees him every now and then, skateboarding and riding his bike like a maniac."

Michelle fell silent. In the hallway came the clatter of rolling wheels.

Sour-faced Mrs. Begbie paused in the doorway, leaning heavily on her IV pole, her own bald head covered by a turquoise hat with wild feathers. "Nurse," she wheezed, "can you get someone to bring my pain shot?"

Brenda glanced at her watch. "I'll go check on it for you, Mrs. B."

Bored, Michelle flicked the TV switch. But that drowned out the guitar. She flicked it off and the screen went blank. Just like she felt. Visiting hours were almost over. Rob wasn't coming.

Suddenly Brenda was back. "C'mon—I'll take you to see Claude. Your admirer. Keep your friend guessing a little, huh?"

Michelle inspected the cool clear tubing that fed sugar water and sometimes, chemo into her arm. "I don't feel like it."

"C'mon, go for it! Put on your wig—you can model it for Dr. Hernandez. He's at the nursing station."

Michelle groaned, then sat up because there was nothing better to do. But she left the wig in the drawer. "This Claude. Is he bald like me?"

"Right on. And he thinks you're gorgeous."

"Oh sure." Wearily Michelle swung her legs over the edge of the bed and let Brenda put slippers on for her. Her knees were bony. And the skimpy hospital gown was too much—even a mannequin would drop dead wearing it. She slid one arm into the hot-pink dressing gown Brenda held ready, but even that looked gimpy with one sleeve dangling because of the IV.

"Glamour!" Brenda's eyes teased her.

"What'd you do with my mink, throw it down the laundry chute?"

"Yep." Brenda's strong arm came around Michelle's waist as she pushed up, grasping the IV pole. "And I'm afraid I've got some bad news. It shrank."

Dr. Hernandez, the young resident, looked up and waved as they inched down the hallway. Michelle waved back, then remembered. Rob hadn't come.

"And here's Claude."

Michelle took one look and wished she could turn and run. Except she was too tired.

Claude was old enough to be her father. His arms were bruised like her own. His bald head gleamed with shiny flesh. A guitar lay in his lap.

Dizzy with exhaustion, Michelle sank into a visitor's chair. Some admirer. What was he, a dirty old man? See if she ever listened to Brenda again!

"So you're Michelle."

"Yeah," she mumbled and looked away.

"We're all pretty proud of Claude," Brenda said. "He's been in and out of this place for eight years now, and each time he comes back, we learn something new."

Eight *years*? And she'd thought eight weeks was torture. "I can hear you in my room," Michelle said hesitantly, since they obviously expected her to talk. "It helps."

Light glowed in the man's dark eyes, and suddenly his face was beautiful. "I taught myself to play in this joint," he said. "Drove everybody nuts." His right hand, splinted to keep the IV needle in place, strummed the guitar with a caressing stroke. A flurry of notes scattered.

"You?" said Brenda. "Never."

Outside, a train rumbled past. Michelle fell silent. Ironic how hospitals ended up in the noisiest parts of town. Ironic how she, once with everything going for her, had so quickly been thrust on a shelf, forgotten, and now by Rob, too. Once cancer cells got their claws into you, none of the old rules applied. You were totally at the mercy of doctors and nurses. And the disease.

"It's not so easy, eh?" Claude's soft voice startled her.

Quickly she forced her face into a polite mask. No point in grasping for the sympathy of somebody just as sick—probably forty, and bald besides. Brenda had disappeared; she guessed it was either be polite and talk, or else try getting back on her own. "No," she said. There was a long pause. Claude's bound fingers gently plucked the guitar. "You've had leukemia for eight *years*?" she burst out.

"Eight years. A long time. It's been pretty hard on the family. But I'm lucky. Most patients my age don't last."

Michelle looked cautiously at Claude, whose shiny bald head had odd bumps and ridges just like hers, who lacked eyelashes and eyebrows. Just as she did. "Do you ever feel like—" She broke off, then barged ahead after a steadying breath: "Like sometimes you'd rather die than be poked by one more needle?"

Claude looked beyond her, out at the night sky. "Sometimes," he said at last. "But we were each given a life. You don't throw that out like garbage."

"I hate it!" Sudden tears trickled down Michelle's cheeks and she wiped at them furiously. "How I look. How I feel. I hate *everything*!" She sniffed hard, blew her nose, but couldn't stop.

"Yeah, it gets that way sometimes." Claude's fingers coaxed more notes out of the guitar, sending music spilling into the hallway. Michelle rested her cheek against the ridge of the bedside table. "I've been there," he went on.

"But you know, we're all in this together."

"Not my friends," she said bitterly.

"You have to be strong inside," he said. "Don't waste yourself fighting the wrong things."

Michelle traced her fingertip along the hard tabletop. At least this man was better than sour Mrs. Begbie, or Mr. Morris who let himself be wheeled around like a big doll. This man had dignity. Did she?

"Michelle?" Brenda's voice penetrated. "I found this guy wandering around the hallway. Is he somebody you know?"

Rob! He stood there in the doorway, still bundled up in his jacket, his face tense.

With a great effort Michelle wiped her eyes. "Hi," she mumbled.

The music stopped. A warm hand rested on her shoulder. "Remember. You've got to fight it."

She managed a wan smile. "Yeah."

"Sorry I'm late," Rob said. "That fog's impossible. I practically had to get out and put my nose on the street just to see the lines."

"Your attention please." The cold voice of the intercom spoke with dismissive finality. "Visiting hours are now over."

"Shush!" Brenda waved her hand at the speaker in the ceiling. "Quick! To your room!"

Shakily Michelle stood up, leaning on her IV pole. Rob moved in to help her. He smelled like fresh air. Which meant she must smell like...the hospital. Sick. Grimly, she kept her legs moving and her grip tight on the pole; she'd already learned how hard it could be to get back up after a fall. But visiting hours were over and now Rob would have to go. Her eyes blurred.

"Who was that guy?" Rob asked.

"He's been sick for eight years." She knew she was wobbly, but it felt as if Rob had just shuddered. Walking took so much of her energy that she couldn't say more. Her bed, freshly made up, looked like heaven. Wearily she sank onto it.

But Brenda was drawing the curtains around her. Rob was pulling up a chair. "She says I can stay half an hour if I promise to be good," he whispered.

Brenda winked and disappeared.

Suddenly Michelle didn't know what to say. Here was Rob, late because of the fog. But his face was still tense and his eyes were guarded. "How was last night?" she mumbled.

"Okay," he said indifferently. "We won the game."

They were not on the same wavelength. Needing to be doing something, Michelle reached for her mirror and studied herself. Her shiny bald head, the bony ridges where her eyebrows had once been. She yanked the wig out of the drawer and pulled it on. Loose hairs caught in her right earring. Furtively she glanced at Rob. "Well?" she demanded. "Am I still ugly?"

Rob sighed.

Might as well forget it. Who wanted a bald girlfriend who couldn't do anything but cry? "I'm ugly compared to Vanessa." She couldn't help the waspish note that sliced into her voice.

"What's the deal about Vanessa?" Rob's fingers tensed as they dangled between his knees. "I only went for something to do. Vanessa's boring, okay? The whole stupid dance was boring. What else do you want to know, what we—"

"Sorry." She felt heat creeping into her face. "When you were so late, I guess I thought..." Out of the corner of her eye she watched him. His jaw was tight, but his green eyes were intent on her. "And then because I'm so ugly and everything, I thought...Oh forget it!" She pulled the wig off and threw it. It landed on her IV bottle and dangled there rakishly.

Michelle bit her lip. It looked so awful she nearly cried—to think she'd hoped Rob might like her better with the wig on. But it didn't look just awful, it looked—*awful*. So awful that...A giggle escaped.

Suddenly Rob lurched to his feet. He bowed to the IV pole. "Allow me, madam, may I have this dance?"

Michelle laughed out loud.

Rob grinned.

Michelle clapped a hand over her mouth, trying to keep her voice down, for suddenly she couldn't stop laughing. But she couldn't let herself get carried away. It was all very well for noble Rob to come to the hospital every day to see poor Michelle, who was so sick with leukemia, *but...*

"You shouldn't feel like you have to come here all the time," she mumbled. "It's no fun for you. I mean, you've been fantastic, really fantastic, but I don't want you to start hating me because I'm such a..." She swallowed hard.

Rob had to be set free. It wasn't fair to expect him to be the knight in shining armour. She had to have the strength to let him go.

"Michelle." His voice was quiet; solemnly he lifted a few strands of hair from the wig, rubbing them between his thumb and fingertips. "What we've got—it's based on a little more than hair, you know?"

She hiccuped, hardly daring to believe what she was hearing.

She had to change gears, fast. Deliberately, she rubbed her hand over her bald head. "Well, at least this never gets tangled." She gulped in a deep breath. "How do you think it would look with flowers painted on it?"

Miraculously, Rob was still there. He was even laughing, and his incredible, world-stopping grin was dawning in his eyes. For the first time in months, Michelle felt a real smile swelling inside.

"Now *that's* the Michelle I know," Rob murmured. He leaned closer.

----

1. RESPONDING TO THE STORY

a. Who is the hero in this story? Explain why you think so.

b. What is the turning point? In what way does Michelle change?

c. What is the overall message and mood?

d. Why is humour an important part of this story?

e. Why do you think Alison Lohans calls her story "The Michelle I Know"?

2. STORY CRAFT   PLOT

Copy the following chart into your notebook. Complete it by adding details from the story.

Elements of Plot	Story Details
Introduction of setting/ major characters	
Conflict	
Rising Action	
Climax	
Conclusion	

Have you read other stories like "The Michelle I Know"? List these stories. How were their plots similar or different? In your notebook, create another column in the chart above to compare one of these stories to "The Michelle I Know."

SELF-ASSESSMENT: What conclusions did you draw about the elements of plot? How can you use these conclusions the next time you write your own short story?

3. WRITING A SHORT STORY

In most good stories the characters undergo a significant change, just as Michelle does. Think about, and jot down, some ideas for a short story about an ordinary person or hero who undergoes a significant change. Which idea would make an entertaining story for an audience of your peers?

Write an outline for your short story, including notes on the following: main character and personality, setting, conflict, rising action, changes, climax, and conclusion. Use this outline to write a first draft. Ask a partner for feedback about improving your story. Revise your draft using this feedback. Before creating a final draft, remember to proofread your story. See the process page on developing plot lines on pages 68–69 to help you develop your story.

4. LANGUAGE CONVENTIONS SENTENCE VARIETY

Reread the first few pages of the story, noting how the author uses sentences of varying lengths and types. Why would an author do this? What effect is created?

Find an example of each of the following in the story:

- a statement
- a question
- an exclamation
- a very short sentence
- a very long sentence

In your notebook, explain the reasons why an author would use a variety of sentences.

SELF-ASSESSMENT: Check the stories in your writing portfolio. Do you think you've used a variety of sentences? How could you change individual sentences to make them more interesting?

Laura Secord

Poem by Raymond Souster

Lady, long part of our history,
would you perhaps have been so eager
that time to drive those silly cows
before you through the forest mile after mile,
risking who knows what indignities
at the hands of the invaders,

had you known you would end up
name on the box for a brand
of over-sweet chocolates?

RESPONDING TO THE POEM

a. During the War of 1812, Laura Secord saved a British garrison from American attack. Using only this statement and the poem for information, write a description of what you think she did.

b. There are two parts to this poem. Why do you think the author divided the poem in this way?

c. The poem is written as one long question. What question is Raymond Souster asking?

d. What do you think he is saying about heroes and heroic deeds?

SELF-ASSESSMENT: In your notebook, describe the message and tone of this poem, explaining why you think so.

GOALS AT A GLANCE

■ Respond critically to a poem.
■ Summarize information.

GOLIATH

Song by
Melanie Doane

From the CD *Adam's Rib*

I've been sleeping
under the beanstalk
and I've been dreaming
of something big
I don't know how
but I could swear
I'm on my way somewhere

Awake the giant
awake, awake

Hey Goliath
oh you're no bigger
You're no bigger than me

I know I've got something
inside of me
Just like I know you've got
something inside of you
It might be hard
but if we dare
we're on our way somewhere

Awake the giant
awake, awake

Hey Goliath
oh you're no bigger
You're no bigger than me

Say the words you have swallowed
See the visions
in your mind's eye
Do what you feel in your heart
Awake the giant in you

I've been waiting
for a signal
for something to tell me
everything's all right
But now I see
it's up to me
No one else can fight this fight

1. RESPONDING TO THE SONG

a. Who is Goliath?

b. What is Goliath's significance in the song?

c. Why does Doane compare Goliath's situation to her own?

d. What is Doane's message about being a hero? Do you agree or disagree with her? Explain.

2. LITERATURE STUDIES ALLUSIONS

Melanie Doane uses several **allusions** in her song. The lyrics lose some meaning if the reader is unaware of the comparisons being made. With a partner, discuss the allusions and their significance to the theme or message of the song.

> An **allusion** is an indirect reference to a person, story, or situation in literature or history.

ROSA PARKS'S HEROISM STILL INSPIRES

On December 1, 1955, Rosa Parks stepped onto a bus in Montgomery, Alabama. During her ride, she made a decision that changed history and made her a hero.

NEWSPAPER ARTICLE BY SANDY BANKS

You would have thought I'd announced a meeting with one of the Spice Girls, from the reaction I got at home.

"I can't believe you get to meet her, in person."

"Please, please, Mom, can I go with you?"

And, to a friend, "You won't believe who my mom is taking us to meet!"

The object of their excitement wasn't a rock diva or movie star.

It was an elderly woman—hardly bigger than my oldest child—who rolled toward us in a wheelchair, climbed out carefully and adjusted her pillbox hat before extending a soft, brown hand to each of my daughters.

"So pleased to meet you," she said, asking each girl her name, gazing straight into their shining eyes. "I'm Mrs. Rosa Parks."

GOALS AT A GLANCE

- Participate in small group discussions to express an opinion.
- Prepare a research report.

I don't recall that I even knew her name as a child, although she's known the world over now as the mother of the civil rights movement.

Martin Luther King Jr. was the reigning hero of the movement-in-progress when I was growing up in the fifties and sixties. But it is Rosa Parks who ignited the indignation of the masses forty-three years ago with her simple act of defiance aboard a Montgomery, Alabama, bus.

Then a middle-aged seamstress, Parks was tired from eight hours on her feet when she boarded the bus that would take her home from work. Blacks were banned from the first four rows, so she settled in the middle section, which could be occupied by either whites or blacks.

But segregationist Jim Crow laws dictated that if a white passenger needed a seat, all the black people seated in those middle rows had to get up and move, so that no white person would have to sit next to a black passenger.

That day, though, as whites filled the bus, Parks merely sighed, slid closer to the window to make room on her seat and told the driver, "I am not going to move."

Police were called and Parks was arrested. She was bailed out of jail by a local civil rights activist, who then enlisted a young minister—a twenty-six-year-old Martin Luther King Jr.—to help organize a boycott of the city's bus line.

The yearlong boycott—which ended when the U.S. Supreme Court ruled that Montgomery's bus segregation laws were unconstitutional—garnered Parks a place in history but cost her her job and forced her and her husband, Raymond, to move north to Detroit to rebuild their lives.

It also made her an international symbol of courage, whose influence reaches to the children of today.

I suppose we were too close to the moment when I was growing up to appreciate the import of what she did. History only becomes historic when you can stand back and view it through the prism of time.

It is different for my daughters—who learn about our struggle

Rosa Parks goes to trial in Alabama.

A statue of Rosa Parks at the Birmingham Civil Rights Institute.

for civil rights as they celebrate Martin Luther King's birthday and study Black History Month in their mostly white schools.

And it is Rosa Parks who represents to them all that was good about that tumultuous period of U.S. history—with an act so straightforward that even my first-grader can understand:

A tired woman on a bus, who simply decided not to get pushed around anymore; whose refusal to stand struck a blow for fairness and freedom, and spoke volumes about courage and righteousness and faith.

There is a majesty in that looming larger for my children than all they have learned about marches on Washington and Supreme Court decisions—mighty events, but beyond their grasp.

It's an overly simplistic view of history, I know—reducing it to one moment, one woman.

But I don't mind.

It is enough to see my daughters glowing with pride, as I snap their photo standing next to this brave eighty-five-year-old woman from their history books.

And to know that Puff Daddy, Leonardo DiCaprio, and the Spice Girls have to move over. They're about to be bumped by a new face on the bedroom wall.

1. RESPONDING TO THE NEWSPAPER ARTICLE

a. What did you already know about the people mentioned in the article before you read it? What did you learn from reading it? What else would you like to learn?

b. What did Rosa Parks do that so upset the townspeople of Montgomery, Alabama? Why did they feel upset?

c. How did Rosa Parks's action ignite the civil rights movement?

d. Reread the article and locate an example of figurative language that you think is particularly effective. Share your example with a partner.

2. ORAL LANGUAGE GROUP DISCUSSION

With a small group, discuss these words
from Martin Luther King Jr.:

> "I have a dream that my four little children will one day live in a nation where they will not be judged by the colour of their skin, but by the content of their character."
>
> *Speech at Civil Rights March,*
> *August 28, 1969*

Do you think the community in which you live has reached this goal? Explain. What can you do to achieve King's "dream"?

3. RESEARCHING RESEARCH REPORT

Work in a group to research an incident of ethnic or religious intolerance in Canada. What were the events leading up to the incident? What were the issues, and how did the people involved feel about them? What, if anything, did the people involved learn from the incident? What did you learn from your research? Decide on how you will present your report, for example, as an oral presentation or in the form of a written paper.

GROUP ASSESSMENT: Did your group
- come to a consensus about the subject and presentation?
- divide group tasks fairly and logically?
- respect the contributions of all members?

For actor and activist Tom Jackson, charitable work isn't a sacrifice— it's a blast!

Tom Jackson

Profile by
Brian Bergman

T om Jackson's imposing six-foot, five-inch frame hunches over the recording studio microphone, his arms outstretched and his fingers clenched like a bird of prey about to pounce. "Silent night, holy night," he sings, wringing every ounce of emotion he can from the familiar refrain. It's just one of dozens of takes, in a session that began at noon and is now racing towards midnight. Jackson is putting the finishing touches on his latest CD *The Huron Carole*, so it can be ready in time for the concert series of the same name, which this year will take him to fifteen Canadian cities. During an outdoors smoke break on a chilly evening in Calgary, Jackson reflects on what makes the effort so rewarding. "You know," he says, "that the end result is going to feed a lot of people for a long time."

GOALS AT A GLANCE

■ Write a profile.
■ Examine the use of quotations.

Jackson is speaking quite literally: all of the proceeds from *The Huron Carole*—now in its eleventh year—go to support Canadian food banks. Last year, the concerts raised over three hundred thousand, which food-bank operators leveraged into six million dollars worth of supplies through discounted bulk purchases. The annual Christmas tour is just one of several philanthropic ventures spearheaded by the fifty-year-old singer and actor, perhaps best known for his role in the long-running CBC series *North of 60*. In the past two years alone, Jackson has performed on behalf of battered women's shelters, raised an estimated three million dollars for Manitoba flood victims, and taken a travelling road show, the Dreamcatcher Tour, to dozens of small northern communities to increase awareness about teenage suicide. Jackson devotes about six months a year to charitable causes—an investment of time he does not begrudge. "People think this is a sacrifice," he says. "It's not. This is what I want to do—and it's a blast."

Jackson traces his impulse to do good to his mother, a woman who he says "could never walk past a person in need." All the same, he only began to follow her example fairly late in life—and after walking down what he calls "some very dark roads." Jackson was born on the One Arrow Reserve near Batoche, Saskatchewan. His mother, Rose, was a Cree; his father, Marshall, was of English descent. After the family moved to Winnipeg in 1963, Jackson dropped out of school at age fifteen. For the next seven years, he lived on the street, playing pool incessantly and discovering what he recalls, paradoxically, as a "wonderful sense of camaraderie."

Jackson left the street in the early 1970s after being invited to sing on a local radio program, which led to a stint as a radio host. By the mid-1980s, Jackson had moved to Toronto and carved out a career as a theatre and television actor. But his personal life was in shambles, the result of immersing himself in what he describes as "every conceivable plague out there," including booze and drugs. He experienced an epiphany of sorts in 1987 when, penniless himself, he watched more than a dozen people walk by a dying man on a downtown Toronto street. Jackson lent a hand—and says he decided from that point on to dedicate his life to "making a difference."

It was about this time that he met his future wife and business partner, Alison (he has four grown children from previous relationships). In their adopted home of Calgary, the couple have built up a successful commercial base—among other things, Jackson is now developing a movie studio—that will free him to do even more charitable work. "I'm addicted to this," laughs Jackson.

1. RESPONDING TO THE PROFILE

a. List words or phrases from the selection that you think best describe Tom Jackson. Use some or all of these words to write your own brief profile of the actor.

b. What does the expression "some very dark roads" mean? Why do you think the author uses this expression instead of telling more about Tom Jackson's early life?

c. In your notebook, explain how you feel when you see a homeless or street person.

d. Would you pass a sick person on the street and not do anything? Why would people not help a street person who was ill?

e. Charity means different things to different people, from contributing money to an organization to putting up refugees in their homes. What does charity mean to you?

f. Would you describe Tom Jackson as a hero? Why or why not?

2. WRITING PROFILES

Profiles are really short biographies that try to give the reader a clear and interesting picture of a person. They don't have to be about someone important or famous. Think of a person you admire or find interesting or someone you consider a hero. Generate a list of words and phrases that describes the person. Use some of the words in your list to write a sentence that best summarizes how you feel about the person. Now use the sentence as the topic sentence for a one-paragraph profile. Share your profile with a small group.

3. EDITOR'S DESK QUOTATIONS IN ARTICLES

Brian Bergman brings Tom Jackson's profile to life by letting the actor speak for himself. Reread the profile and locate three quotations that you think help you understand Tom Jackson better. Reread the profile you've just written. Could you improve it by using a quotation? Revise your profile, including at least one quotation.

SELF-ASSESSMENT: Read over your profile and ask yourself these questions. Is the opening paragraph clear? Will the reader have a clear idea of how I feel about my subject? Do the quotations improve the profile?

HOW TO

CONDUCT AN INTERVIEW

Goals at a Glance
• Conduct an interview. • Write an article.

In an interview you go right to the source to find the answers you need. First-hand information makes a topic come alive, both for you and your readers. An interview is also a great way to report information.

Watch the Pros

Watch television personalities as they interview their subjects. Evaluate their styles and the techniques they use.

• What body language shows they are interested and listening attentively?
• Do they move from question to question, or do they ask for clarification and elaboration of answers?
• Do they refer to their notes?
• What qualities do the best interviewers have in common?

Be Prepared

Find out what you can about your topic and subject. You'll be able to ask better questions and get better answers if you've done some background research.

1. Ask yourself what you would like to know about the topic and subject, and generate a list of questions. Can you find the answers from other sources? If so, think of questions that only your subject can answer.
2. Choose ten questions and evaluate them. Do they make sense? Are they asking for facts or opinions? (Depending on your topic, you might want either or both. Just be aware of what your question is asking.) Avoid questions with yes/no answers. Instead of "Do you like being involved in this community project?" ask "What do you find most rewarding about being involved in this project?"
3. Practise saying the questions aloud.
4. Contact your subject to schedule a meeting or phone interview. Be able to explain the purpose for the interview in one sentence. If you're planning to tape the interview, get permission.
5. Practise using the tape recorder and ensure that it is in working order.

PROCESS

Tips and Techniques

1. Arrive a few minutes early for the interview so you can be set up and ready.
2. Remind yourself that people enjoy talking about themselves and their work. Relax and don't be shy about asking questions.
3. Take notes during the interview even if you're taping it. These notes will give you a summary in case of a mechanical failure. Use abbreviations and your own shorthand. You can ask your subject to pause if there is an important point you want to get down exactly.
4. Listen to the answers. Make note of interesting points. Be flexible and ready to follow up on new ideas. If the conversation seems to be wandering, return to your prepared questions. If an answer doesn't make sense, ask for clarification.
5. Jot down a description of your subject. These details can add a human interest element to your story later on.
6. Quickly review your notes for any additional questions or points you need to clarify. Check the spelling of any names with your subject.
7. End the interview on time. Thank your subject and ask whether you may contact him or her later if you have any other questions or information gaps.

Writing Your Article

Immediately after the interview, read over your notes, clarify any scribbles or abbreviations, and jot down new ideas and questions. Look for any themes running through it.

1. Input or rewrite your notes clearly. Listen to the tape and transcribe the sections you wish to use. You may need to re-order the questions.
2. Write your story.
   - Develop a **lead** that sums up the story.
   - Use **quotations** from your subject. You may want to leave out part of the quote. Use ellipsis points to show information has been left out, but be careful how you edit the subject's words. Don't misrepresent what he or she has said.

Add the Finishing Touches

At the revision stage, you have the chance to improve your story.
- Describe your subject. This will add an important human interest element.
- Examine the focus of the interview. Is the lead clearly stated?
- Are the facts, dates, and names accurate?

Self-Assessment

Use the following checklist to assess the interview process.
- ❏ I asked relevant, useful questions.
- ❏ I listened attentively to the answers.
- ❏ I asked follow-up questions.
- ❏ I used my note-taking skills.
- ❏ I represented my subject's ideas accurately.

PROCESS

What does it take to be a hero?
Strength? Courage? Or something
as simple as...

An Open Heart

Personal Essay
by Judith Mackenzie

When I was eight years old, my father, a union organizer in the forties and fifties, was blacklisted, accused of communist activities. It meant no work—with a vengeance. My mother, then in her forties, had twin boys that spring—premature, and in pre-medicare times you can imagine the devastating costs for their care. I was hungry that year, hungry when I got up, hungry when I went to school, hungry when I went to sleep. In November I was asked to leave school because I only had boys' clothes to wear—hand-me-downs from a neighbour. I could come back, they said, when I dressed like a young lady.

The week before Christmas, the power and gas were disconnected. We ate soup made from carrots, potatoes, cabbage, and grain meant to feed chickens, cooked on our wood garbage burner. Even as an eight-year-old, I knew the kind of hunger we had was nothing compared to that of some people in India and Africa. I don't think we could have died in our middle-class Vancouver suburb. But I do know that the pain of hunger is intensified and brutal when you live in the midst of plenty. As Christmas preparations increased, I felt more and more isolated, excluded, set apart. I felt a deep, abiding hunger for more than food. Christmas Eve day came, grey and full of the bleak sleety rain of a west-coast winter. Two women, strangers,

38

struggled up our driveway, loaded down with bags. They left before my mother answered the door. The porch was full of groceries—milk, butter, bread, cheese, and Christmas oranges. We never knew who they were, and after that day, pride being what it was, we never spoke of them again. But I'm forty-five years old, and I remember them well.

Since then I've crafted a life of joy and independence, if not financial security. Several years ago, living in Victoria, my son and I were walking up the street, once more in west-coast sleet and rain. It was just before Christmas and we were, as usual, counting our pennies to see if we'd have enough for all our festive treats, juggling these against the necessities. A young man stepped in front of me, very pale and carrying an old sleeping bag, and asked for spare change—not unusual in downtown Victoria. No, I said, and walked on. Something hit me like a physical blow about a block later. I left my son and walked back to find the young man. I gave him some of our Christmas luxury money—folded into a small square and tucked into his hand. It wasn't much, only ten dollars, but as I turned away, I saw the look of hopelessness turned into amazement and then joy. Well, said the rational part of my mind, Judith, you are a fool, you know he's just going up the street to the King's Hotel and spend it on drink or drugs. You've taken what belongs to your family and spent it on a frivolous romantic impulse. As I was lecturing myself on gullibility and sensible charity, I noticed the young man with the sleeping bag walking quickly up the opposite side of the street, heading straight for the King's. Well, let this be a lesson, said the rational Judith. To really rub it in, I decided to follow him. Just before the King's, he turned into a corner grocery store. I watched through the window, through the poinsettias and the stand-up Santas. I watched him buy milk, butter, bread, cheese, and Christmas oranges.

Now, I have no idea how that young man arrived on the street in Victoria, nor will I ever have any real grasp of the events that led my family to a dark and hungry December. But I do know that charity cannot be treated as an RRSP. There is no best-investment way to give, no way to insure value for our dollar. Like the Magi, these three, the two older women struggling up the driveway and the young man with the sleeping bag, gave me, and continue to give me, wonderful gifts—the reminder that love and charity come most truly and abundantly from an open and unjudgmental heart. ◆

1. RESPONDING TO THE PERSONAL ESSAY

a. With a small group, discuss this essay's message. Is the message conveyed effectively?

b. What is the author saying about charity? Do you agree?

c. *Sympathy* means to share someone else's sorrow. *Empathy* is to imagine how someone else feels. Which word best describes the author's reaction to the street person? Explain.

d. Compare the idea of charity in this selection to the idea of charity in "Tom Jackson." What similarities and differences do you find? Is there only one kind of charity?

e. Why would this personal essay be included in a unit called "What Makes a Hero?"

2. WRITING POINT OF VIEW

Since "An Open Heart" is a personal essay, the point of view is the author's. Assume that you are the street person she gave ten dollars to. Write a brief essay about the incident from your (the street person's) point of view. How does it feel to be without money and hungry? What is it like to have no home to go to? What are you thinking when someone passes you by without helping you? How does it feel to receive charity? What are your hopes for the future?

3. VISUAL COMMUNICATION PORTRAY SETTING

Reread the first two paragraphs. With a partner, discuss the various images the author uses to bring the setting to life. What is the setting? How is it different from a contemporary setting? With your partner, discuss how you could create a visual that represents this setting—both in time and place. You could use a drawing, collage, poster, visual, or video. Share your completed visual with another pair of classmates, explaining how and why it was done.

PEER ASSESSMENT: Ask those classmates to give you some constructive feedback on your work—its composition, message, and mood.

4. LANGUAGE CONVENTIONS SUFFIXES AND PREFIXES

Reread the essay, locating words that use a suffix or prefix. List these words, sorting them into suffixes or prefixes. List the root word and its meaning. What is the meaning of each prefix and suffix on the list?

Sally knew her father's words were special.
If only she had the key to their meaning!

The Conversation of Birds

Short Story by Jean Yoon

I promised to go and there was no getting out of it now. I tried rubbing my face awake but it still felt numb around the edges. Six-fifteen in the morning. My room was blue with dawn.

"Sally-ah!! Are you coming?" Mom's voice raked like nails across my neck.

"Yeah, yeah, yeah."

My father said nothing when I came downstairs in jeans and a windbreaker. He adjusted and re-adjusted his tie. Mom pursed her lips but she didn't say anything either. She was wearing a beige skirt and her blue lace collar blouse. Silk.

"What?" I said. "Are we going to church or something?"

In the car, Mom broke out the thermos of coffee. She poured only a bit out at a time, cooled it with her breath and passed the mug to Dad who gulped it down at each red light then passed the mug back. Cocooned in a sleeping bag, I tried to doze in the back seat. I didn't say much but Mom and Dad spoke quietly, mostly in Korean but sometimes in English, trying consciously not to exclude me.

"About forty people were coming, but not many young people. Reverend Lee said he was coming, didn't he? There should be more young people. It was horrible all those students in Kwang Joo stood up and here hardly any young people cared if they were dead or in jail." My mother sighed and passed more coffee to my Dad.

"Is your speech ready?" she asked. My father nodded.

"I think so."

So I was the token young person. I didn't mind really. It was important to Dad and he was going to make a speech. Not that I would be able to understand it, but he was my father. There was something knotted in his face as he was writing out his speech. I asked him what was going on. He said there were student protests in Kwang Joo against martial rule. It was his home town and he had to do something. All these students were being killed for something as simple as a fair vote. Evil never makes sense but I thought of Kent State because I'd seen something about it on TV so I told him I'd go along to this memorial service if he really wanted me to.

"*Chal-haet-da!*" he said rubbing my back. "That's good."

Dad parked the car, then we walked about ten minutes into the park. The morning was new and wet so after a few minutes, Mom's dress shoes were muddied up the heel and my ankles were damp and cold. Dad walked briskly ahead, his short legs slicing through heavy grass. I waited while Mom stopped to straighten her skirt. She pulled a hair brush from her purse and made to brush my hair.

"MOM!" I pulled away and slapped her hand down.

"What? What did I do wrong?" We stood for a moment, mother and daughter, perfectly in balance. It would be so easy to turn away and not talk about it.

Somewhere outside of us, people were talking. Voices like fog between naked trees.

"Sorry," I said.

I took the brush from her hand and gave my hair a few quick strokes. I looked to my father expecting to see him watching our little war, saying nothing, revealing nothing, but he was far ahead of us now. He disappeared through the trees where the voices were.

Mom tucked the brush back into her purse and straightened the collar of my adidas wind breaker.

"You look neat, anyways."

"Say '*anyong-ha say-yoh*' to Mr. Im." Mom was smiling but she looked miserable and cold. Her ears were red and all the powder in the world wouldn't take the shine off her nose. Mr. Im reminded me of Mr. Layton, my Grade Three school teacher who would purposely ask me questions about geography. The one subject I could never get straight!

"What province is St. John's in?" The whole class was looking at me. All I could do was guess, jump off a cliff, and hope I'd land in sand.

"Ahm. London?" Mr. Layton rolled the stick of chalk in his hand like a cigarette.

"What province." It wasn't in London but some bigger place.

"Oh, England." The chalk snapped.

"Sally, there's a big difference between England and Canada." Mr. Layton turned away like a lawyer who had proved his point. I was growing smaller and smaller.

I looked from Mom to Mr. Im.

"Hi." I hooked my fingers in the loops of my pants and stood, legs apart, like a cowboy. They both laughed nervously.

"Mr. Im teaches Korean classes at the Church on Sundays."

"Oh, really. That sounds cool."

"You are very bad not to speak Korean." Mr. Im crossed his arms across his chest. My mother looked down and sniffed at the grass.

"Well, yeah. I guess."

"You must come to school. I have a special class for older students too." Thanks but no thanks, I thought. I'd be in the dummy class again. Mom would be poking me to see if I'd done my homework and Mr. Im would be pointedly correct. That was the last thing I needed.

A small crowd of forty husbands and wives arranged themselves in a circle. The sun was angled sharply white just over the black branches of trees. Knots of unformed green brightened in the morning light. I stood by my mother with my back to the sun. It was warm.

It was Dad's turn to speak now. He looked towards us nervously. I gave him a wink. He grinned but his hands were shaking as he unfolded the speech he had written last night. It was quiet, just the rattle of papers, the conversation of birds. A cough.

This was my Dad. The arbitrator of family squabbles. Dad who goes to work, comes home, and in the hours when he is invisible does work that is too big to explain. Dad who, in his spare time, patches all the little cracks in the walls, and keeps the house leak-proof, like an ark.

From what I could tell, the start of Dad's speech was conventional.

"Speak up," a man shouted in Korean.

"*Mooyo?*"

"We can't hear you," a woman said loudly. Dad looked down at his papers and started again, this time louder. I tried to follow what he was saying but all I could catch were names I already knew. Pak Chung Hee, Chun Doo Hwan, Kwang Joo, Seoul Tae Hak Kyo. Something was wrong. Dad stopped, crumpled up the papers he had laboured over and just stood there. He was crying. Speaking now with fire and hurt and something I didn't know a name for.

I had only seen Dad cry twice before. Once when he and Mom were fighting. She was screaming and slamming doors. The house shook and I huddled in my room waiting for a truce. When I came out, Mom was gone and Dad was sitting in the living room without any lights on. The TV was still on but he didn't seem to notice.

The other time was much later. The phone rang and Dad listened for a moment. His voice was as strong as green wood, but his face twisted up. His stepmother had just died. He never liked her and she never liked him. That's what I guessed. But then, I don't know. There are things he never talks about.

Dad didn't have any kleenex. He kept sniffling and wiping his nose with his fingers. When he finished, there was applause. Dad bowed, turning away his face and came over to Mom and me. Mom hugged Dad and told him she was proud he spoke from the heart, but when he turned to me, I had nothing to say. I hadn't understood a word of it.

I stayed on the edge of things while people came by to shake Dad's hand and say how moved they were by his speech. If there was anything they could do, please call and let them know. He wiped his nose with his sleeve then tucked his arm at his side. He said thank you and looked to my Mom who was talking with the handful of people who were left in the clearing. The rest were already on their way home or to work. Voices scattered in all directions. A man shouted to his wife that he would wait for her at the car. She shouts back in Korean, she's coming, she's coming.

I tugged Dad's jacket and the two of us started down through the park.

"What did you say, Dad?"

"Nothing special." He was embarrassed. Mom caught up and the three of us walked through the damp morning in silence.

I tried asking him again later. He smiled this time and made a face.

"You know," he said. "Just the same old thing." ◆

1. RESPONDING TO THE STORY

a. With a small group, discuss the story's theme and message.

b. Reread "The Conversation of Birds" and find where the title occurs in the story. Why do you think the author chose this phrase for the title?

c. In speaking of his speech, the father says that it was "just the same old thing." What does he mean by that?

d. How do you know that the author feels that it is important to speak out against injustice and human suffering? What else can people do to stop human rights violations?

e. Who is the hero in this story? What makes him or her a hero?

2. ORAL LANGUAGE SPEECH

The speech Sally's father gives is not the one he has written. It is spoken "from the heart" with "fire and hurt." In your notebook, describe a time when you felt like speaking out against an injustice. To a partner, give a short spontaneous speech about the subject "from the heart." Tape your speech. Listen to it, and decide if speaking from the heart is sometimes more effective than preparing a formal speech.

3. LITERATURE STUDIES COMPARISONS

Reread the story and, in your notebook, list all the examples of **similes**. Briefly explain what you think each one means. Notice that the author doesn't use many of these comparisons. Why do you think this is so?

SELF-ASSESSMENT: Examine some of your writing from your portfolio. Do you use similes? Do they make your writing clearer or harder to understand?

> **Simile** is a comparison that uses the words "like" or "as," for example, "Voices like fog between naked trees."

4. MEDIA MESSAGES NEWS REPORTS

With a small group of classmates, discuss how TV news programs report human rights violations. Do they give all sides of a story? Do they spend enough time fully explaining the issues? Do TV news programs influence the way you think about national and world issues?

5. RESEARCHING LOCATING INFORMATION

Research an example of a human rights violation from any country at any point in time (perhaps one of those referred to in the story). Find one article or information piece from each of these sources:

- a book
- a newspaper article
- a magazine feature
- a Web site

Compare what you've learned from each source. Is the information the same? If there are differences in facts and explanations, how can you tell which is correct? Do you think it's possible to discover what really happened? Why is it important to use more than one resource when researching a topic?

Caesar is dead! And now the Romans must decide if his assassins are heroes of the republic or power-hungry traitors.

Julius Caesar

An excerpt from Act 3, Scene 2

Play by William Shakespeare

PREVIOUS TO THE RISE OF JULIUS CAESAR, THE CITY-STATE OF ROME HAD BEEN A DEMOCRATIC REPUBLIC FOR ALMOST FIVE HUNDRED YEARS. MOST PATRIOTIC ROMANS WERE PROUD OF THIS TRADITION AND ABHORRED THE IDEA OF BEING RULED BY A KING. IN 44 B.C., CAESAR ANNOUNCED TO THE ROMAN SENATE THAT HE WISHED TO BE DECLARED KING. IN AN ATTEMPT TO PRESERVE FREEDOM AND ROME'S DEMOCRATIC TRADITIONS, A GROUP OF SENATORS, LED BY BRUTUS AND CASSIUS, ASSASSINATED JULIUS CAESAR. THE FOLLOWING SCENE TAKES PLACE IMMEDIATELY AFTER CAESAR'S MURDER.

Rome. The Forum.
Enter a group of angry citizens, accompanied by Brutus.

1. satisfied - given a full explanation

CITIZENS: We will be satisfied! Let us be satisfied!
BRUTUS: Then follow me, and give me audience friends...
And public reasons shall be rendered
Of Caesar's death.
CITIZEN 1: I will hear Brutus speak...
CITIZEN 3: The noble Brutus is ascended! Silence!
BRUTUS: Be patient till the last.
Romans, countrymen, and lovers, hear me for my

GOALS AT A GLANCE

■ Respond critically.
■ Model the selection to write a parody.

cause, and be silent, that you may hear. Believe me for
mine honour, and have respect to mine honour, that you   10
may believe. Censure me in your wisdom, and awake
your senses, that you may the better judge. If there be
any in this assembly, any dear friend of Caesar's, to him
I say, that Brutus's love to Caesar was no less than his. If
then, that friend demand, why Brutus rose against Caesar,
this is my answer: Not that I loved Caesar less, but
that I loved Rome more. Had you rather Caesar were living,
and die all slaves, than that Caesar were dead, to
live all free men? As Caesar loved me, I weep for him;
as he was fortunate, I rejoice at it; as he was valiant, I   20
honour him. But, as he was ambitious, I slew him. There
is tears for his love, joy for his fortune, honour for
his valour, and death for his ambition. Who is here
so base that would be a bondman? If any, speak, for him
have I offended. Who is here so rude, that would not
be a Roman? If any, speak, for him have I offended. Who
is here so vile that will not love his country? If any,
speak, for him have I offended. I pause for a reply.
ALL: None, Brutus, none!
BRUTUS: Then none have I offended. I have done no   30
more to Caesar than you shall do to Brutus. The question
of his death is enroll'd in the Capitol. His glory not
extenuated, wherein he was worthy, nor his offences enforced,
for which he suffered death.

Enter Mark Antony, with Caesar's body.

Here comes his body, mourn'd by Mark Antony, who,
though he had no hand in his death, shall receive the benefit
of his dying, a place in the commonwealth, as which of
you shall not? With this I depart, that as I slew my best
lover for the good of Rome, I have the same dagger for
myself, when it shall please my country to need my death.   40
ALL: Live, Brutus! Live! Live!
CITIZEN 1: Bring him with triumph home unto his house!
CITIZEN 2: Give him a statue with his ancestors!
CITIZEN 3: Let him be Caesar!
CITIZEN 1: We'll bring him to his house,

11. *censure* - judge

12. *senses* - good sense

15. *demand* - ask

20. *fortunate* - successful (in military campaigns)

24. *bondman* - slave

25. *rude* - common, uncivilized

31. *question of* - justification for

32. *enroll'd* - recorded

33. *extenuated* - understated

33. *enforced* - overstated

37. *commonwealth* - free state of Rome

42. *triumph* - great joy

43. *ancestors* - one of Brutus' ancestors was responsible for driving the last of the tyrant kings out of Rome and establishing the republic

With shouts and clamours!

BRUTUS: My countrymen,—

CITIZEN 2: Peace, silence, Brutus speaks!

CITIZEN 1: Peace, ho!

BRUTUS: Good countrymen, let me depart alone,   50

And, for my sake, stay here with Antony.

Do grace to Caesar's corpse, and grace his speech

Tending to Caesar's glories, which Mark Antony,

By our permission, is allow'd to make.

I do entreat you, not a man depart,

Save I alone, till Antony have spoke.

Exit Brutus.

CITIZEN 1: Stay, ho, and let us hear Mark Antony.

CITIZEN 3: Let him go up into the public chair.

We'll hear him! Noble Antony, go up.

ANTONY: For Brutus's sake, I am beholding to you.   60

CITIZEN 4: What does he say of Brutus?

CITIZEN 3: He says, for Brutus's sake

He finds himself beholding to us all.

CITIZEN 4: 'Twere best he speak no harm of Brutus here!

CITIZEN 1: This Caesar was a tyrant.

CITIZEN 3: Nay, that's certain.

We are blest that Rome is rid of him.

CITIZEN 2: Peace, let us hear what Antony can say.

ANTONY: You gentle Romans.

CITIZENS: Peace, ho! Let us hear him.   70

ANTONY: Friends, Romans, countrymen, lend me your ears!

I come to bury Caesar, not to praise him.

The evil that men do, lives after them,

The good is oft interred with their bones.

So let it be with Caesar. The noble Brutus,

Hath told you Caesar was ambitious.

If it were so, it was a grievous fault,

And grievously hath Caesar answer'd it.

Here, under leave of Brutus, and the rest,

For Brutus is an honourable man,   80

So are they all, all honourable men,

Come I to speak in Caesar's funeral.

He was my friend, faithful, and just to me;
But Brutus says he was ambitious,
And Brutus is an honourable man.
He hath brought many captives home to Rome,
Whose ransoms, did the general coffers fill.

Did this in Caesar seem ambitious?
When that the poor have cried, Caesar hath wept.
Ambition should be made of sterner stuff,   90
Yet Brutus says, he was ambitious,
And Brutus is an honourable man.

You all did see, that on the Lupercal,
I thrice presented him a kingly crown,
Which he did thrice refuse. Was this ambition?
Yet Brutus says, he was ambitious,
And sure he is an honourable man.
I speak not to disprove what Brutus spoke,
But here I am to speak what I do know.
You all did love him once, not without cause.   100
What cause withholds you then, to mourn for him?
O judgment! Thou art fled to brutish beasts,
And men have lost their reason. Bear with me.
My heart is in the coffin there with Caesar,
And I must pause till it come back to me.

[Mark Antony pauses and pretends to weep.]

CITIZEN 1: Methinks there is much reason in his sayings.
CITIZEN 2: If thou consider rightly of the matter,
Caesar has had great wrong.
CITIZEN 3: Has he masters? I fear there will a worse come
in his place.   110
CITIZEN 4: Marked ye his words? He would not take the crown,
Therefore 'tis certain, he was not ambitious.

CITIZEN 1: If it be found so, some will dear abide it.
CITIZEN 2: Poor soul! His eyes are red as fire with weeping.
CITIZEN 3: There's not a nobler man in Rome than Antony. ◆

1. RESPONDING TO THE PLAY

a. What reasons does Brutus offer the people for killing Caesar? According to Brutus, how should they feel about his actions?

b. How do the people respond to Brutus's speech?

c. In his speech, how does Marc Antony convince the people that Brutus is not an honourable man?

d. Marc Antony claims that he is not an orator. Do you agree? Explain fully.

e. How does Antony incite the people to "rise and mutiny"?

f. Based on this excerpt, what conclusions can you draw about the citizens of Rome?

g. Do you think either Brutus or Antony have any qualities of a hero?

2. WRITING A SHORT ESSAY

In Scene 2, Shakespeare suggests a number of ideas about the nature of leaders and heroes. He also reminds us of the dangers of being manipulated by eloquent speakers. Write a short essay exploring one of these ideas about heroes and leaders. As you develop your essay remember to

- include an opening statement or thesis stating your view
- use specific details and references from the scene to support your thesis
- end with a concluding statement that sums up your ideas

3. ORAL LANGUAGE DELIVER A SPEECH

Develop a **parody** of Antony's "Friends, Romans, Countrymen" speech. Rather than "burying Caesar," you may choose to focus on a habit or behaviour, a school subject, a sport, or a TV program. To develop your parody, follow the basic structure of Antony's speech and include some of the key phrases or words used in it.

> A **parody** is a humorous imitation of a serious piece of writing. It makes fun by imitating.

Perform your speech, focussing on your tone, volume, and gestures. How can you use these techniques to give a convincing and persuasive performance?

PEER ASSESSMENT: Ask for feedback from your audience. Was the focus clear? Was the delivery effective? Were your tone, volume, and gestures appropriate? What would they advise to improve your performance?

In the world of professional sports, you don't necessarily have to be a hero to be a star.

Man,
You're a Great Player!

SATIRE BY GARY LAUTENS

O ccasionally I run into sports figures at cocktail parties, on the street, or on their way to the bank.

"Nice game the other night," I said to an old hockey-player pal.

"Think so?" he replied.

"You've come a long way since I knew you as a junior."

"How's that?"

"Well, you high-stick better for one thing—and I think the way you clutch sweaters is really superb. You may be the best in the league."

He blushed modestly. "For a time," I confessed, "I never thought you'd get the hang of it."

"It wasn't easy," he confided. "It took practice and encouragement. You know something like spearing doesn't come naturally. It has to be developed."

"I'm not inclined to flattery but, in my book, you've got it made. You're a dirty player."

"Stop kidding."

"No, no," I insisted. "I'm not trying to butter you up. I mean it. When you broke in, there were flashes of dirty play—but you weren't consistent.

GOALS AT A GLANCE

■ Model selection to write a satire.
■ Analyse and use jargon.

53

That's the difference between a dirty player and merely a colourful one."

"I wish my father were alive to hear you say that," he said quietly. "He would have been proud."

"Well, it's true. There isn't a player in the league who knows as many obscene gestures."

"I admit I have been given a few increases in pay in recent years. Management seems to be treating me with new respect."

"You're selling tickets," I said. "You're a gate attraction now—not some bum who only can skate and shoot and the rest of it. Your profanity is beautiful."

"C'mon."

"No, I'm serious. I don't think anyone in the league can incite a riot the way you can."

"I've had a lot of help along the way. You can't make it alone," he stated generously.

"No one does," I said.

"Take that play where I skate up to the referee and stand nose-to-nose with my face turning red. It was my old junior coach who taught me that. He was the one who used to toss all the sticks on the ice and throw his hat into the stands and pound his fist on the boards."

"You were lucky to get that sort of training. A lot of players never learn the fundamentals."

"I think there are a few boys in the league who can spit better than me."

"Farther, perhaps, but not more accurately," I corrected.

"Well, thanks anyway. I've always considered it one of my weaknesses."

"That last brawl of yours was perfectly executed. Your sweater was torn off, you taunted the crowd, you smashed your stick across the goalposts. Really a picture Donnybrook."

"The papers gave me a break. The coverage was outstanding."

"Do you ever look back to the days when you couldn't cut a forehead or puff a lip or insult an official?"

"Everyone gets nostalgic," he confessed. "It's a good thing I got away from home by the time I was fifteen. I might never have been any more than a ham-and-egger, you know, a twenty-goal man who drifts through life unnoticed."

"What was the turning point?"

"I had heard prominent sports experts say that nice guys finish last, and that you have to beat them in the alley if you hope to beat them in the rink. But it didn't sink in."

"Nobody learns overnight."

"I wasted a few years learning to play my wing and to check without using the butt of the stick. But I noticed I was being passed by. I skated summers to keep in shape, exercised, kept curfew."

"Don't tell me. They said you were dull."

"Worse than that. They said I was clean. It's tough to live down that sort of reputation."

I nodded.

"Anyway, during a game in the sticks, I was skating off the ice—we had won five-one and I had scored three goals. The home crowd was pretty listless and there was some booing. Then it happened."

"What?"

"My big break. My mother was in the stands and she shouted to me. I turned to wave at her with my hockey stick and I accidentally caught the referee across the face. He bled a lot—took ten stitches later."

"Is that all?"

"Well, someone pushed me and I lost my balance and fell on the poor man. A real brawl started. Luckily, I got credit for the whole thing—went to jail overnight, got a suspension. And, talk about fate! A big league scout was in the arena. He offered me a contract right away."

"It's quite a success story," I said.

"You've got to get the breaks," he replied, humbly. ◆

1. RESPONDING TO THE SATIRE

a. In this article, Gary Lautens uses **satire** to make a point about hockey. What is the author's real message?

b. When did you realize that Lautens was not being serious? Did the teaser or title give you any clues? Explain.

c. What features make "Man, You're a Great Player!" a satire rather than a realistic sports piece?

> A **satire** is a type of writing that uses humour and irony to point out the shortcomings of an organization, person, situation, or society.

d. Lautens was a journalist known for writing satiric humorous pieces. Would his message be more effective if he had written a typical sports column? Explain your view.

e. Is this hockey player a hero? Why or why not? Think about the selections you've read in this unit. With a small group, discuss "What Makes a Hero?"

2. WRITING A SATIRIC ARTICLE

Read the definition of satire above and discuss with a partner how Lautens uses it to express his message. How does Lautens establish, develop, and conclude his satire? Is the satire effective? Why or why not? How does an audience know a piece of writing is satiric rather than serious?

Choose another aspect of sports that you and your partner both criticize. Work together to write a satiric article. Begin by jotting down the message you want to convey. Then think about how you can use satire to deliver your message. What supporting statements can you add?

Exchange articles with another pair of classmates and ask for feedback.

SELF-ASSESSMENT: Did you maintain a satiric tone throughout the article? Did your audience understand the *real* message of your satire?

3. WORD CRAFT JARGON

The language of sports writers is full of **jargon**. Gary Lautens cleverly uses some of that sports jargon in his satire. Reread the article and list examples of jargon. Choose three examples from your list and explain what each means. If you were to rewrite this article in the form of a short story, would you include these examples of jargon? Why or why not?

> **Jargon** is the language of a particular group or profession.

REFLECTING ON THE UNIT

SELF-ASSESSMENT: LANGUAGE CONVENTIONS

As you worked on the activities in this unit, what did you learn about
• jargon?
• active and passive voice?
• suffixes and prefixes?
• quotations in non-fiction?

LITERATURE STUDIES EXPLORE VIEWPOINTS

Think about the selections you've read. What does each one say about being a heroic person? Choose two selections that explore different viewpoints and write a paragraph for each one summarizing these views. Which view do you think is more realistic or accurate? In one or two paragraphs, explain your choice. Use examples from the selection to support your opinion.

MEDIA MESSAGES PERSONALITIES

Many of today's heroes are media personalities, for example, movie and TV actors, sports figures, even politicians. What media personality do you admire? In a few sentences, briefly explain your reasons.

SHORTSTORIES

A moment's insight
is sometimes worth
a life's experience.
Oliver Wendell Holmes

SHORT STORIES
INSIGHTS

Have you ever helped an adult get a date?
It sure isn't easy!

The Crystal Stars Have Just Begun to Shine

Short Story
BY MARTHA BROOKS

Lisa Barnett, moving down the halls, books clasped against her chest, tosses tawny hair away from her eyes in one fluid motion.

How does she do that? Just once I'd like to be able to do that. I have this wild frizzy hair that my boyfriend, Brad, says drives him crazy with unrequited passion, and then he leans me back in his arms and his bicycle topples to the ground. Brad's hair is black with a dyed green stripe down the centre. Brad is half Japanese.

My Dad is Jamaican. His hair is more agreeable than mine—always soft, like he's just been caught in the rain. My Mom's hair, I can see in photos, is much like Lisa Barnett's, although it could be any colour now. Who knows? I don't remember her except for the photos. She was young and pretty when she checked out.

A thought strikes! Lisa Barnett could look like my half-sister. The one I've never met.

Daddy is sometimes a terrible yeller and sometimes a hugger. In between times, he's quite reserved. At night, he sits alone in his armchair and watches reruns of $M*A*S*H$. He gets up every morning and goes to a job he hates. He buys the best of everything he can afford for us and has an aversion to leftovers. So I always eat them cold for breakfast before I go to school; this helps ease my sense of guilt.

I feel guilty a lot. I sometimes even feel guilty about that because after he's yelled, when I'm bent over homework and stuffing my face with a snack, he comes up behind me, wraps his arms around my shoulders, and mumbles parental anguish. I'm gumming a mouthful of chips and there he is, rocking me cheek to cheek, telling me I'm all he's got.

It's murder being loved by someone who spends his whole miserable life just looking after you. I wish he had a girlfriend. But he rarely goes out, that's how much of a rut he's in. A couple of years ago I came home from a movie and he and this woman were sitting in the living room, all cuddled up on the couch with the TV blaring. She was a redhead. She smiled at me and I immediately liked her. I was so relieved to see him with somebody. But he was embarrassed. As if a parent, for pete's sake, isn't supposed to have feelings like the rest of us mortals. After that night, I didn't see the redhead again. I was so disgusted with him, I never asked who she was or where she'd come from.

Brad, my boyfriend, says it's probably just that he's too old now to enjoy women.

I tell him, "He's only forty-six!"

"So," he shrugs, "let's fix him up with somebody."

"Like who?"

"I dunno. We must know somebody who's as old as him."

Daddy's sparkling social life suggests a handful of possibilities. We start eliminating the implausibles and what remains is Rita, the over-permed checkout lady at Payfair. She looks to be about his age and is friendly, kind, divorced, and available. I have, however, one reservation. She's rather flabby. I feel that if we're going to set my father up with a woman, she's got to be in good shape.

"Why?" says Brad. "I don't see your dad out jogging and he drives a bus all day long."

"He's perfectly fit," I say protectively.

"He's got a paunch," Brad says cruelly, and smiles. He has these marvellous eyebrows, like wings; they move about at will. When he's excited, his whole face looks as if at any moment it'll take off somewhere.

"You have to face facts, Deirdre," he says, leaning over the counter in his mother's kitchen, where we're sitting on high stools as we pig out on Calamato olives and oatmeal biscuits that Brad himself has made. He plants me with a nice cozy kiss. "Look," he continues, "Rita doesn't exactly make *me* sweat. But who knows what she'll do for your father?"

"Maybe he'd be better off with Auntie Eulie's friend Ginny after all," I muse. "She's better looking. Besides, she's black. A change, they say, is as good as a rest."

"Ginny, as we have already discussed, is wacko," says Brad. "She's desperate and totally unstable. Would you want her for a stepmother?"

In spite of Brad's green hair, he's really a very straight-ahead guy. He thinks all love relationships should end happily in marriage. His Italian mother and Japanese father have been married over twenty-three years. He says from the minute he laid eyes on me he knew we were right for each other. He had his mother work out our astrological signs, and according to the reading ours would be a marriage made in heaven. I told him to quit talking that way, we're only fourteen. He responded, wiggling his eyebrows, "In seven years I'm going to marry you, Deirdre, so don't argue with Destiny."

My father does most of our grocery shopping at Payfair. Sometimes I go with him. He shops every Thursday evening after supper. He makes a list, carefully marking off with a little red tick each of the specials he's seen advertised at other stores. Then he can comparison shop. At the store, he checks prices according to units instead of weight. When he shops he looks like the male version of a bag lady. He is one very drab dude. You have to imagine a skinny balding black man (with a *slight* paunch) in a shapeless camel coat (Zellers special, 1979), wine-coloured polyester slacks, and black rubber galoshes.

"You're going to have to do something about the clothes, Deirdre," says Brad. "Doesn't he own anything that looks modern?"

"I gave him jeans for Christmas last year. He never wears them," I say, suddenly discouraged.

"Make him wear the jeans Thursday night. And does he own a decent sweater—or anything?"

"Only a navy turtleneck Auntie Eulie gave him to go with the jeans," I say. "He's never worn that either."

Thursday night I make dinner and invite Brad to stay. Daddy gets home and kisses my forehead and asks Brad if he's ever considered dying his green stripe orange. He laughs all the way to the bathroom, where he washes up. Then he goes to his bedroom to change. I go and tap lightly on his door. "Daddy," I say, "please don't wear those purple pants tonight."

"What's wrong with the purple pants?" he says from behind the door.

"They're so tacky."

"They're perfectly fine, I wear them all the time," he says indignant and ready to yell.

"Exactly," I snap back. "And I get tired of looking at you in them. It's time you changed your image. Get reckless." Sometimes, if I state my mind firmly enough, he comes through.

Dead silence from behind the door. Then a suspicious, "Why are you all of the sudden so concerned about the way I look?"

"The jeans," I say. "Okay?"

"They're obscenely tight, Deirdre," he says coldly.

"They're supposed to be tight. That's how they're worn. Are you going to wear those purple pants until you drop dead? I'll have to bury you in them."

"All right," he mutters, "all right."

I stay by the door, breathing.

"What else?" he says.

"Else?"

"What else do you want me to wear. With the tight jeans."

"Oh," I say, as casually as possible, "well, what about that nice sweater Auntie Eulie gave you?"

Another silence.

"It itches," he whines.

"Wear an undershirt," I say, and quickly leave.

He appears, five minutes later, looking uncomfortable and handsome.

Brad stares at him, obviously amazed. Daddy gives him the cold eye and flares up. "What're you gawking at? It's my fashion statement."

"Terrific," says Brad. Later, in the car, he whispers out of the corner of his mouth. "Make sure he takes off that coat when we get there."

Rita smiles warmly as we trail snow through the door. She doesn't appear to be busy tonight. She's running through a litre of milk for an old lady with an English accent.

"Hi Rita!" Brad and I say, almost in unison. Daddy scurries off to get his cart. He hasn't even acknowledged her.

"Love in bloom," says Brad sarcastically, as we traipse after Daddy.

"I'll attend to his coat," I say, ignoring this. "Your job is the candies."

In the produce section, Daddy pauses over bags of celery. He lifts several, checking each for weight. Light celery is stringy, heavy celery is succulent. He frowns, decides against buying celery this week, and moves on to the broccoli, where he scrutinizes the heads through his half-glasses. Brad has disappeared. I imagine him whisking back down Aisle Two so he'll come out directly in front of Rita's till. Now, he's reaching into his jacket. He produces a heart-shaped box of chocolates he bought earlier in the day at the drug-store. It didn't look too fresh, but what can you do? This is November and they're probably a holdover from last Valentine's day. But the heart shape was absolutely essential, you see, because older ladies really like that kind of stuff.

"They sure keep this store hot, don't they?" I say to Daddy.

"Huh?" He's carefully shaking out a plastic produce bag.

"Want me to hold your coat?"

"Why would I want you to hold my coat?" He eases two stalks of broccoli into the bag.

I see I'm going to have to be more forceful. "Daddy, for heaven's sake, you look like a bag lady in that coat. What will people think? Do you want to embarrass me?"

He takes off his glasses, waves them impatiently around.

"Deirdre, what on earth are you talking about? What people? Do you see any people in this store? There are no people. None."

"Well…there could be. There might be. *Anybody* could walk through that door, right now."

"Tsk!" says Daddy, scowling. But he unbuttons the coat before moving on to the apples. His sweater and jeans are at least visible.

Brad slips up behind me just as we progress to the canned goods.

"That took long enough," I whisper tensely.

We hang back like a couple of thieves. Daddy is checking out the canned tomatoes.

"She's terrific!" says Brad, eyebrows poised for liftoff. "I mean, up until now I must admit I've totally overlooked her personality and her eyes. She's got great eyes! But if I was an older man—yeah! I'd take a chance on her myself."

"I want to know her reaction, Brad."

"Shock."

"Good or bad?" I say, watching his face carefully.

"At first it was hard to tell. She just froze with this blank expression. I then told her he was too shy to give them to her himself but that she could thank him personally when she rang up his groceries."

"What'd she say?"

"Nothing. Believe it or not, she smiled like she'd just been handed a ticket to Florida. Your father has something I've missed." He waves at Daddy who, cautious, still scowling, holds aloft a large can of stewed tomatoes.

"I don't see why you're so surprised," I say haughtily. One down. One to go. Please God, let him be smiling when he gets to Rita's till. If you do, I'll eat cold pork every morning for the next month.

Fifteen minutes before closing, Daddy has finally put the last item in his cart. He wheels over to Rita's till. She nods and smiles enigmatically.

"Evening Rita," he says, throwing down a large tub of margarine.

She rings it through. I notice she's freshly applied dark pink lipstick. My father makes a remark about the weather and stares dismally past her shoulder out the window at the snow that is singing against the glass.

Wordlessly, Rita rings through the rest of the groceries. I've never noticed how much better she looks up close than far away. Up close you really *can* see that her best feature is her eyes. They're pale amber with thick lashes. Her nose is perhaps too big, her skin sort of saggy. But those eyes! She really talks with them. Too bad all this seems to be lost on Daddy. If he'd only look directly at her he'd see what's there.

Just when I think we're never going to get this show on the road, she rings up the bill and, as Daddy hands her three twenty-dollar bills, sort of leans into him and whispers, practically in his ear, "Thanks for the box of chocolates, Elliot. It really made my day."

Daddy doesn't move. He seems paralysed, except for his eyes, which shift upward to her, back to us, then dart wildly about the store as he processes this information. Finally, he takes off his glasses, seems about to say something, and can't. He looks back at her, smiles. She smiles back. Her eyes do a bit of talking. Daddy's eyes start doing their own talking.

I never knew this would be so embarrassing! I can't watch them anymore so I turn around to Brad who still is. Mesmerized, he wears a foolish smile.

I wish somebody would say something out loud. Nobody does. Eventually we leave, each holding onto bags of groceries. Our warm breath hits the outside air and searches out the night. Overhead the crystal stars have just begun to shine.

----

1. RESPONDING TO THE STORY

a. What is the problem Martha Brooks introduces at the beginning of the story? What conflict does it produce? How are the problem and conflict resolved?

b. Have you ever tried to get an adult to do something he or she didn't want to do? Was it difficult? embarrassing? Discuss the situation with a partner.

c. What do you think the story's title refers to? Why do you think Brooks chose this title?

d. What do you think will happen between Elliot and Rita after the story ending?

e. Which of the characters could you identify with? Do you think the story offers a realistic portrayal of family life in Canadian society?

2. STORY CRAFT ANALYSE THEME

The subject of this story is how a daughter tries to make her father happy by finding him a partner. The **theme**, however, is what the main character, or the reader, discovers about life or people by the end of the story. In your opinion, what is the theme of "The Crystal Stars Have Just Begun to Shine?" Discuss your thoughts with a partner.

The **theme** of a story is what the protagonist discovers about life. Common examples of theme include the horror of war, loneliness, betrayal, and the importance of family.

3. WRITING FIRST-PERSON NARRATOR

Some of the stories in this unit are narrated by one of the characters. This is called writing in the *first person*. The author uses *I* and *me* instead of the third person *he* or *she*.

Think of something that recently happened to you. Use the first person to describe the event or situation. Now rewrite your piece in the third person. What are the differences in tone and vocabulary between the two versions? Explain which version you prefer.

4. LANGUAGE CONVENTIONS VERB TENSES IN FICTION

Most short stories and novels are written in the past tense. The reasoning is that the action and events have taken place before the author began to write. Brooks, however, uses the present tense. Reread the story. Did you even notice this tense on your first reading? What effect does using the present tense have? What tone or mood is created? Do you think the present tense would work as well for other types of stories, such as historical fiction, fantasy, or science fiction?

Choose a paragraph from the story and rewrite it in the past tense. What are the differences between the two versions? Discuss whether you think the present tense is more effective for this story.

SELF-ASSESSMENT: Look through your writing portfolio for a short story that you want to revise. Consider whether changing the verb tense could improve the story. You might also change the narrative voice.

5. LITERATURE STUDIES ANALYSE REVIEWS

Book reviews can help the undecided reader by giving him or her a preview of a book and an opinion of its merits and faults.

With a group of classmates, examine book reviews from your local newspaper. How are they set up? What are the different elements of these reviews? Using these reviews as a model, write your own review of "The Crystal Stars Have Just Begun to Shine."

HOW TO

DEVELOP A PLOT

Goals at a Glance

● Structure a narrative using story elements. ● Create an outline.

Developing a good plot is perhaps the most important part of writing a good story. It can also be the most difficult thing to achieve. But there are some pre-writing steps you can take to help develop a well-crafted plot.

Understanding Plot

The **plot** is the narrative action of a story (as opposed to the characters, setting, mood, or theme). It is the sum of all the events in the story. A good plot line carries readers eagerly along as the characters try to solve conflicts or overcome problems. You could almost say that the plot *is* the story.

Classic plots have the following five stages, although creative writers give their own original twists to the "rules."

1. The **initial incident** sets the plot in motion. Readers are introduced to the major characters and the problem they have to solve.

2. The **rising action** occurs as events and tension build up. The characters meet further challenges and obstacles.

3. The **climax** is the point of highest intensity in the plot. All the action leads to a culminating event.

4. During the **falling action**, the characters react to the events of the climax. An explanation of problems or conflicts may be offered.

5. The **conclusion** or **denouement** brings the plot to a close by resolving conflicts and revealing the fate of the characters.

Create a Plot Outline

Begin by making an outline of your plot. Build your plot according to the five stages listed above. At each stage, your characters should come closer to resolving the conflict.

PROCESS

Deepen the Plot

- Think about the sequence of events in the plot. Will you tell everything in chronological order? Or will you begin with a climactic event, work backwards to explain how it happened, and then move forward again to the conclusion?
- Try one of these techniques to vary the sequence of events: use **foreshadowing** to give clues as to what will happen next, or **flashbacks** to reveal events that took place in the past.
- **Conflict** is central to the plot. To develop conflict, ask yourself, "What does my main character want to achieve, and why? What obstacles stand in the way?"
- Skim through short stories that you've read and enjoyed. Examine how the authors have developed their plots, and use some of these techniques in your own writing.

Write a Story: First Draft

Forget your outline, and let the words flow onto the page. Don't try to correct spelling, grammar, or awkward-sounding sentences. Besides plot, there are all the other essential story elements:

- **Characters:** Make them vivid and appealing. Their decisions and actions should usually shape the events.
- **Setting:** Your readers should be able to picture the specific time and place in your story.
- **Mood:** The feeling and atmosphere your story creates are important in engaging and keeping your readers' interest.
- **Theme:** Do you have a message you want to convey to your readers? How will your story accomplish this?

Revise Your Story

At the revision stage you have a chance to improve your story. Read it aloud to yourself or a partner, and rewrite parts that seem weak to you. Think about the major story elements— plot, characters, setting, mood, and theme— and decide if they are working. Finally, look at the language you've used. Try varying your sentence structure, using more striking verbs, and correcting any errors.

Self-Assessment

Use the questions below to reflect on the process you followed to develop the plot of your story.

- ❏ Did my plot outline help me to construct a well-crafted story?
- ❏ Will the opening of the story (the initial incident) grab the readers' attention?
- ❏ Do the events of the rising action build tension and conflict? Is the conflict believable?
- ❏ Does the story have an exciting or unexpected climax?
- ❏ Do the falling action and conclusion give the story a satisfying ending?

Do you think you really understand why adults do the things they do?

War

SHORT STORY BY TIMOTHY FINDLEY

That's my dad in the middle. We were just kids then, Bud on the right and me on the left. That was taken just before my dad went into the army.

Some day that was.

It was a Saturday, two years ago. August, 1940. I can remember I had to blow my nose just before that and I had to use my dad's hankie because mine had a worm in it that I was saving. I can't remember why; I mean, why I was saving that worm, but I can remember why I had to blow my nose, all right. That was because I'd had a long time crying. Not exactly because my dad was going away or anything—it was mostly because I'd done something.

I'll tell you what in a minute, but I just want to say this first. I was ten years old then and it was sort of the end of summer. When we went back to school I was going into the fifth grade and that was pretty important, especially for me because I'd skipped Grade Four. Right now, I can't even remember Grade Five except that I didn't like it. I should have gone to Grade Four. In Grade Five, everyone was a genius and there was a boy called Allan McKenzie.

Anyway, now that you know how old I was and what grade I was into, I can tell you the rest.

It was the summer the war broke out and I went to stay with my friend, Arthur Robertson. Looking back on it, Arthur seems a pretty silly name for Arthur Robertson because he was so small. But he was a nice kid and his dad had the most enormous summer cottage you've ever seen. In Muskoka, too.

It was like those houses they have in the movies in Beverly Hills. Windows a mile long—pine trees outside and then a lake and then a red canoe tied up with a yellow rope. There was a Native man, too, who sold little boxes made of birchbark and porcupine quills. Arthur Robertson and I used to sit in the red canoe and this man would take us for a ride out to

the raft and back. Then we'd go and tell Mrs. Robertson or the cook or someone how nice he was and he'd stand behind us and smile as though he didn't understand English and then they'd have to buy a box from him. He certainly was smart, because it worked about four times. Then one day they caught on and hid the canoe.

Anyway, that's the sort of thing we did. And we swam too, and I remember a book that Arthur Robertson's nurse read to us. It was about dogs.

Then I had to go away because I'd only been invited for two weeks. I went on to this farm where the family took us every summer when we were children. Bud was already there, and his friend, Teddy Hartley.

I didn't like Teddy Hartley. It was because he had a space between his teeth and he used to spit through it. Once I saw him spit two-and-a-half yards. Bud paced it out. And then he used to whistle through it, too, that space, and it was the kind of whistling that nearly made your ears bleed. That was what I didn't like. But it didn't really matter, because he was Bud's friend, not mine.

So I went by train and Mr. and Mrs. Currie met me in their truck. It was their farm.

Mrs. Currie got me into the front with her while Mr. Currie put my stuff in the back.

"Your mum and dad aren't here, dear, but they'll be up tomorrow. Buddy is here—and his friend."

Grownups were always calling Bud "Buddy." It was all wrong.

I didn't care too much about my parents not being there, except that I'd brought them each one of those birchbark boxes. Inside my mother's there was a set of red stones I'd picked out from where we swam. I thought maybe she'd make a necklace out of them. In my dad's there was an old golf ball, because he played golf. I guess you'd have to say I stole it, because I didn't tell anyone I had it—but it was just lying there on a shelf in Mr. Robertson's boathouse, and he never played golf. At least, I never saw him.

I had these boxes on my lap because I'd thought my mum and dad would be there to meet me, but now that they weren't I put them into the glove compartment of the truck.

We drove to the farm.

Bud and Teddy were riding on the gate, and they waved when we drove past. I couldn't see too well because of the dust but I could hear them shouting. It was something about my dad. I didn't really hear exactly what it was they said, but Mrs. Currie went white as a sheet and said: "Be quiet," to Bud.

Then we were there and the truck stopped. We went inside.

And now—this is where it begins.

After supper, the evening I arrived at the Curries' farm, my brother Bud and his friend Teddy Hartley and I all sat on the front porch. In a hammock.

This is the conversation we had.

BUD: (to me) Are you all right? Did you have a good time at Arthur
    Robertson's place? Did you swim?
ME: (to Bud) Yes.
TEDDY HARTLEY: I've got a feeling I don't like Arthur Robertson.
    Do I know him?
BUD: Kid at school. Neil's age. (He said that as if it were dirty to be my age.)
TEDDY HARTLEY: Thin kid? Very small?
BUD: Thin and small—brainy type. Hey Neil, have you seen Ted spit?
ME: Yes—I have.
TEDDY HARTLEY: When did you see me spit? I never spat for you.

ME: Yes, you did. About three months ago. We were still in school.
  Bud—he did too, and you walked it out, too, didn't you?
BUD: I don't know.
TEDDY HARTLEY: I never spat for you yet! Never!
ME: Two yards and a half.
TEDDY HARTLEY: Can't have been me. I spit four.
ME: Four YARDS!!
TEDDY HARTLEY: Certainly.
BUD: Go ahead and show him. Over the rail.
TEDDY HARTLEY: (Standing up) Okay. Look, Neil. Now watch…
  Come on, WATCH!!
ME: All right—I'm watching.
  (Teddy Hartley spat. It was three yards and a half by Bud's feet.
  I saw Bud mark it myself.)
BUD: Three yards and a half a foot.
TEDDY HARTLEY: Four yards. (Maybe his feet were smaller or
  something.)
BUD: Three-and-foot. Three and *one* foot. No, no. A *half*-a-one.
  Of a foot.
TEDDY HARTLEY: Four.
BUD: Three!
TEDDY HARTLEY: Four! Four! Four!
BUD: One-two-three-and-a-half-a-foot!!
TEDDY HARTLEY: My dad showed me. It's four! He showed me, and
  he knows. My dad knows. He's a mathematical teacher—yes, yes, yes,
  he showed me how to count a yard. I saw him do it. And he knows,
  my dad!!
BUD: Your dad's a crazy man. It's three yards and a half a foot.
TEDDY HARTLEY: (All red in the face and screaming) You called my dad
  a nut! You called my dad a crazy-man-nut-meg! Take it back, you. Bud
  Cable, you take that back.
BUD: Your dad is a matha-nut-ical nutmeg tree.
TEDDY HARTLEY: Then your dad's a…your dad's a…your dad's an Insane!
BUD: Our dad's joined the army.

That was how I found out.
  They went on talking like that for a long time. I got up and left. I
started talking to myself, which is a habit I have.
  "Joined the army? Joined the army? Joined the ARMY! Our dad?"
  Our dad was a salesman. I used to go to his office and watch him selling

things over the phone sometimes. I always used to look for what it was, but I guess they didn't keep it around the office. Maybe they hid it somewhere. Maybe it was too expensive to just leave lying around. But whatever it was, I knew it was important, and so that was one thing that bothered me when Bud said about the army—because I knew that in the army they wouldn't let my dad sit and sell things over any old phone—because in the army you always went in a trench and got hurt or killed. I knew that because my dad had told me himself when my uncle died. My uncle was his brother in the first war, who got hit in his stomach and he died from it a long time afterwards. Long enough, anyway, for me to have known him. He was always in a big white bed, and he gave us candies from a glass jar. That was all I knew—except that it was because of being in the army that he died. His name was Uncle Frank.

So those were the first two things I thought of: my dad not being able to sell anything any more—and then Uncle Frank.

But then it really got bad, because I suddenly remembered that my dad had promised to teach me how to skate that year. He was going to make a rink too, in the backyard. But if he had to go off to some old trench in France, then he'd be too far away. Soldiers always went in trenches—and trenches were always in France. I remember that.

Well, I don't know. Maybe I just couldn't forgive him. He hadn't even told me. He didn't even write it in his letter that he'd sent me at Arthur Robertson's. But he'd told Bud—he'd told Bud, but I was the one he'd promised to show how to skate. And I'd had it all planned how I'd really surprise my dad and turn out to be a skating champion and everything, and now he wouldn't even be there to see.

All because he had to go and sit in some trench.

I don't know how I got there, but I ended up in the barn. I was in the hayloft and I didn't even hear them, I guess. They were looking all over the place for me, because it started to get dark.

I don't know whether you're afraid of the dark, but I'll tell you right now, I am. At least, I am if I have to move around in it. If I can just sit still, then I'm all right. At least, if you sit still you know where you are. And that's awful. You never know what you're going to step on next and I always thought it would be a duck. I don't like ducks—especially in the dark or if you stepped on them.

Anyway, I was in the hayloft in the barn and I heard them calling out— "Neil, Neil"—and "Where are you?" But I made up my mind right then I wasn't going to answer. For one thing, if I did, then I'd have to go down to them in the dark—and maybe I'd step on something. And for another, I didn't really want to see anyone anyway.

It was then that I got this idea about my father. I thought that maybe if I stayed hidden for long enough, then he wouldn't join the army. Don't ask me why—right now I couldn't tell you that—but in those days it made sense. If I hid then he wouldn't go away. Maybe it would be because he'd stay looking for me or something.

The trouble was that my dad wasn't even there that night, and that meant that I either had to wait in the hayloft till he came the next day— or else that I had to go down now, and then hide again tomorrow. I decided to stay where I was because there were some ducks at the bottom of the ladder. I couldn't see them but I could tell they were there.

I stayed there all night. I slept most of the time. Every once in a while they'd wake me up by calling out "Neil! Neil!"—but I never answered.

I never knew a night that was so long, except maybe once when I was in the hospital. When I slept I seemed to sleep for a long time, but it never came to morning. They kept waking me up but it was never time.

Then it was.

I saw that morning through a hole in the roof of the hayloft. The sun-light came in through cracks between the boards and it was all dusty; the sunlight, I mean.

They were up pretty early that morning, even for farmers. There seemed to be a lot more people than I remembered—and there were two or three cars and a truck I'd never seen before, too. And I saw Mrs. Currie holding onto Bud with one hand and Teddy Hartley with the other. I remember thinking, "If I was down there, how could she hold onto me if she's only got two hands and Bud and Teddy Hartley to look after?" And I thought that right then she must be pretty glad I wasn't around.

I wondered what they were all doing. Mr. Currie was standing in the middle of a lot of men and he kept pointing out the scenery around the farm. I imagined what he was saying. There was a big woods behind the house and a cherry and plum tree orchard that would be good to point out to his friends. I could tell they were his friends from the way they were listening. What I couldn't figure out was why they were all up so early— and why they had Bud and Teddy Hartley up, too.

Then there was a police car. I suppose it came from Orillia or some-where. That was the biggest town near where the farm was. Orillia.

When the police got out of their car, they went up to Mr. Currie. There were four of them. They all talked for quite a long time and then everyone started going out in all directions. It looked to me as though Bud and Teddy

Hartley wanted to go, too, but Mrs. Currie made them go in the house. She practically had to drag Bud. It looked as if he was crying and I wondered why he should do that.

Then one of the police officers came into the barn. He was all alone. I stayed very quiet, because I wasn't going to let anything keep me from going through with my plan about my dad. Not even a police officer.

He urinated against the wall inside the door. It was sort of funny, because he kept turning around to make sure no one saw him, and he didn't know I was there. Then he did up his pants and stood in the middle of the floor under the haylofts.

"Hey! Neil!"

That was the police officer.

He said it so suddenly that it scared me. I nearly fell off from where I was, it scared me so much. And I guess maybe he saw me, because he started right up the ladder at me.

"How did you know my name?"

I said that in a whisper.

"They told me."

"Oh."

"Have you been here all night?"

"Yes."

"Don't you realize that *everyone* has been looking for you all over the place? Nobody's even been to sleep."

That sort of frightened me—but it was all right, because he smiled when he said it.

Then he stuck his head out of this window that was there to let the air in (so that the barn wouldn't catch on fire)—and he yelled down, "He's all right—I've found him! He's up here."

And I said: "What did you go and do that for? Now you've ruined everything."

He smiled again and said, "I had to stop them all going off to look for you. Now,"—as he sat down beside me—"do you want to tell me what is it you're doing up here?"

"No."

I think that sort of set him back a couple of years, because he didn't say anything for a minute—except "Oh."

Then I thought maybe I had to have something to tell the others anyway, so I might as well make it up for him right now.

"I fell asleep," I said.

"When—last night?"

"Yes."

I looked at him. I wondered if I could trust a guy who did that against walls, when all you had to do was go in the house.

"Why did you come up here in the first place?" he said.

I decided I could trust him because I remembered once when I did the same thing. Against the wall.

So I told him.

"I want to hide on my dad," I said.

"Why do you want to do that? And besides, Mrs. Currie said your parents weren't even here."

"Yes, but he's coming today."

"But why hide on him? Don't you like him, or something?"

"Sure I do," I said.

I thought about it.

"But he's...he's...Do you know if it's true, my dad's joined the army?"

"I dunno. Maybe. There's a war on, you know."

"Well, that's why I hid."

But he laughed.

"Is that why you hid? Because of the war?"

"Because of my dad."

"You don't need to hide because of the war—the Germans aren't coming over here, you know."

"But it's not that. It's my dad." I could have told you he wouldn't understand.

I was trying to think of what to say next when Mrs. Currie came into the barn. She stood down below.

"Is he up there, officer? Is he all right?"

"Yes, ma'am, I've got him. He's fine."

"Neil dear, what happened? Why don't you come down and tell us what happened to you?"

Then I decided that I'd really go all out. I had to, because I could tell they weren't going to—it was just *obvious* that these people weren't going to understand me and take my story about my dad and the army and everything.

"Somebody chased me."

The police officer looked sort of shocked and I could hear Mrs. Currie take in her breath.

"Somebody chased you, eh?"

"Yes."

"Who?"

I had to think fast.

"Some man. But he's gone now."

I thought I'd better say he was gone, so that they wouldn't start worrying.

"Officer, why don't you bring him down here? Then we can talk."

"All right, ma'am. Come on, Neil, we'll go down and have some breakfast."

They didn't seem to believe me about that man I made up.

We went over to the ladder.

I looked down. A lot of hay stuck out so that I couldn't see the floor.

"Are there any ducks down there?"

"No, dear, you can come down—it's all right."

She was lying, though. There was a great big duck right next to her. I think it's awfully silly to tell a lie like that. I mean, if the duck is standing right there it doesn't even make sense, does it?

But I went down anyway and she made the duck go away.

When we went out, the police officer held my hand. His hand had some sweat on it but it was a nice hand, with hair on the back. I liked that. My dad didn't have that on his hand.

Then we ate breakfast with all those people who'd come to look for me. At least, they ate. I just sat.

After breakfast, Mr. and Mrs. Currie took me upstairs to the sitting room. It was upstairs because the kitchen was in the cellar.

All I remember about that was a vase that had a potted plant in it. This vase was made of putty and into the putty Mrs. Currie had stuck all kinds of stones and pennies and old bits of glass and things. You could look at this for hours and never see the same kind of stone or glass twice. I don't remember the plant.

All I remember about what they said was that they told me I should never do it again. That routine.

Then they told me my mother and my dad would be up that day around lunch time.

What they were really sore about was losing their sleep, and then all those people coming. I was sorry about that—but you can't very well go down and make an announcement about it, so I didn't.

At twelve o'clock, I went and sat in Mr. Currie's truck. It was in the barn. I took out those two boxes I'd put in the glove compartment and looked at them. I tried to figure out what my dad would do with an old box like that in the army. And he'd probably never play another game of golf as long as he lived. Not in the army, anyway. Maybe he'd use the box for his bullets or something.

Then I counted the red stones I was going to give my mother. I kept seeing them around her neck and how pretty they'd be. She had a dress they'd be just perfect with. Blue. The only thing I was worried about was how to get a hole in them so you could put them on a string. There wasn't much sense in having beads without a string—not if you were going to wear them, anyway—or your mother was.

And it was then that they came.

I heard their car drive up outside and I went and looked from behind the barn door. My father wasn't wearing a uniform yet like I'd thought he would be. I began to think maybe he really didn't want me to know about it. I mean, he hadn't written or anything, and now he was just wearing an old blazer and some grey pants. It made me remember.

I went back and sat down in the truck again. I didn't know what to do. I just sat there with those stones in my hand.

Then I heard someone shout, "Neil!"

I went and looked. Mr. and Mrs. Currie were standing with my parents by the car—and I saw Bud come running out of the house, and then Teddy Hartley. Teddy Hartley sort of hung back, though. He was the kind of person who's only polite if there are grownups around him. He sure knew how to pull the wool over their eyes, because he'd even combed his hair. Wildroot-cream-oil-Charlie.

Then I noticed that they were talking very seriously and my mother put her hand above her eyes and looked around. I guess she was looking for me. Then my dad started toward the barn.

I went and hid behind the truck. I wasn't quite sure yet what I was going to do, but I certainly wasn't going to go up and throw my arms around his neck or anything.

"Neil. Are you in there, son?"

My dad spoke that very quietly. Then I heard the door being pushed open, and some chicken had to get out of the way, because I heard it making that awful noise chickens make when you surprise them doing something. They sure can get excited over nothing—chickens.

I took a quick look behind me. There was a door there that led into the part of the barn where the haylofts were and where I'd been all night. I decided to make a dash for it. But I had to ward off my father first—and so I threw that stone.

I suppose I'll have to admit that I meant to hit him. It wouldn't be much sense if I tried to fool you about that. I wanted to hit him because when I stood up behind the truck and saw him then I suddenly got mad. I thought about how he hadn't written me, or anything.

It hit him on the hand.

He turned right around because he wasn't sure what it was or where it came from. And before I ran, I just caught a glimpse of his face. He'd seen me and he sure looked peculiar. I guess that now I'll never forget his face and how he looked at me right then. I think it was that he looked as though he might cry or something. But I knew he wouldn't do that, because he never did.

Then I ran.

From the loft I watched them in the yard. My dad was rubbing his hands together and I guess maybe where I'd hit him it was pretty sore. My mother took off her handkerchief that she had round her neck and put it on his hand. Then I guess he'd told them what I'd done, because this time they *all* started toward the barn.

I didn't know what to do then. I counted out the stones I had left and there were about fifteen of them. There was the golf ball, too.

I didn't want to throw stones at all of them. I certainly didn't want to hit my mother—and I hoped that they wouldn't send her in first. I thought then how I'd be all right if they sent in Teddy Hartley first. I didn't mind the thought of throwing at him, I'll tell you that much.

But my dad came first.

I had a good view of where he came from. He came in through the part where the truck was parked, because I guess he thought I was still there. And then he came on into the part where I was now—in the hayloft.

He stood by the door.

"Neil."

I could only just see his head and shoulders—the rest of him was hidden by the edge of the loft.

"Neil, aren't you even going to explain what you're angry about?"

I thought for a minute and then I didn't answer him after all. I looked at him, though. He looked worried.

"What do you want us to do?"

I sat still.

"Neil?"

Since I didn't answer, he started back out the door—I guess to talk to my mother or someone.

I hit his back with another stone. I had to make sure he knew I was there.

He turned around at me.

"Neil, what's the matter? I want to know what's the matter."

He almost fooled me, but not quite. I thought that perhaps he really didn't know for a minute—but after taking a look at him I decided that he did know, all right. I mean, there he was in that blue blazer and everything—just as if he hadn't joined the army at all.

So I threw again and this time it really hit him in the face.

He didn't do anything—he just stood there. It really scared me. Then my mother came in, but he made her go back.

I thought about my rink, and how I wouldn't have it. I thought about being in the fifth grade that year and how I'd skipped from Grade Three. And I thought about the Native man who'd sold those boxes that I had down in the truck.

"Neil—I'm going to come up."

You could tell he really would, too, from his voice.

I got the golf ball ready.

To get to me he had to disappear for a minute while he crossed under the loft and then when he climbed the ladder. I decided to change my place while he was out of sight. I began to think that was pretty clever and that maybe I'd be pretty good at that war stuff myself. Field Marshal Cable.

I put myself into a little trench of hay and piled some up in front of me. When my dad came up over the top of the ladder, he wouldn't even see me and then I'd have a good chance to aim at him.

The funny thing was that at that moment I'd forgotten why I was against him. I got so mixed up in all that Field Marshal stuff that I really forgot all about my dad and the army and everything. I was just trying to figure out how I could get him before he saw me—and that was all.

I got further down in the hay and then he was there.

He was out of breath and his face was all sweaty, and where I'd hit him there was blood. And then he put his hand with my mother's hankie up to his face to wipe it. And he sort of bit it (the handkerchief). It was as if he was confused or something. I remember thinking he looked then just like I'd felt my face go when Bud had said our dad had joined the army. You know how you look around with your eyes from side to side as though maybe you'll find the answer to it somewhere near you? You never do find it, but you always look anyway, just in case.

Anyway, that's how he was just then, and it sort of threw me. I had that feeling again that maybe he didn't know what this was all about. But then, he had to know, didn't he? Because he'd done it.

I had the golf ball ready in my right hand and one of those stones in the other. He walked toward me.

I missed with the golf ball and got him with the stone.

And he fell down. He really fell down. He didn't say anything—he didn't even say "ouch," like I would have—he just fell down.

In the hay.

I didn't go out just yet. I sat and looked at him. And I listened.

Nothing.

Do you know, there wasn't a sound in that whole place? It was as if everything had stopped because they knew what had happened.

My dad just lay there and we waited for what would happen next.

It was me.

I mean, I made the first noise.

I said: "Dad?"

But nobody answered—not even my mother.

So I said it louder. *"Dad?"*

It was just as if they'd all gone away and left me with him, all alone.

He sure looked strange lying there—so quiet and everything. I didn't know what to do.

"Dad?"

I went over on my hands and knees.

Then suddenly they all came in. I just did what I thought of first. I guess it was because they scared me—coming like that when it was so quiet.

I got all the stones out of my pockets and threw them, one by one, as they came through the door. I stood up to do it. I saw them all running through the door, and I threw every stone, even at my mother.

And then I fell down. I fell down beside my dad and pushed him over on his back because he'd fallen on his stomach. It was like he was asleep.

They came up then and I don't remember much of that. Somebody picked me up, and there was the smell of perfume and my eyes hurt and I got something in my throat and nearly choked to death and I could hear a lot of talking. And somebody was whispering, too. And then I felt myself being carried down and there was the smell of oil and gasoline and some chickens had to be got out of the way again and then there was sunlight.

Then my mother just sat with me, and I guess I cried for a long time. In the cherry and plum tree orchard—and she seemed to understand because she said that he would tell me all about it and that he hadn't written me because he didn't want to scare me when I was all alone at Arthur Robertson's.

And then Bud came.

My mother said that he should go away for a while. But he said: "I brought something" and she said: "What is it, then?" and now I remember where I got that worm in my handkerchief that I told you about.

It was from Bud.

He said to me that if I wanted to, he'd take me fishing on the lake just before the sun went down. He said that was a good time. And he gave me that worm because he'd found it.

So my mother took it and put it in my hankie and Bud looked at me for a minute and then went away.

The worst part was when I saw my dad again.

My mother took me to the place where he was sitting in the sun and we just watched each other for a long time.

Then he said: "Neil, your mother wants to take our picture because I'm going away tomorrow to Ottawa for a couple of weeks, and she thought I'd like a picture to take with me."

He lit a cigarette and then he said: "I would, too, you know, like that picture."

And I sort of said: "All right."

So they called to Bud, and my mother went to get her camera.

But before Bud came and before my mother got back, we were alone for about ten hours. It was awful.

I couldn't think of anything and I guess he couldn't either. I had a good look at him, though.

He looked just like he does right there in that picture. You can see where the stone hit him on his right cheek—and the one that knocked him out is the one over the eye.

Right then the thing never got settled. Not in words, anyway. I was still thinking about that rink and everything—and my dad hadn't said anything about the army yet.

I wish I hadn't done it. Thrown those stones and everything. It wasn't his fault he had to go.

For another thing, I was sorry about the stones because I knew I wouldn't find any more like them—but I did throw them, and that's that.

They both got those little boxes, though—I made sure of that. And in one there was a string of red beads from Orillia and in the other there was a photograph.

There still is. ◆

1. Responding to the Story

a. Whose war does the author refer to in the title? Support your view with examples from the story.

b. With a small group, discuss whether you think the way Neil reacts to his father leaving is typical of a ten-year-old boy. Why do you think he throws the stones?

c. Like most short stories, the action builds up to an event that's the high point or **climax**. What is the climax of "War"? Explain whether you think the conflict is resolved at the end.

> The **climax** of a story is the greatest moment of intensity.

2. Writing Explore Personal Feelings

Have you ever felt so strongly about something that you lost control of your emotions or the way you acted? What event or situation in your life made you lose control? Jot down in note form what happened, how you felt at the time, how you felt afterwards, and how the situation was resolved.

Use your notes to write a story about that incident. You might use a structure similar to "War." The beginning could introduce the main characters and the problem or situation. The middle section could explore how everyone tried to deal with this problem. The climax could occur when you (or your character) lose control. The end could briefly describe how everything was resolved.

3. Literature Studies Conversation in Stories

Reread the conversation between Bud, Teddy, and Neil that is in the form of a script. Rewrite it using paragraphs and quotations. Try to add some descriptive information about how the characters are speaking and what they might be doing and thinking. Compare the two versions. Which one is easier to read? Which one gives the most information about what's happening in the story? Why do you think the author chose this format to write this scene?

Self-Assessment: When you write a story, how do you write conversations between characters? Could your style be improved? How?

It's the 1920s, and Dublin's streets have become a battlefield in Ireland's struggle for independence.

The Sniper

Short Story
by Liam O'Flaherty

GOALS AT A GLANCE

- Assume a role to write a factual report.
- Analyse the use of vivid verbs.

The long June twilight faded into night. Dublin lay enveloped in darkness but for the dim light of the moon that shone through fleecy clouds, casting a pale light as of approaching dawn over the streets and the dark waters of the Liffey. Around the beleaguered Four Courts the heavy guns roared. Here and there through the city, machine guns and rifles broke the silence of the night, spasmodically, like dogs barking on lone farms. Republicans and Free Staters were waging civil war.

On a rooftop near O'Connell Bridge, a Republican sniper lay watching. Beside him lay his rifle and over his shoulders were slung a pair of field glasses. His face was the face of a student, thin and ascetic, but his eyes had the cold gleam of the fanatic. They were deep and thoughtful, the eyes of a man who is used to looking at death.

He was eating a sandwich hungrily. He had eaten nothing since morning. He had been too excited to eat. He finished the sandwich, and taking a flask of whisky from his pocket, he took a short draught. Then he returned the flask to his pocket. He paused for a moment, considering whether he should risk a smoke. It was dangerous. The flash might be seen in the darkness, and there were enemies watching. He decided to take the risk.

Placing a cigarette between his lips, he struck a match, inhaled the smoke hurriedly, and put out the light. Almost immediately, a bullet flattened itself against the parapet of the roof. The sniper took another whiff and put out the cigarette. Then he swore softly and crawled away to the left.

Cautiously he raised himself and peered over the parapet. There was a flash and a bullet whizzed over his head. He dropped immediately. He had seen the flash. It came from the opposite side of the street.

He rolled over the roof to a chimney stack in the rear, and slowly drew himself up behind it, until his eyes were level with the top of the parapet. There was nothing to be seen—just the dim outline of the opposite housetop against the blue sky. His enemy was under cover.

Just then an armoured car came across the bridge and advanced slowly up the street. It stopped on the opposite side of the street, forty-five metres ahead. The sniper could hear the dull panting of the motor.

His heart beat faster. It was an enemy car. He wanted to fire, but he knew it was useless. His bullets would never pierce the steel that covered the grey monster.

Then round the corner of a side street came an old woman, her head covered by a tattered shawl. She began to talk to the man in the turret of the car. She was pointing to the roof where the sniper lay. An informer.

The turret opened. A man's head and shoulders appeared, looking toward the sniper. The sniper raised his rifle and fired. The head fell heavily on the turret wall. The woman darted toward the side street. The sniper fired again. The woman whirled round and fell with a shriek into the gutter.

Suddenly from the opposite roof a shot rang out and the sniper dropped his rifle with a curse. The rifle clattered to the roof. The sniper thought the noise would wake the dead. He stopped to pick the rifle up. He couldn't lift it. His forearm was dead. "I'm hit," he muttered.

Dropping flat onto the roof, he crawled back to the parapet. With his left hand he felt the injured right forearm. The blood was oozing through the sleeve of his coat. There was no pain—just a deadened sensation, as if the arm had been cut off.

Quickly he drew his knife from his pocket, opened it on the breastwork of the parapet, and ripped open the sleeve. There was a small hole where the bullet had entered. On the other side there was no hole. The bullet had lodged in the bone. It must have fractured it. He bent the arm below the wound. The arm bent back easily. He ground his teeth to overcome the pain.

Then taking out his field dressing, he ripped open the packet with his knife. He broke the neck of the iodine bottle and let the bitter fluid drip into the wound. A paroxysm of pain swept through him. He placed the cotton wadding over the wound and wrapped the dressing over it. He tied the ends with his teeth.

Then he lay still against the parapet, and, closing his eyes, he made an effort of will to overcome the pain.

In the street beneath, all was still. The armoured car had retired speedily over the bridge, with the machine gunner's head hanging lifeless over the turret. The woman's corpse lay still in the gutter.

The sniper lay still for a long time nursing his wounded arm and planning escape. Morning must not find him wounded on the roof. The enemy on the opposite roof covered his escape. He must kill that enemy and he could not use his rifle. He had only a revolver to do it. Then he thought of a plan.

Taking off his cap, he placed it over the muzzle of his rifle. Then he pushed the rifle slowly upward over the parapet, until the cap was visible from the opposite side of thc street. Almost immediately, there was a report, and a bullet pierced the centre of the cap. The sniper slanted the rifle forward. The cap slipped down into the street. Then catching the rifle in the middle, the sniper dropped his left hand over the roof and let it hang, lifelessly. After a few moments he let the rifle drop to the street. Then he sank to the roof, dragging his hand with him.

Crawling quickly to the left, he peered up at the corner of the roof. His ruse had succeeded. The other sniper, seeing the cap and rifle fall, thought that he had killed his man. He was now standing before a row of chimney pots, looking across, with his head clearly silhouetted against the western sky.

The Republican sniper smiled and lifted his revolver above the edge of the parapet. The distance was about forty-five metres—a hard shot in the dim light, and his right arm was paining him like a thousand angry knives. He took a steady aim. His hand trembled with eagerness. Pressing his lips together, he took a deep breath through his nostrils and fired. He was almost deafened with the report and his arm shook with the recoil.

Then when the smoke cleared he peered across and uttered a cry of joy. His enemy had been hit. He was reeling over the parapet in his death agony. He struggled to keep his feet, but he was slowly falling forward, as if in a dream. The rifle fell from his grasp, hit the parapet, fell over, bounded off the pole of a barber's shop beneath and then clattered on the pavement.

Then the dying man on the roof crumpled up and fell forward. The body turned over and over in space and hit the ground with a dull thud. Then it lay still.

The sniper looked at his enemy falling and he shuddered. The lust of battle died in him. He became bitten by remorse. The sweat stood out in beads on his forehead. Weakened by his wound and the long summer day of fasting and watching on the roof, he revolted from the sight of the shattered mass of his dead enemy. His teeth chattered, he began to gibber to himself, cursing the war, cursing himself, cursing everybody.

He looked at the smoking revolver in his hand, and with an oath he hurled it to the roof at his feet. The revolver went off with the concussion and the bullet whizzed past the sniper's head. He was frightened back to his senses by the shock. His nerves steadied. The cloud of fear scattered from his mind and he laughed.

Taking the whisky flask from his pocket, he emptied it at a draught. He felt reckless under the influence of the spirit. He decided to leave the roof now and look for his company commander, to report. Everywhere around was quiet. There was not much danger in going through the streets. He picked up his revolver and put it in his pocket. Then he crawled down through the skylight to the house underneath.

When the sniper reached the laneway on the street level, he felt a sudden curiosity as to the identity of the enemy sniper whom he had killed. He decided that he was a good shot, whoever he was. He wondered did he know him. Perhaps he had been in his own company before the split in the army. He decided to risk going over to have a look at him. He peered around the corner into O'Connell Street. In the upper part of the street there was a heavy firing, but around here all was quiet.

The sniper darted across the street. A machine gun tore up the ground around him with a hail of bullets, but he escaped. He threw himself face downward beside the corpse. The machine gun stopped.

Then the sniper turned over the dead boy and looked into his brother's face. ◆

1. RESPONDING TO THE STORY

a. Reread the first paragraph. What details in the author's description of the setting establish the tone or atmosphere of the story?

b. What message about this civil war is Liam O'Flaherty trying to convey? How does his message compare to the theme in "War"?

c. List words and phrases the author uses to describe the sniper and what he's doing. Write your own description of him, using some or all of these words.

d. The sniper is the only character the author describes in great deal. Why do you think the author chose to do that?

e. Were you surprised by the ending? Why or why not? Did you find it a powerful ending?

f. Do you think such a story could occur in Canada? Give reasons for your opinion.

2. WRITING A FACTUAL REPORT

Imagine you are the main character in "The Sniper." You've just returned to your company and have been asked to write a report about what happened. List the events in the story in the order they occurred. Use a complete sentence for each event. Because this is an official report, leave out how you felt or what you thought—just include the facts as you saw them.

3. EDITOR'S DESK VIVID VERBS

Words are all an author can use to create images and events in the reader's mind. Verbs are especially useful because they help the reader to picture the action. Here are two examples from "The Sniper." The verbs are underlined.

- Almost immediately, a bullet <u>flattened</u> itself against the parapet of the roof.
- Then taking out his field dressing, he <u>ripped</u> open the packet with his knife.

Why is the first example more vivid than simply writing "...a bullet hit the parapet of the roof"? What does "ripped" in the second example tell you about the state of the sniper's mind?

Choose a short story from your writing portfolio that you would like to revise. Rewrite it using verbs that create a clear and direct image. Keep in mind, however, that too many vivid verbs can make a story difficult to read or make the language sound too forced and artificial. Look over your rewrite. Is it clear? Is it better or worse than your first version?

STRATEGIES

4. ORAL LANGUAGE DEBATE AN ISSUE

Although Ireland has gained independence since the events of the story, Northern Ireland continues to be a place of conflict, which can be viewed in at least two ways:

- Northern Ireland should remain separate from Ireland.
- Ireland should become *one* country without a north and south division.

Work in a group to debate these two opposing viewpoints. First, use the print and media resources in your library to research this conflict. Then decide on a statement to debate; for example, *Northern Ireland should remain a separate country.* Divide into two groups, one for and one against, and then prepare to debate with your classmates. Use the following guidelines as you prepare:

- review the facts in your research
- think about your opinion or the position you'll be taking
- prepare a persuasive argument about two minutes in length
- work co-operatively with others on your team to develop three arguments that support, but don't repeat, each other
- revise your argument
- memorize and practise delivering your argument
- during the debate listen carefully to the opposing team's arguments
- prepare your *rebuttal* (your response to the argument of an opposing team member)

SELF-ASSESSMENT: Evaluate the debate process you've gone through and think about these questions:

- Did you prepare a clear and logical argument?
- Did you present your argument clearly?
- Did you listen carefully to other arguments?
- Did you present a rebuttal based on an opposing argument?

Blue Against White

Short Story by Jeannette C. Armstrong

Lena walked up the steep hill toward her mother's house. She could see the bright blue door. It stood out against the stark white of the house. It was the only house with a door like that on the hill. All the houses on that part of the reserve looked a lot alike, the colours ranging from mostly white to off-white to grey, and a few with light pastel colours. All the doors matched the houses.

Thinking of it now, Lena realized that it was funny how she had always thought of it as her mother's house rather than her father's house, though it had been his idea to paint the door a bright blue. He had said that the houses up there up on the hill all looked too much alike. He had said that their home would be easy to see because of the door. He was right, but there was a question that had always been silent: "Who would have a problem?" She had known that all the Natives in a thousand-kilometre radius knew each other and that they didn't find their way to each other by the description of their houses.

As she walked toward the house, she realized that she had kept that door in her mind all the years she had been away. It had been there as always, a bright blue against the white. A blue barrier against the cold north wind. A cool blue shield against the summer heat. She remembered having hated the door and having wished it would just be white like the rest of the house. But while she was away, it had been the part of the house that had been a constant clear image. Behind that door, warm smells and laughter mixed into a distinct impression of the way it was back home. Her mother, long braids tied together in the back, smiled at her from behind that door.

GOALS AT A GLANCE

■ Analyse symbols.
■ Create a photo essay.

Now, she walked up the hill toward the house carrying the one bag that held her things. She felt light, weightless, and somehow insubstantial like the last fluffseeds still clinging shakily to the milkweeds that lined the narrow dirt road gutted with deep, dry ruts. In this country, the summer rains left cracked mud tracks which froze in the fall and stayed hidden under the snow and ice in winter.

At this moment, she felt she could easily be lifted to float up and away from those deep earth gashes, to move across the land with the dry fall drifting of seeds and leaves. She had hated this dirt road and the mud in the spring and the dust in the summer, the ruts in the fall, and the ungraded snow in the winter. She had mostly hated the dry milkweeds crowding together everywhere. As always, on this road the lumps of soil were uneven and slow to travel over. She felt like turning and bolting back to the bus to catch it before it could leave her here, but running was hard on this broken ground.

The door seemed to loom ahead of her, though the house was no taller than the rest. She hated the way all the cheap government houses on the row facing the road were so close together and had paint peeling and dry weedy yards with several mangy dogs. She turned to look back at the road winding steeply down to the crossroad where the bus stopped momentarily to drop off or pick up people from the reserve. The freeway stretched away into a hazy purple distance where night was beginning to shadow the land. Only the white line dividing those coming from those going was visible after a certain point. The red lights of the bus were fading straight into that shadow line between sky, asphalt, and the darkened earth.

Turning, she faced the rest of the climb. A single black crow cawed at her from its perch on the steeple cross of the village church, raising a ruckus in the quiet. It screeched and flapped its wings, dove over her mother's house, and then flew lazily overhead, looking down at her as it passed, flying over the dirt road toward the crossroad in the direction of the twilight.

She watched the crow disappear into dark blue. She knew his name from the old stories. She wanted to laugh and say it. She knew he hung around only in the summer months and then flew away when the shadows in the fall grew long and the days short. She wanted to say, "You, old pretender, you don't fool me. You're not going to preach to me, too, are you? You're no smarter than me!" Instead, she found tears wetting her cheeks.

Her tears brought the memory of a dream from the week before she had started the long bus ride home. In her dream, she had been in a large building with many bright lights and shiny reflections. Although there was a lot of noise, she couldn't see anyone. She felt totally alone as she walked down a long white hallway. She remembered looking, one by one, at the doors she passed, feeling like the only thing behind each one was a patch of sky. In the dream, she remembered feeling something like dizziness as she saw how many doors there were and how they seemed to stretch into darkness on and on without end. She recalled running and stumbling past the doors and calling out. When she awoke, she had been crying.

She was almost at the top of the hill now. She stopped and put down her bag. A couple of reserve dogs barked at her and then wagged their tails, trotting toward her, making greeting noises in their throats. She looked down at the one that was obviously a lady dog with her sagging dry milk sacs and she stroked her ear. She thought of the city she had left behind and said, "Mamma dogs don't just walk around free there, you know. You're pretty lucky to be here." The lady dog sat down and thumped her tail against some of the weeds, sending puffs of seed floating with each excited wave.

Behind the houses farther up into the dark hills, she heard the high, faraway yipping of a coyote. She saw the dogs' ears perk up. She saw the way their eyes glowed a deeper orange as they forgot her and pointed their noses toward the hills above them, a low, crooning echo rumbling deep in their throats. She, too, looked up there and whispered, "How are you, brothers?" in the language. She knew them, too.

She thought of that one coyote in the papers, in some city, that had got trapped in a hallway after coming in from an alley door. How somebody mistaking it for a dog had opened an elevator for it and how it had ridden to the roof of an apartment building and ran around crazily, and then jumped to its death rather than run back through the elevator door and ride back down into the hallway and out the alley door. She had known that it hadn't been a matter of animal stupidity, because a coyote always remembered where it had come from. She had secretly known that it had more to do with the quick elevator door and the long lonely ride up to the top. She thought of the coyotes hanging around in the cities these days. Nobody wanted them there, so nobody made friends with them, but once in a while they made the papers when they did something wrong or showed up, trotting along Broadway, cool as could be.

Lena thought about all the time she had spent away from this place of hard, cracked earth, seed pods, and clean coyote prints in the new snow up in the hills. She looked up at the bright blue surface directly in front of her, waiting to open, and felt the bone-aching, deep tiredness of long journeys over the hard even surface of freeways into alley and white hallways. As she reached for the doorknob she looked down and realized that the freeway's white line and the mud ruts ended here, right at her mother's door. The door that her dad had painted bright blue so that it stood out clearly against the white. ◆

1. RESPONDING TO THE STORY

a. Do you think Lena is happy or not to be returning home? Use examples from the story to support your answer.

b. The image of a door keeps repeating itself in this story. List words and phrases the author uses about doors.

c. The "Blue" in the title is the colour of Lena's parents' door. What does "White" represent? Why do you think the author uses these two contrasting colours in the story's title?

d. Write a paragraph describing how Lena feels about the differences between living in the city and living on the reserve. Use examples from the story to support your ideas.

e. Think of an incident when you were young that still seems vivid to you. Briefly describe it. Why do you still remember what happened?

2. STORY CRAFT ANALYSE SYMBOLS

Use some of the examples you listed in **b** to describe what you think the "door" represents in the story. What does a "door" symbolize to you? What other **symbols** are used in the story? What do you think the symbols mean to Lena? What do they represent to you?

> A **symbol** is a person, place, thing, or event that stands for or represents something else. For example, a flag is a symbol of a nation.

SELF-ASSESSMENT: Reread some of your short stories. Did you use symbols? If so, what are some examples? Did you consciously or unconsciously use these symbols in your writing? Do you think symbols are an important part of a good story? Why or why not?

3. VISUAL COMMUNICATION PHOTO ESSAY

Jeannette Armstrong's story can be seen in the mind's eye as a series of vivid photos that bring back childhood memories. Create a collection of photos from your family albums which represent your most vivid childhood memories. Try to include photos with a symbolic meaning or strong colours. Arrange these images and give the photo essay a title. Discuss your photo essay with friends and family members.

What do you think: does this princess possess the key to happiness?

SVAYAMVARA*

Short, Short Story
by Sunita Namjoshi

Once upon a time there was a little princess who was good at whistling. "Don't whistle," said her mother. "Don't whistle," said her father, but the child was good at it and went on whistling. Years went by and she became a woman. By this time, she whistled beautifully. Her parents grieved. "What man will marry a whistling woman?" said her mother dolefully. "Well," said her father, "we will have to make the best of it. I will offer half my kingdom and the princess in marriage to any man who can beat her at whistling." The king's offer was duly proclaimed, and soon the palace was jammed with suitors whistling. It was very noisy. Most were terrible and a few were good, but the princess was better and beat them easily. The king was displeased, but the princess said, "Never mind, father. Now let me set a test and perhaps some good will come of it." Then she turned to the suitors, "Do you acknowledge that you were beaten fairly?" "No," they all roared, all except one, "we think it was magic or some sort of trick." But one said, "Yes." "Yes," he said, "I was beaten fairly." The princess smiled and turning to her father she pointed to this man. "If he will have me," she said, "I will marry him." ◆

---

*Svayamvara: the choosing of a husband by the bride herself. (Sanskrit dictionary)

GOALS AT A GLANCE

■ Respond critically.
■ Write an advice column.

1. RESPONDING TO THE STORY

a. The way "Svayamvara" is written is different from most story formats. What is different about it? Why do you think the author chose this way to write the story?

b. Explain why "Svayamvara" can be described as an updated fairy tale.

c. What type of husband are the king and queen looking for? What type of husband is the princess looking for?

d. If whistling were to be considered a symbol in this story, what would it stand for?

e. What is the message of the story? Do you agree with it? Why or why not?

2. MEDIA MAKER WRITE AN ADVICE COLUMN

Some newspapers have advice columns. Collect some examples and note the way they are written. Write an imaginary letter to one of these columns asking for advice on how to find a good husband or wife. Exchange letters with a partner and write a response to your partner's letter. Does your partner agree with what you have written? Do you agree with your partner's answer? Discuss which is easier, to give advice or accept it from others?

As you develop your letter consider the following suggestions:

- Begin by addressing the expert; for example, "Dear Mr. Know-How."
- Keep the letter as brief as possible. Explain the situation or problem, describe how you feel about it, and then ask for advice.
- You could end by restating the problem.

To write the response to your partner's letter, think about the tone of the writer's request. Is it serious or humourous? You should respond in the same tone. Offer your opinion of the problem, and give some practical advice.

*You're soaking wet,
it's fifty below, and
you've just lost
your last match...*

To Build a Fire

Short Story by Jack London

Day had broken cold and grey, exceedingly cold and grey, when the man turned aside from the main Yukon trail and climbed the high earth-bank, where a dim and little-travelled trail led eastward through the fat spruce timber-land. It was a steep bank, and he paused for breath at the top, excusing the act to himself by looking at his watch. It was nine o'clock. There was no sun nor hint of sun, though there was not a cloud in the sky. It was a clear day, and yet there seemed an intangible pall over the face of things, a subtle gloom that made the day dark, and that was due to the absence of sun. This fact did not worry the man. He was used to the lack of sun. It had been days since he had seen the sun, and he knew that a few more days must pass before that cheerful orb, due south, would just peep above the skyline and dip immediately from view.

The man flung a look back along the way he had come. The Yukon River lay a mile wide and hidden under three feet of ice. On top of this ice there were as many feet of snow. It was all pure white, rolling in gentle undulations where the ice-jams of the freeze-up had formed. North and south, as far as his eye could see, it was unbroken white, save for a dark hairline that curved and twisted from around the spruce-covered island to the south, and that curved and twisted away into the north, where it disappeared behind another spruce-covered island. This dark hairline was the trail—the main trail—that led south five hundred miles to the Chilcoot Pass, Dyea, and salt water; and that led north seventy miles to Dawson, and still on to the north a thousand miles to Nulato, and finally to St. Michael on the Bering Sea, a thousand miles and half a thousand more.

GOALS AT A GLANCE

■ Develop an essay.
■ Research and evaluate information.

99

But all this—the mysterious, far-reaching hairline trail, the absence of sun from the sky, the tremendous cold, and the strangeness and weirdness of it all—made no impression on the man. It was not because he was long used to it. He was a newcomer in the land, a *cheechako*, and this was his first winter. The trouble with him was that he was without imagination. He was quick and alert in the things of life, but only in the things, and not in the significances. Fifty degrees below zero* meant eighty-odd degrees of frost.** Such fact impressed him as being cold and uncomfortable, and that was all. It did not lead him to meditate upon his frailty as a creature of temperature, and upon people's frailty in general, able only to live within certain narrow limits of heat and cold; and from there on, it did not lead him to the conjectural field of immortality and one's place in the universe. Fifty degrees below zero stood for a bite of frost that hurt and must be guarded against by the use of mittens, ear-flaps, warm moccasins, and thick socks. Fifty degrees below zero was to him just precisely fifty degrees below zero. That there should be anything more to it than that was a thought that never entered his head.

---

fifty degrees below zero: equals -45°C.
**eighty-odd degrees of frost:* 80 Fahrenheit degrees below the freezing point.

As he turned to go on, he spat speculatively. There was a sharp, explosive crackle that startled him. He spat again. And again, in the air, before it could fall to the snow, the spittle crackled. He knew that at fifty below spittle crackled on the snow, but this spittle had crackled in the air. Undoubtedly, it was colder than fifty below—how much colder he did not know. But the temperature did not matter. He was bound for the old claim on the left fork of Henderson Creek, where the boys were already. They had come over across the divide from the Indian Creek country, while he had come the roundabout way to take a look at the possibilities of getting out logs in the spring from the islands in the Yukon. He would be in to camp by six o'clock; a bit after dark, it was true, but the boys would be there, a fire would be going, and a hot supper would be ready. As for lunch, he pressed his hand against the protruding bundle under his jacket. It was also under his shirt, wrapped up in a handkerchief and lying against the naked skin. It was the only way to keep the biscuits from freezing. He smiled agreeably to himself as he thought of those biscuits, each cut open and sopped in bacon grease, and each enclosing a generous slice of fried bacon.

He plunged in among the big spruce trees. The trail was faint. A foot of snow had fallen since the last sled had passed over, and he was glad he was without a sled, travelling light. In fact, he carried nothing but the lunch wrapped in the handkerchief. He was surprised, however, at the cold.

It certainly was cold, he concluded, as he rubbed his numb nose and cheekbones with his mittened hand. He was a warm-whiskered man, but the hair on his face did not protect the high cheekbones and the eager nose that thrust itself aggressively into the frosty air.

At the man's heels trotted a dog, a big native husky, the proper wolf-dog, grey-coated and without any visible or temperamental difference from its brother, the wild wolf. The animal was depressed by the tremendous cold. It knew that it was no time for travelling. Its instinct told it a truer tale than was told to the man by the man's judgment. In reality, it was not merely colder than fifty below zero; it was colder than sixty below, than seventy below. It was seventy-five below zero.* Since the freezing point is thirty-two above zero, it meant that one hundred and seven degrees of frost** obtained. The dog did not know anything about thermometers. Possibly in its brain there was no sharp consciousness of a condition of very cold such as was in the man's brain. But the brute had its instinct. It experienced a vague but menacing apprehension that subdued it and made it slink along at the man's heels, and that made it question eagerly every unwonted movement of the man as if expecting him to go into camp or to seek shelter somewhere and build a fire. The dog had learned fire, and it wanted fire, or else to burrow under the snow and cuddle its warmth away from the air.

The frozen moisture of its breathing had settled on its fur in a fine powder of frost, and especially were its jowls, muzzle, and eyelashes whitened by its crystalled breath. The man's red beard and moustache were likewise frosted, but more solidly, the deposit taking the form of ice and increasing with every warm moist breath he exhaled. Also, the man was chewing tobacco, and the muzzle of ice held his lips so rigidly that he was unable to clear his chin when he expelled the juice. The result was that a crystal beard of the colour and solidity of amber was increasing its length on his chin. If he fell down it would shatter itself, like glass, into brittle fragments. But he did not mind the appendage. It was the penalty all tobacco-chewers paid in that country, and he had been out before in two cold snaps. They had not been so cold as this, he knew, but by the spirit thermometer at Sixty Mile he knew they had been registered at fifty below and at fifty-five.

---

*seventy-five degrees below zero: equals -59°C.
**one hundred and seven degrees of frost: 107 Fahrenheit degrees below the freezing point.

He held on through the level stretch of woods for several miles, crossed a wide flat of bulrushes, and dropped down a bank to the frozen bed of a small stream. This was Henderson Creek, and he knew he was ten miles from the forks. He looked at his watch. It was ten o'clock. He was making four miles an hour, and he calculated that he would arrive at the forks at half-past twelve. He decided to celebrate that event by eating his lunch there.

The dog dropped in again at his heels, with a tail drooping discouragement, as the man swung along the creek-bed. The furrow of the old sled-trail was plainly visible, but a dozen inches of snow covered the marks of the last runners. In a month no one had come up or down that silent creek. The man held steadily on. He was not much given to thinking, and just then particularly he had nothing to think about save that he would eat lunch at the forks and that at six o'clock he would be in camp with the boys. There was nobody to talk to; and, had there been, speech would have been impossible because of the ice-muzzle on his mouth. So he continued monotonously to chew tobacco and to increase the length of his amber beard.

Once in a while the thought reiterated itself that it was very cold and that he had never experienced such cold. As he walked along, he rubbed his cheekbones and nose with the back of his mittened hand. He did this automatically, now and again changing hands. But rub as he would, the instant he stopped his cheekbones went numb, and the following instant the end of his nose went numb. He was sure to frost his cheeks; he knew that, and experienced a pang of regret that he had not devised a nose-strap of the sort Bud wore in cold snaps. Such a strap passed across the cheeks, as well, and saved them. But it didn't matter much, after all. What were frosted cheeks? A bit painful, that was all; they were never serious.

Empty as the man's mind was of thoughts, he was keenly observant, and he noticed the changes in the creek, the curves and bends and timber-jams, and always he sharply noted where he placed his feet. Once, coming around a bend, he shied abruptly, like a startled horse, curved away from the place where he had been walking, and retreated several paces back along the trail. The creek he knew was frozen clear to the bottom—no creek could contain water in that arctic winter—but he knew also that there were springs that bubbled out from the hillsides and ran along under the snow and on top the ice of the creek. He knew that the coldest snaps never froze these springs, and he knew likewise their danger. They were traps. They hid pools of water under the snow that might be three inches deep, or three feet. Sometimes a skin of ice half an inch thick covered them, and in turn was covered by the snow. Sometimes there were alternate layers of water and ice-skin, so that when one broke through he kept on breaking through for a while, sometimes wetting himself to the waist.

That was why he had shied in such panic. He had felt the ground give under his feet and heard the crackle of a snow-hidden ice-skin. And to get his feet wet in such a temperature meant trouble and danger. At the very least it meant delay, for he would be forced to stop and build a fire, and under its protection to bare his feet while he dried his socks and moccasins. He stood and studied the creek-bed and its banks, and decided that the flow of water came from the right. He reflected a while, rubbing his nose and cheeks, then skirted to the left, stepping gingerly and testing the footing for each step. Once clear of the danger, he took a fresh chew of tobacco and swung along at his four-mile gait.

In the course of the next two hours, he came upon several similar traps. Usually the snow above the hidden pools had a sunken, candied appearance that advertised the danger. Once again, however, he had a close call; and once, suspecting danger, he compelled the dog to go on in front. The dog did not want to go. It hung back until the man shoved it forward, and then it went quickly across the white, unbroken surface. Suddenly it broke through, floundered to one side, and got away to firmer footing. It had wet its forefeet and legs, and almost immediately the water that clung to it turned to ice. It made quick efforts to lick the ice off its legs, then dropped down in the snow and began to bite out the ice that had formed between the toes. This was a matter of instinct. To permit the ice to remain would mean sore feet. It did not know this. It merely obeyed the mysterious prompting that arose from the deep crypts of its being. But the man knew, having achieved a judgment on the subject, and he removed the mitten from his right hand and helped tear out the ice-particles. He did not expose his fingers more than a minute, and was astonished at the swift numbness that smote them. It certainly was cold. He pulled on the mitten hastily, and beat the hand savagely across his chest.

At twelve o'clock the day was at its brightest. Yet the sun was too far south on its winter journey to clear the horizon. The bulge of the earth intervened between it and Henderson Creek, where the man walked under a clear sky at noon and cast no shadow. At half-past twelve, to the minute, he arrived at the forks of the creek. He was pleased at the speed he had made. If he kept it up, he would certainly be with the boys by six. He unbuttoned his jacket and shirt and drew forth his lunch. The action consumed no more than a quarter of a minute, yet in that brief moment the numbness laid hold of the exposed fingers. He did not put the mitten on, but, instead, struck the fingers a dozen sharp smashes against his leg. Then he sat down on a snow-covered log to eat. The sting that followed upon the striking of his fingers against his leg ceased so quickly that he was startled. He had had no chance to take a bite of biscuit. He struck the fingers repeatedly and returned them to the mitten, baring the other hand for the purpose of eating. He tried to take a mouthful, but the ice-muzzle prevented. He had forgotten to build a fire and thaw out. He chuckled at his foolishness, and as he chuckled he noted the numbness creeping into the exposed fingers. Also, he noted that the stinging which had first come to his toes when he sat down was already passing away. He wondered whether the toes were warm or numb. He moved them inside the moccasins and decided that they were numb.

He pulled the mitten on hurriedly and stood up. He was a bit frightened. He stamped up and down until the stinging returned into the feet. It certainly was cold, was his thought. That man from Sulphur Creek had spoken the truth when telling how cold it sometimes got in the country. And he had laughed at him at the time! That showed one must not be too sure of things. There was no mistake about it, it was cold. He strode up and down, stamping his feet and threshing his arms, until reassured by the returning warmth. Then he got out matches and proceeded to make a fire. From the undergrowth, where high water of the previous spring had lodged a supply of seasoned twigs, he got his firewood. Working carefully from a small beginning, he soon had a roaring fire, over which he thawed the ice from his face and in the protection of which he ate his biscuits. For the moment, the cold of space was outwitted. The dog took satisfaction in the fire, stretching out close enough for warmth and far enough away to escape being singed.

When the man had finished, he filled his pipe and took his comfortable time over a smoke. Then he pulled on his mittens, settled the ear-flaps of his cap firmly about his ears, and took the creek trail up the left fork. The dog was disappointed and yearned back toward the fire. This man did not know cold. Possibly all the generations of his ancestry had been ignorant of cold, of real cold, of cold one hundred and seven degrees below freezing point. But the dog knew; all its ancestry knew, and it had inherited the knowledge. And it knew that it was not good to walk abroad in such fearful cold. It was the time to lie snug in a hole in the snow and wait for a curtain of cloud to be drawn across the face of outer space whence this cold came. On the other hand, there was no keen intimacy between the dog and the man. The one was the toil-slave of the other, and the only caresses it had ever received were the caresses of the whiplash and of harsh and menacing throat-sounds that threatened the whiplash. So the dog made no effort to communicate its apprehension to the man. It was not concerned in the welfare of the man; it was for its own sake that it yearned back toward the fire. But the man whistled, and spoke to it with the sound of whiplashes, and the dog swung in at the man's heel and followed after.

The man took a chew of tobacco and proceeded to start a new amber beard. Also, his moist breath quickly powdered with white his moustache, eyebrows, and lashes. There did not seem to be so many springs on the left fork of the Henderson, and for half an hour the man saw no signs of any. And then it happened. At a place where there were no signs, where the soft, unbroken snow seemed to advertise solidity beneath, the man broke through. It was not deep. He wet himself halfway to the knees before he floundered out to the firm crust.

He was angry, and cursed his luck aloud. He had hoped to get to camp with the boys at six o'clock, and this would delay him an hour, for he would have to build a fire and dry out his footgear. This was imperative at that low temperature—he knew that much; and he turned aside to the bank, which he climbed. On top, tangled in the underbrush about the trunks of several small spruce trees, was a high water deposit of dry firewood—sticks and twigs, principally, but also larger portions of seasoned branches and fine, dry, last-year's grasses. He threw down several large pieces on top of the snow. This served for a foundation and prevented the young flame from drowning itself in the snow it otherwise would melt. The flame he got by touching a match to a small shred of birchbark that he took from his pocket. This burned even more readily than paper. Placing it on the foundation, he fed the young flame with wisps of dry grass and with the tiniest of dry twigs.

He worked slowly and carefully, keenly aware of his danger. Gradually, as the flame grew stronger, he increased the size of the twigs with which he fed it. He squatted in the snow, pulling the twigs out from their entanglement in the brush and feeding directly to the flame. He knew there must be no failure. When it is seventy-five below zero, a man must not fail in his first attempt to build a fire—that is, if his feet are wet. If his feet are dry, and he fails, he can run along the trail for half a mile and restore his circulation. But the circulation of wet and freezing feet cannot be restored by running when it is seventy-five below. No matter how fast he runs, the wet feet will freeze the harder.

All this the man knew. The old-timer on Sulphur Creek had told him about it the previous fall, and now he was appreciating the advice. Already all sensation had gone out of his feet. To build a fire, he had been forced to remove his mittens, and the fingers had quickly gone numb. His pace of four miles an hour had kept his heart pumping blood to the surface of his body and to all the extremities. But the instant he stopped, the action of the pump eased down. The cold of space smote the unprotected tip of the planet, and he, being on that unprotected tip, received the full force of the blow. The blood of his body recoiled before it. The blood was alive, like the dog, and like the dog it wanted to hide away and cover itself up from the fearful cold. So long as he walked four miles an hour, he pumped that blood, willy-nilly, to the surface; but now it ebbed away and sank down into the recesses of his body. The extremities were the first to feel its absence. His wet feet froze the faster, and his exposed fingers numbed the faster, though they had not yet begun to freeze. Nose and cheeks were already freezing, while the skin of all his body chilled as it lost its blood.

But he was safe. Toes and nose and cheeks would be only touched by the frost, for the fire was beginning to burn with strength. He was feeding it with twigs the size of his finger. In another minute, he would be able to feed it with branches the size of his wrist, and then he could remove his wet footgear, and, while it dried, he could keep his naked feet warm by the fire, rubbing them at first, of course, with snow. The fire was a success. He was safe. He remembered the advice of the old-timer on Sulphur Creek, and smiled. The old-timer had been very serious in laying down the law that no man must travel alone in the Klondike after fifty below. Well, here he was; he had had the accident; he was alone; and he had saved himself. Those old-timers were rather soft, some of them, he thought. All a man had to do was to keep his head, and he was all right. Any man who was a man could travel alone. But it was surprising, the rapidity with which his cheeks and nose were freezing. And he had not thought his fingers could go lifeless in so short a time. Lifeless they were, for he could scarcely make them move together to grip a twig, and they seemed remote from his body and from him. When he touched a twig, he had to look and see whether or not he had hold of it. The wires were pretty well down between him and his finger-ends.

All of which counted for little. There was the fire, snapping and crack-ling and promising life with every dancing flame. He started to untie his moccasins. They were coated with ice; the thick German socks were like sheaths of iron halfway to the knees; and the moccasin strings were like rods of steel all twisted and knotted as by some conflagration. For a moment, he tugged with his numb fingers, then, realizing the folly of it, he drew his sheath-knife.

But before he could cut the strings, it happened. It was his own fault or, rather, his mistake. He should not have built the fire under the spruce tree. He should have built it in the open. But it had been easier to pull the twigs from the brush and drop them directly on the fire. Now the tree under which he had done this carried a weight of snow on its boughs. No wind had blown for weeks, and each bough was fully freighted. Each time he had pulled a twig he had communicated a slight agitation to the tree— an imperceptible agitation, so far as he was concerned, but an agitation sufficient to bring about the disaster. High up in the tree one bough capsized its load of snow. This fell on the boughs beneath, capsizing them. This process continued, spreading out and involving the whole tree. It grew like an avalanche, and it descended without warning upon the man and the fire, and the fire was blotted out! Where it had burned was a mantle of fresh and disordered snow.

The man was shocked. It was as though he had just heard his own sentence of death. For a moment, he sat and stared at the spot where the fire had been. Then he grew very calm. Perhaps the old-timer on Sulphur Creek was right. If he had only had a trail-mate he would have been in no danger now. The trail-mate could have built the fire. Well, it was up to him to build the fire over again, and this second time there must be no failure. Even if he succeeded, he would most likely lose some toes. His feet must be badly frozen by now, and there would be some time before the second fire was ready.

Such were his thoughts, but he did not sit and think them. He was busy all the time they were passing through his mind. He made a new foundation for a fire, this time in the open, where no treacherous tree could blot it out. Next, he gathered dry grasses and tiny twigs from the high water flotsam. He could not bring his fingers together to pull them out, but he was able to gather them by the handful. In this way, he got many rotten twigs and bits of green moss that were undesirable, but it was the best he could do. He worked methodically, even collecting an armful of the larger branches to be used later when the fire gathered strength. And all the while the dog sat and watched him, a certain yearning wistfulness in its eyes, for it looked upon him as the fire-provider, and the fire was slow in coming.

When all was ready, the man reached in his pocket for a second piece of birchbark. He knew the bark was there, and, though he could not feel it with his fingers, he could hear its crisp rustling as he fumbled for it. Try as he would, he could not clutch hold of it. And all the time, in his consciousness, was the knowledge that each instant his feet were freezing. This thought tended to put him in a panic, but he fought against it and kept calm. He pulled on his mittens with his teeth, and threshed his arms back and forth, beating his hands with all his might against his sides. He did this sitting down, and he stood up to do it; and all the while the dog sat in the snow, its wolf-brush of a tail curled around warmly over its forefeet, its sharp wolf-ears pricked forward intently as it watched the man. And the man, as he beat and threshed with his arms and hands, felt a great surge of envy as he regarded the creature that was warm and secure in its natural covering.

After a time, he was aware of the first faraway signals of sensation in his beaten fingers. The faint tingling grew stronger till it evolved into a stinging ache that was excruciating, but which the man hailed with satisfaction. He stripped the mitten from his right hand and fetched forth the birchbark. The exposed fingers were quickly going numb again. Next, he brought out his bunch of sulphur matches. But the tremendous cold had already driven the life out of his fingers. In his effort to separate one match from the others, the whole bunch fell in the snow. He tried to pick it out of the snow, but failed. The dead fingers could neither touch nor clutch. He was very careful. He drove the thought of his freezing feet, and nose, and cheeks, out of his mind, devoting his whole soul to the matches. He watched, using the sense of vision in place of that of touch, and when he saw his fingers on each side the bunch, he closed them—that is, he willed to close them, for the wires were down, and the fingers did not obey. He pulled the mitten on the right hand, and beat it fiercely against his knee. Then, with both mittened hands, he scooped the bunch of matches, along with much snow, into his lap. Yet he was no better off.

After some manipulation, he managed to get the bunch between the heels of his mittened hands. In this fashion, he carried it to his mouth. The ice crackled and snapped when by a violent effort he opened his mouth. He drew the lower jaw in, curled the upper lip out of the way, and scraped the bunch with his upper teeth in order to separate a match. He succeeded in getting one, which he dropped on his lap. He was no better off. He could not pick it up. Then he devised a way. He picked it up in his teeth and scratched it on his leg. Twenty times he scratched before he succeeded in lighting it. As it flamed he held it with his teeth to the birchbark. But the burning brimstone went up his nostrils and into his lungs, causing him to cough spasmodically. The match fell into the snow and went out.

The old-timer on Sulphur Creek was right, he thought in the moment of controlled despair that ensued: after fifty below, a man should travel with a partner. He beat his hands, but failed in exciting any sensation. Suddenly he bared both hands, removing the mittens with his teeth. He caught the whole bunch between the heels of his hands. His arm muscles not being frozen enabled him to press the heels of his hands tightly against the matches. Then he scratched the bunch along his leg. It flared into flame, seventy sulphur matches at once! There was no wind to blow them out. He kept his head to one side to escape the strangling fumes, and held the blazing bunch to the birchbark. As he so held it, he became aware of sensation in his hand. His flesh was burning. He could smell it. Deep down below the surface he could feel it. The sensation developed into pain that grew acute. And still he endured it, holding the flame of the matches clumsily to the bark that would not light readily because his own burning hands were in the way, absorbing most of the flame.

At last, when he could endure no more, he jerked his hands apart. The blazing matches fell sizzling into the snow, but the birchbark was alight. He began laying dry grasses and the tiniest twigs on the flame. He could not pick and choose, for he had to lift the fuel between the heels of his hands. Small pieces of rotten wood and green moss clung to the twigs, and he bit them off as well as he could with his teeth. He cherished the flame carefully and awkwardly. It meant life, and it must not perish. The withdrawal of blood from the surface of his body now made him begin to shiver, and he grew more awkward. A large piece of green moss fell squarely on the little fire. He tried to poke it out with his fingers, but his shivering frame made him poke too far, and he disrupted the nucleus of the little fire, the burning grasses and tiny twigs separating and scattering. He tried to poke them together again, but in spite of the tenseness of the effort, his shivering got away with him, and the twigs were hopelessly scattered. Each twig gushed a puff of smoke and went out. The fire-provider had failed. As he looked apathetically about him, his eyes chanced on the dog, sitting across the ruins of the fire from him, in the snow, making restless, hunching movements, slightly lifting one forefoot and then the other, shifting its weight back and forth on them with wistful eagerness.

The sight of the dog put a wild idea into his head. He remembered the tale of the man, caught in a blizzard, who killed a steer and crawled inside the carcass, and so was saved. He would kill the dog and bury his hands in the warm body until the numbness went out of them. Then he could build another fire. He spoke to the dog, calling it to him; but in his voice was a strange note of fear that frightened the animal, who had never known the man to speak in such way before. Something was the matter, and its suspicious nature sensed danger—it knew not what danger, but somewhere, somehow, in its brain arose an apprehension of the man. It flattened its ears down at the sound of the man's voice, and its restless, hunching movements and liftings and shiftings of its forefeet became more pronounced;

but it would not come to the man. He got on his hands and knees and crawled toward the dog. This unusual posture again excited suspicion, and the animal sidled mincingly away.

The man sat up in the snow for a moment and struggled for calmness. Then he pulled on his mittens, by means of his teeth, and got upon his feet. He glanced down at first in order to assure himself that he was really standing up, for the absence of sensation in his feet left him unrelated to the earth. His erect position in itself started to drive the webs of suspicion from the dog's mind; and when he spoke peremptorily, with the sound of whiplashes in his voice, the dog rendered its customary allegiance and came to him. As it came within reaching distance, the man lost his control. His arms flashed out to the dog, and he experienced genuine surprise when he discovered that his hands could not clutch, that there was neither bend nor feeling in the fingers. He had forgotten for the moment that they were frozen and that they were freezing more and more. All this happened quickly, and before the animal could get away, he encircled its body with his arms. He sat down in the snow, and in this fashion held the dog, while it snarled and whined and struggled.

But it was all he could do, hold its body encircled in his arms and sit there. He realized that he could not kill the dog. There was no way to do it. With his helpless hands, he could neither draw nor hold his sheath-knife nor throttle the animal. He released it, and it plunged wildly away, with tail between its legs, and still snarling. It halted forty feet away and surveyed him curiously, with ears sharply pricked forward. The man looked down at his hands in order to locate them, and found them hanging on the ends of his arms. It struck him as curious that one should have to use his eyes in order to find out where his hands were. He began threshing his arms back and forth, beating the mittened hands against his sides. He did this for five minutes, violently, and his heart pumped enough blood up to the surface to put a stop to his shivering. But no sensation was aroused in the hands. He had an impression that they hung like weights on the ends of his arms, but when he tried to run the impression down, he could not find it.

A certain fear of death, dull and oppressive, came to him. This fear quickly became poignant as he realized that it was no longer a mere matter of freezing his fingers and toes, or of losing his hands and feet, but that it was a matter of life and death with the chances against him. This threw him into a panic, and he turned and ran up the creek-bed along the old, dim trail. The dog joined in behind and kept up with him. He ran blindly, without intention, in fear such as he had never known in his life. Slowly, as he plowed and floundered through the snow, he began to see things again—the banks of the creek, the old timber-jams, the leafless aspens, and the sky. The running made him feel better. He did not shiver. Maybe, if he ran on, his feet would thaw out; and, anyway, if he ran far enough, he would reach camp and the boys. Without doubt, he would lose some fingers and toes and some of his face; but the boys would take care of him, and save the rest of him when he got there. And at the same time there was another thought in his mind that said he would never get to the camp and the boys; that it was too many miles away, that the freezing had too great a start on him, and that he would soon be stiff and dead. This thought he kept in the background and refused to consider. Sometimes it pushed itself forward and demanded to be heard, but he thrust it back and strove to think of other things.

It struck him as curious that he could run at all on feet so frozen that he could not feel them when they struck the earth and took the weight of his body. He seemed to himself to skim along above the surface, and to have no connection with the earth. Somewhere he had once seen a winged Mercury, and he wondered if Mercury felt as he felt when skimming over the earth.

His theory of running until he reached camp and the boys had one flaw in it: he lacked the endurance. Several times he stumbled, and finally he tottered, crumpled up, and fell. When he tried to rise, he failed. He must sit and rest, he decided, and next time he would merely walk and keep on going. As he sat and regained his breath, he noted that he was feeling quite warm and comfortable. He was not shivering, and it even seemed that a warm glow had come to his chest and trunk. And yet, when he touched his nose or cheeks, there was no sensation. Running would not thaw them out. Nor would it thaw out his hands and feet. Then the thought came to him that the frozen portions of his body must be extending. He tried to keep this thought down, to forget it, to think of something else; he was aware of the panicky feeling that it caused, and he was afraid of the panic. But the thought asserted itself, and persisted, until it produced a vision of his body totally frozen. This was too much, and he made another wild run along the trail. Once he slowed down to a walk, but the thought of the freezing extending itself made him run again.

And all the time the dog ran with him, at his heels. When he fell down a second time, it curled its tail over its forefeet and sat in front of him, facing him, curiously eager and intent. The warmth and security of the animal angered him, and he cursed it till it flattened down its ears appeasingly. This time the shivering came more quickly upon the man. He was losing in his battle with the frost. It was creeping into his body from all sides. The thought of it drove him on, but he ran no more than a hundred feet, when he staggered and pitched headlong. It was his last panic. When he had recovered his breath and control, he sat up and entertained in his mind the conception of meeting death with dignity. However, the conception did not come to him in such terms. His idea of it was that he had been making a fool of himself, running around like a chicken with its head cut off—such was the simile that occurred to him. Well, he was bound to freeze anyway, and he might as well take it decently. With this newfound peace of mind came the first glimmerings of drowsiness. A good idea, he thought, to sleep off to death. It was like taking an anaesthetic. Freezing was not so bad as people thought. There were lots worse ways to die.

He pictured the boys finding his body next day. Suddenly, he found himself with them, coming along the trail and looking for himself. And, still with them, he came around a turn in the trail and found himself lying in the snow. He did not belong with himself any more, for even then he was out of himself, standing with the boys and looking at himself in the snow. It certainly was cold, was his thought. When he got back to the States, he could tell the folks what real cold was. He drifted on from this to a vision of the old-timer on Sulphur Creek. He could see him quite clearly, warm and comfortable, and smoking a pipe.

"You were right, old hoss; you were right," the man mumbled to the old-timer of Sulphur Creek.

Then the man drowsed off into what seemed to him the most comfortable and satisfying sleep he had ever known. The dog sat facing him and waiting. The brief day drew to a close in a long, slow twilight. There were no signs of a fire to be made, and, besides, never in the dog's experience had it known a man to sit like that in the snow and make no fire. As the twilight drew on, its eager yearning for the fire mastered it, and with a great lifting and shifting of forefeet, it whined softly, then flattened its ears down in anticipation of being chidden by the man. But the man remained silent. Later, the dog whined loudly. And still later it crept close to the man and caught the scent of death. This made the animal bristle and back away. A little longer it delayed, howling under the stars that leaped and danced and shone brightly in the cold sky. Then it turned and trotted up the trail in the direction of the camp it knew, where were the other food-providers and fire-providers. ◆

1. RESPONDING TO THE STORY

a. The author writes of the main character, "The trouble with him was that he was without imagination." Why would it be important to have imagination living and travelling in a harsh climate? What other characteristics or qualities does the man have? How are these demonstrated?

b. When did you first suspect that the man was going to die? How is his death **foreshadowed**?

c. Who or what is the "enemy" in this story? How did the man deal with this enemy? What type of conflict is developed in this story?

> **Foreshadowing** occurs when the author gives hints about what will happen in the story.

d. Why do you think Jack London gave no name to the man or dog?

e. What examples in the story can you find that tell you it was written a long time ago? Could the events in this story occur today? Why or why not?

2. LITERATURE STUDIES SHORT STORY THEME

In "To Build a Fire," Jack London not only tells his story convincingly, and entertainingly, he also expresses his feelings about the North and how people react to it.

In a sentence, write what you think the author's theme is. List three examples from the story to support your view. For each example, write a sentence that explains why it supports the author's theme.

PEER ASSESSMENT: Share one of your sentences with a group of students. Do they agree with your understanding of the story's theme?

3. WRITING AN ESSAY

Look over the notes you made above. What you have written is a rough outline for an essay about the story's theme.

- The sentence you wrote about the author's theme is your *thesis*. This is a statement or viewpoint you are trying to prove or explain.
- The sentences you wrote for the examples are similar to the topic sentences you might write for the body of your essay. They develop and prove your thesis.

Have a partner review your notes. Is your thesis sentence clear and easy to understand? Do your examples support your thesis or do they stray from its topic? Revise your sentence outline.

Now write a five-paragraph essay. The first paragraph will be your intro-duction and include your thesis sentence. Write a paragraph for each of your topic sentences. End your essay with a one-paragraph summary or conclusion. Work with a partner to edit and revise your essay.

4. RESEARCHING GATHER FACTS

"To Build a Fire" takes place in the Yukon. Use print and media resources to find out more about the first large settlement in the Yukon during the Klondike Gold Rush. List each fact you discover on a separate piece of paper or card. Be sure to include a complete list of sources for the information you collect.

Divide your facts into categories, for example, the type of people who went there, or how people travelled to the gold fields. Using these categories as guidelines, write a brief report.

REFLECTING ON THE UNIT

SELF-ASSESSMENT: STORY CRAFT

As you worked on the activities in this unit, what did you learn about
• story themes?
• first- and third-person narratives?
• plot?
• symbols?
• foreshadowing?
• conflict?

Do you feel that analysing literary techniques can deepen your understanding of short stories?

WRITING REVIEW

Choose a short story that you especially enjoyed, or one that you didn't think was very good. For your choice, write a three-paragraph review. For example, you might follow this outline:

• **First Paragraph**—Give the name and author of the story. Say whether you think it is or isn't a good piece of writing.
• **Second Paragraph**—Support your opinion with a few examples from the story or book.
• **Third Paragraph**—Conclude with your recommendation. Explain why you think it is or isn't something others should read.

MEDIA

PROD. N

SCEN

From the Inside

The Product Is Nothing™

Magazine Article by Hilary Keever

Fiona Jack of Auckland, New Zealand is getting Nothing done. One-third of Auckland's population have viewed her advertisements, but no one's buying. No upper management complains, no share prices fall, no lack of demand for the project exists. What exactly isn't selling? Nothing™.

Jack, a twenty-four-year-old graphic designer, launched the Nothing™ campaign hoping to raise awareness about why we buy. "I was thinking about advertising and all its strangeness. Its coercive ability to sell the most completely bizarre things to people who usually don't need them," explained Jack. "I realized that the ultimate non-existent product would be nothing. To actually call a product *nothing* and try and market it."

GOALS AT A GLANCE

■ Develop ideas for a new product.
■ Analyse how products are advertised.

After conceptualizing Nothing™, Jack approached New Zealand billboard companies to sponsor the campaign, promoting it under the auspices of an art project. The Outdoor Advertising Association of New Zealand chose Jack's advertisements for a market research campaign to assess the effectiveness of billboard advertising. Jack received the use of twenty-seven billboards at no cost, although OAANZ imposed a gag order for the duration of the campaign.

Both parties declare the Nothing™ campaign a success. OAANZ's statistics suggest over a third of Aucklanders viewed the billboards. The company also received phone calls from viewers asking where they could buy Nothing™—viewers knowledgeable of a brand but not a product.

Jack's campaign flourished when the OAANZ billboard campaign ended: she could start talking. Three out of four New Zealand TV stations covered her story, along with national newspapers, radio, and magazines. "I think the Nothing™ campaign proved the point that you can market anything if there's enough money behind it, that money is basically the main thing that's required to convince the public of something these days," emphasized Jack.

Some critics challenged Jack for accepting the deal with OAANZ, saying if the results were successful, her campaign would encourage more advertising. "That my anti-advertising message got completely funded by one of the biggest advertising organizations in New Zealand is ironic," said Jack. "I think it's perfect. The whole campaign is full of irony and absurdity." ◆

1. RESPONDING TO THE MAGAZINE ARTICLE

a. What is **ironic** about the Nothing™ campaign?

b. What is a *gag order* and why do you think it was used?

> **Irony** is the use of an idea, word, or phrase to mean the opposite of its normal meaning.

c. Explain why you agree or disagree with this statement from the article:

> "Some critics challenged Jack for accepting the deal with OAANZ, saying if the results were successful, her campaign would encourage more advertising."

d. This selection was originally printed in a magazine called *Adbusters*. Find a copy of this magazine in your local library. With a partner, discuss the magazine's purpose, audience, and content.

e. With a partner, discuss the purpose of an ad campaign.

2. MEDIA MAKER DEVELOPING PRODUCT IDEAS

This is not the first time "nothing" has been advertised and sold. There have been books and music albums promoted and sold that have been blank inside. Think of your own example of a "nothing" product that people might be persuaded to buy. What is it? How would you advertise it? Why might people buy it?

3. MEDIA MESSAGES ANALYSE ADVERTISING

With a small group, brainstorm the different types of advertising, such as bill-boards or radio ads. Each group member can choose one type and research it, finding out how successful this type of advertising is at selling products. For example, you might investigate magazine articles on advertising, search the Internet for ad agency sites, or talk to family and friends. Summarize what you have learned in one or two paragraphs. As a group, compile your summaries, producing a report on advertising. Work together to revise, edit, and proofread the report.

SELF-ASSESSMENT: Do you listen to others when they offer comments and criticisms? Do other people's comments help you improve your work? Do you offer comments to others in a fair, non-judgmental way?

*Are you aware of the techniques
advertisers use to persuade consumers?*

Market Savvy Teens

Newspaper Article

by Kathy Friedman

and Lauren Krugel

Almost two hundred youths weighed in on the subject of marketing to teens in the first Young People's Press and *The Toronto Star* Internet forum.

The strongest response: They are torn between two opposing forces. One tells them, "Be who you want to be." The other tells them, "Be who *we* want you to be."

Most said they were trying to decide whether to follow the way the media represents "coolness" or follow their own ideals and principles.

And they had a lot to say about how the media use implicit yet powerful techniques to make a profit.

Tim's response was caustic. "Instead of 'Be young, have fun, drink Pepsi,' why [don't advertisers] say it in plain English: 'You're stupid! Give us all your money!'"

There was a lot of agreement that the media simply do not give young people enough credit for realizing what's going on.

Others said the media know how important it is for adolescents to feel accepted and they exploit it.

"The media play upon people's insecurities, especially [those of] women," says Molly Bell. "They make us feel as if we aren't 'good enough' unless we have that certain product."

Although youth know companies feed on the inner workings of their psyches, they admit savvy marketing professionals are tremendously difficult to resist.

"It seems like my whole teenage life has been shaped by what the advertisers tell me is cool and what's not," says Camren A.

"It's automatic now, if it's on TV, I want it. I'm eighteen and I find it hard to pass a Gap store without thinking of the song 'They call me Mellow Yellow.'"

It was a strong theme—the media are there, the media affect what they choose to buy, and there's absolutely nothing they can do about it.

Young people said they are in constant conflict between their own values and those portrayed by the media.

Since finding one's identity is so important to teens, they look to role models for answers. That makes celebrity endorsements probably the most manipulative way to get teens to buy products, they said.

"I think for younger children, it's normal to wear clothes that a celebrity wears. At that age, celebrities are like heroes," reflects Jennifer-Ashley Kendall. "When you reach a certain age you become more opinionated and you realize you like a certain style. You don't care if someone else doesn't like it, it's not theirs—it's yours."

However, others admitted they still rely on celebrities to help them create an identity even as they get older.

When asked his definition of *cool*, Matthew replied, "I can tell, because the stars wear it, so it's cool."

Teens like to feel like they are part of something—and to many, seeing their idols promoting products helped them feel better.

"I think that celebrity endorsement is cool because if you have the hat Tiger Woods does, you might feel as if you are part of the game," Brian Lewis said.

Respondents also said that discovering how to be cool is a difficult and lonely process, especially since no one seems to agree what cool actually is.

What is cool?

Many argued coolness is about being true to yourself. That's easier said than done, they admitted, because the process of growing older is about finding out who you are—and many young people aren't there yet.

Sarah Leroux spoke for many when she said: "All these teens feel stereotyped and are basically putting down the media, yet they're still buying the latest fads."

Teens must always be on top of what is "in" to make sure they are accepted. "Yes, I do find myself wanting the goods I see in commercials because I do not want to be the only one not wearing FuBu or Nike," said Brian Lewis.

WHAT'S COOL? IT DEPENDS ON WHERE YOU'RE COMING FROM.

Other young people admitted to dressing like their friends, listening to the same music, and having the same interests as a way of defining cool.

As E. Phillips put it, "To me cool is what's in. Not cool is if you're not like everyone else."

Then again, people who hang out with carbon copies of themselves often risk being stereotyped, and that's definitely not cool.

There's a familiar cast of characters in a typical high school, said Nicole Mulholland: "You have the preppies, goths, ravers, skaters, rockers,...hip-hoppers, coolies, and, of course, the outcasters."

Why such sharply defined categories? Many young people seem to feel it comes from wanting to create an easily definable identity.

According to Camille R., this is because of media influence. "Our identity now seems to be defined by what we wear, what we listen to, and so on. There seems to be so many advertisements that pressure us teenagers into believing that image is everything. We are so pressured that we often confuse image with identity."

Image is our external appearance, she said, and identity is who we really are.

Not everyone falls into a category, though, despite the pressure.

"That's what makes us cool— not following the in-crowd," Laura wrote. "When people look at me, it's exciting in a way. When people dress all the same, it's boring and sort of depressing."

Each cultural group also embraces its own ideals of what is acceptable. According to the teens, the media have managed to exploit this as well.

Christos wrote: "Sure I'm a black guy with oversized clothing, with a Walkman blarin' Noreaga & Mobb Deep, but how can [the media define me] by these characteristics only? I live in a white suburban neighbourhood and I work in a men's suit store. So what does that make me?"

"COOL IS JUST CONFORMITY WRAPPED IN THE GUISE OF SELF-EXPRESSION."

For some, the word *cool* is an illusion, used by advertisers to convince teens to buy their products.

"In the corporate sense, cool is really just conformity wrapped in the guise of self-expression," said Adi Persuad. A cool person embodies "individuality, leadership, confidence, rebelliousness, and faith in one's own beliefs," whereas a mass-marketed version of coolness is about conformity—the complete opposite.

Media pressure is not just confined to advertising. TV programs aimed at teens often present an unrealistic image of what their lives *should* be like. According to these shows, all cool teens have lots of gorgeous friends, wake up fully made-up or perfectly coiffed, and always have a girlfriend or boyfriend.

Yes, teens can tell reality from TV fantasy, but it's hard to resist the fantasy when all TV teens act and look a certain way. Anastasia Koshkin wrote: "Through these shows, I find out how other people my age should/often live."

And other youth found that the issues that some TV shows raise have helped them deal with problems in their own lives, issues like drugs, pregnancy, and sexual harassment.

Product placement in movies and TV shows is increasingly blurring the distinction between commerce and entertainment, bringing us back to the days of early TV when actors regularly endorsed products during their shows. Many youth admitted being seduced by this process, saying they felt more in touch with the actors if that actor ate a chocolate bar they liked.

"TO ME, COOL IS WHAT'S IN. NOT COOL IS IF YOU'RE NOT LIKE EVERYONE ELSE."

Bombarded with media images, it is increasingly difficult for many teens to find out who they really are. The majority of youth revealed in the YPP forum that they are aware of the effect the media have on them, yet they feel powerless to stop it.

Sha-awn Marcano wrote that even though wearing the best brand names may seem shallow, "you just can't change something that the whole media has clearly brain-washed you into thinking is right."

How can teens remove themselves from the trap of a pre-packaged, mass-marketed perception of individuality?

"You just have to grow, mature, and understand WHO YOU ARE before you can break free of the cool pressure," wrote one youth.

"If you are defining yourself by a subculture, by the music you listen to, or by what brand of pants you wear, you haven't discovered who you are yet...so keep searching...and keep the faith. YOU are somewhere in there. Explore."

----

1. RESPONDING TO THE NEWSPAPER ARTICLE

a. In small groups, discuss the meaning of the following quotation from the article:

"Image is our external appearance, identity is who we are."

Which idea—image or identity—do you think is most important? Explain.

b. How does the article define cool? What is your definition of cool?

c. What person mentioned in this article is most like you? least like you? Explain your choices.

d. Who has the greatest influence over you? friends? family? media personalities? your "inner voice"? Give reasons for your choice.

2. MEDIA MESSAGES ADVERTISING ESSAY

The article raises a number of questions about advertising and teens. What questions do you have about advertising and the way it may influence people's lives? Jot down a list and then choose one of your questions and use it as the basis for an essay about the influence of advertising on teenagers. Before you begin, develop a good thesis sentence and essay outline. Ask a partner to help you edit and revise your first draft.

STRATEGIES

3. MEDIA MAKER A NEWSPAPER ARTICLE

This selection reports on an Internet survey conducted by *The Toronto Star*. Reread the article, noting its features and organization. Use this selection as a model to write a newspaper article about how people feel about some aspect of media. You could write about role models, celebrity endorsements, product placement in movies, or another topic of your choice.

Begin by surveying friends, school mates, and family about your topic. How do they feel about it? What makes them angry? What do they appreciate about it? What would they like to see changed? Have they ever complained about it? Develop your questions into a questionnaire, passing out this form to the survey participants. Like *The Toronto Star*, you could post your survey on the Internet. If you do so, you may want to limit your participants to a certain age group.

Analyse the results of your survey. Write an article, reporting the results of your survey, including some statistics, as well as quotations from the participants. Include any conclusions you can draw from the results. Remember to use the features and organization of "Market Savvy Teens" as a model for your article.

Use a computer to give your newspaper article a design that is similar to other newspaper articles. Publish it on the school's Web site, in the school newspaper, or share it with your classmates.

SELF-ASSESSMENT: In your notebook, describe those elements of writing an article that worked well. What writing skills do you need to work on? What would you do differently next time?

Check out how these advertisers use advertising techniques to persuade their audience.

The Purpose Is Persuasion

Print Ads from Canadian Magazines

GOALS AT A GLANCE

- Respond personally and critically to ads.
- Model the selection to create print ads.

Take the friendliest of people

Cover with a rain forest dressing

Adorn with gorgeous scenery

And serve with a scattering
of National Parks

COSTA RICA
NO ARTIFICIAL INGREDIENTS
1•800•343•6332
http://www.tourism-costarica.com
ICT-COSTA RICA TOURIST BOARD

----

1. RESPONDING TO THE PRINT ADS

a. Which ad gives you the most information about what it is promoting? the least? Which ad do you prefer? Why?

b. Which ad (or ads) is designed to appeal to your emotions? to your intellect? to your sense of humour? Why would advertisers choose these methods? (Read activity 2 to see other methods an advertiser might choose. Have any of these methods been used in the ads?)

c. Which ad (or ads) depends upon you having some background knowledge? What are the advantages and disadvantages to this kind of advertising?

d. For one of the ads, explain why you think the ad agency chose its image and message.

2. MEDIA MAKER CREATE A PRINT AD

Think of a product (real or imagined) that you could create a print ad for. For whom is the product intended? This group will be your target market or audience, and you should consider its needs and interests as you design a print ad. The purpose of your ad is to persuade this target market to buy your product.

As you design the ad think of how you can combine text and visuals effectively. The text should describe the product in a clever or humorous way, and may include a **slogan**. Use photos or drawings, and perhaps a **logo**, to create visuals for the ad. Here are a few examples of the types of ads that are commonly used:

> A **slogan** is a short, catchy phrase most often used by a business or company to advertise its product or service. A **logo** is an identifying symbol or image used in advertising, for example, Nike's swoosh.

- Ads that show famous people—If it's good enough for me, it's good enough for you.
- Ads that offer comfort—Toilet paper so soft you can use it to blow your nose.
- Ads that offer great value—Buy one, get one almost free. (Some conditions apply.)
- Ads that offer factual "proof"—Nine out of ten people choose Bix Bits for breakfast.
- Ads that show beautiful people—If you buy this car, you'll be a supermodel, too.
- Ads that play on emotions—One day you may have this disease, so give generously now.

Use one of the above methods, or a method of your own, to develop your ad. You could use publishing and design software, if they are available, to put a final copy of your ad together. Share your ad with a small group, explaining the effect you hoped to achieve.

SELF-ASSESSMENT: Does your ad successfully combine text and images? Does your ad provide your target market with enough information about the product? Is your ad persuasive? Would you buy this product?

*In the 500-channel universe, the appearance of a brand new
broadcaster could go unnoticed—
unless it's something really special.*

Tuning in to
Aboriginal
TV

Article
by Marie
Verdun

In September, 1999, a remarkable event unfolded on TV
screens across Canada—the
launch of the Aboriginal
Peoples Television Network.
Broadcast live from the APTN
studio in Winnipeg, Manitoba,
the launch featured a three-
hour celebration complete with
speeches, storytellers, singers,
and dancers in traditional dress.

At first glance, viewers
might have assumed that
Canada's fourth network was
launched overnight. In reality,
however, the APTN had been in the making for more than twenty
years. That's how long it took for the Aboriginal communities and the

GOALS AT A GLANCE

- Explore ideas for a new TV specialty channel.
- Debate a media issue.

network's founders to convince the media powers-that-be that a Canadian TV network dedicated to programming by, for, and about Aboriginal peoples was both necessary and practical.

The final result was a triumphant opening show—and the beginning of lots of hard work.

If you tune in to Aboriginal Peoples TV (APT in your broadcast guide), what can you expect to see and hear? The range of programming is similar to that on other networks: a wide range of choices such as documentaries, news magazines, dramas, entertainment specials, children's series, cooking shows, and educational programs.

Our People is a series of hour-long shows profiling Aboriginal people, places, and events. It also imports specials of Aboriginal interest from other countries such as the United States, Australia, and New Zealand. Other programs such as *Spirit of the Land* and *Tribal Journeys* investigate the experiences and beliefs of First Nations people, Métis, and Inuit from the West Coast to the east.

Takuginai, which means "look here" in Inuktitut, is a program from Nunavut aimed at five to seven year olds. Hosted by a mix of young people and puppets (look for "Johnny" the lemming), the show explores cultural values through fun and games. It also teaches Inuktitut numbers and symbols.

A popular show for teens is *Qaujisaut*, meaning "to see, to find out." It's a fast-paced program that deals with issues faced by Inuit youth who sometimes feel caught between two cultures, between new ways and traditional lifestyles. The show is broadcast in Inuktitut with occasional English.

Which brings us to another question: What language will you hear when you click on APTN? It varies: sixty percent of the network shows are in English, fifteen percent in French, and twenty-five percent in a variety of Native languages such as Cree, Mi'kmaq, Ojibwa, and Inuktitut. In other words, the network is definitely accessible to both Native and non-Native viewers.

OBJECTIVES OF THE APTN

The APTN strives "to reflect the Aboriginal community and give Aboriginal people a sense of pride in their history and their culture," says Jennifer David, the network's spokesperson. "Our other objective is to ensure that Canadians have access to our stories so they will see accurate portrayals of our people."

Creating eighteen hours of programming each day keeps everyone at the Winnipeg broadcast centre very busy. With a permanent staff of only forty, the network relies heavily on shows created by freelance writers, producers, and directors. The Program Selection Committee is the group that considers and selects proposals for new programs.

Program proposals may be submitted by people of any cultural or racial background, but the network's licence (granted by the CRTC—Canadian Radio and Television Commission) suggests that preference be given to Aboriginal producers. The idea is always to promote the original vision and objectives of the network.

Although the hands-on programming is all centred in Winnipeg, the APTN's corporate offices are in Ottawa. Two of the important people working there are Chief Operating Officer Abraham Tagalik and Board Member Alanis Obomsawin.

Obomsawin is an award-winning documentary filmmaker who has been directing documentaries for twenty-five years at the National Film Board of Canada. After lobbying hard for the creation of an Aboriginal broadcast network, she has remained very involved in the direction of the APTN and all its ventures. Obomsawin acted as host for the spectacular launch of the network.

Tagalik handles the business issues of APTN. He spent twenty years as a radio announcer, TV producer, and network manager with the Inuit Broadcasting Corporation. Tagalik stresses that APTN is not just another specialty channel but a network like CBC or CTV, offering a full range of programs. In other words, it's an ongoing challenge.

Aboriginal broadcasting is definitely on an upswing, and Canadians have said they approve. In January, 1998, an Angus Reid poll concluded that two of every three Canadians supported the idea of a national Aboriginal TV network.

In the past, Aboriginal people have felt both underrepresented and misrepresented on TV. With the addition of APTN to the channel line-up, Canadian audiences—Native and non-Native—have a long overdue opportunity to see and hear the stories of our Aboriginal peoples, told by the people themselves. We should all reap the benefits.

APTN was twenty years in the making. What will the next twenty years bring?

1. RESPONDING TO THE ARTICLE

a. Is the article objective or subjective? Support your opinion.

b. What did you learn from the article about how a TV network is organized?

c. What TV channel do you watch most often? Why do you watch it? What purpose do you think the channel serves?

d. What do these words and phrases from the article mean: *ventures, Angus Reid poll,* and *on an upswing?* Add any other unfamiliar or interesting words from the article to your personal word list.

2. MEDIA MAKER SPECIALTY CHANNELS

Cable TV has introduced a number of specialty channels that concentrate on a theme or a subject area, for example, Much Music and Arts and Entertainment. Think of a new specialty channel you would like to see on TV. List at least ten programs it might have. Write program guide listings for your programs, including a brief summary, length of the show, and the time of day or night when it is on. Be sure to give your specialty channel a name.

3. ORAL LANGUAGE DEBATE AN ISSUE

Most TV channels are brought directly to homes by way of cable wires, and cable companies charge a monthly fee for this service. Originally TV shows were broadcast free, and were paid for by commercial or government sponsors. In small groups, debate whether everyone, rich or poor, should have the same access to TV programs.

SELF-ASSESSMENT: During the debate, did you listen to the opinions and ideas of others? Did you support your own opinions with facts?

4. LANGUAGE CONVENTIONS ABBREVIATIONS

Reread the article, locating the **abbreviations**. Record these abbreviations, with their definitions, in your notebook. With a partner, discuss the purpose, advantages, and disadvantages of abbreviations. List some common media abbreviations—like *CBC* or *sfx*—that are important to know as you work on a media unit.

> An **abbreviation** is a short form of a longer word.

On *the* Box

The Forecast

Poem by Dan Jaffe

Perhaps our age has driven us indoors.
We sprawl in the semi-darkness, dreaming sometimes
Of a vague world spinning in the wind.
But we have snapped our locks, pulled down our shades,
Taken all precautions. We shall not be disturbed.
If the earth shakes, it will be on a screen;
And if the prairie wind spills down our streets
And covers us with leaves, the weatherman will tell us.

TOSHIBA

GOALS AT A GLANCE

- Respond personally and critically to poetry.
- Use communication skills in small group discussions.

Reflections Dental

Poem by Phyllis McGinley

How pure, how beautiful, how fine
Do teeth on television shine!
No flutist flutes, no dancer twirls,
But comes equipped with matching pearls.
Gleeful announcers all are born
With sets like rows of hybrid corn.
Clowns, critics, clergy, commentators,
Ventriloquists and roller skaters,
M.C.s who beat their palms together,
The girl who diagrams the weather,
The crooner crooning for his supper—
All flash white treasures, lower and upper.
With miles of smiles the airwaves teem,
And each an orthodontist's dream.

'Twould please my eye as gold a miser's—
One charmer with uncapped incisors.

- -

1. RESPONDING TO THE POEMS

What two viewpoints are presented in the poems? What is the opinion
of each poet about TV? What's your opinion of TV? Do you think it's an
important medium that enriches people's lives? Do you think it's an escape
from reality that makes it difficult for people to cope with real life? Explain.

2. POET'S CRAFT POETIC DEVICES

With a small group, discuss both poems. What is the tone
of each poem? How do the poets use poetic devices like
alliteration, simile, or rhyme, effectively? Choose an
image from each poem and explain what you think the
author means. Read aloud lines that you find particularly
effective, explaining why you like them.

> **Alliteration** involves the
> repetition of the same first
> sounds in a group of words or
> line of poetry; for example,
> "He clasped the crag with
> crooked hands."

How can you tell if you're a bad driver?
Red Green asks an expert, Dougie, for the answer.

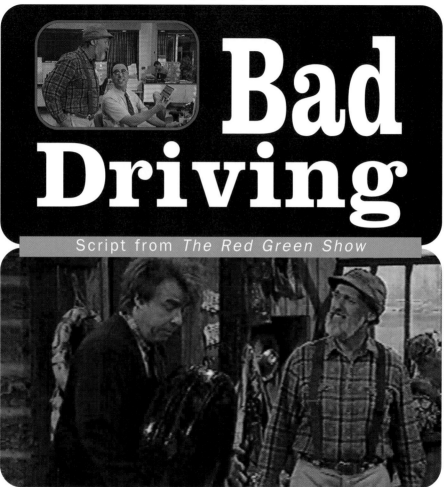

Bad Driving

Script from *The Red Green Show*

HAROLD: Our Car Buffs today are my Uncle Red and his best friend, Dougie Franklin. We've received a letter that reads: "Dear Car Buffs. I consider myself to be an above-average driver. However, the judge who took my licence away suggested I may not be as good as I think. Exactly how do you tell if you're a bad driver?"

RED: Well, Dougie, bad driving is certainly your area of expertise.

DOUGIE: No kidding, Red. You want to know about bad drivers, I'm your man. I must run into one of those bad drivers every month or so. Usually head-on. Okay, first of all, I blame our driver education system.

GOALS AT A GLANCE

- Present a script.
- Develop a script modelled on the selection.

RED: Yep. You're right there. I agree.

DOUGIE: I mean a kid spends four years at school learning how to control a pencil, which has no moving parts, could never go more than about a kilometre an hour, and won't burst into flame if you roll it over. Then they spend a few weeks learning to drive a two-tonne ball of metal, glass, and rubber, which goes a hundred and fifty clicks an hour down the highway.

RED: A hundred and fifty?

DOUGIE: And them driving instructors spend hours teaching kids how to parallel park and basically no time on stuff like avoiding high-speed collisions. How much danger can there be while you're parallel parking?

RED: Well, Dougie, remember that time you parallel parked into the tanker truck and...

DOUGIE: That was a freak accident, Red. My point is that there's all this time on parking and nothing on high-speed collisions. And speaking for myself, I parallel park maybe once a month, whereas I'm always avoiding high-speed collisions.

RED: Not always, Dougie. Remember that load of cabbages...

DOUGIE: That was a freak accident, Red. The fact remains that we're not teaching kids right. And how can we? The teachers are talking theory. You've gotta learn from someone who's been there. Like my own family. We've had every kind of automobile accident there is. Sideswipe, roll over, head-on, rear-ender, T-bone. We're the ones who should be teaching the kids. You get me, my dad, and my brother in front of a classroom and I guarantee ya it'd bring down the number of bad drivers on the road.

RED: Yeah. By three.

----

1. RESPONDING TO THE SCRIPT

a. Why could this segment of *The Red Green Show* be called a *satire*? What is the point of this satire? Does it provide the reader with any helpful factual information? Explain.

b. What do you find humorous in this script? Why? What is the punch line? Briefly define *humour*.

c. *The Red Green Show* is a popular Canadian TV show. Based on this script, explain why you think it might be popular.

d. In a paragraph, describe what makes a bad driver.

2. ORAL LANGUAGE PRESENT A SCRIPT

With two classmates, prepare a performance of this script. Think about how the words should be spoken. Practise performing the script, experimenting with volume, tone, expressions, pauses, and gestures. When you think your delivery is just right, present the script to your class. You may want to video-tape your presentation.

GROUP ASSESSMENT: Was your performance smooth and flawless? Did each group member present his or her lines in sync with the others? Did you work well together? Why or why not? If you work together again, what would you do differently?

3. MEDIA MAKER DEVELOP A TV SCRIPT

Assume that you're a writer on *The Red Green Show*. You've been asked to develop another short skit involving Red, Harold, and Dougie. Work alone, or with a partner, to develop this script. Your script should be at least a page long, and should include at least three funny points, including a punch line.

 Watch a few episodes of the show or reread "Bad Driving" to find out more about these characters. Note how the writers use punctuation, repetition, slang, and colloquial language.

*Would you like to know how to build a career
from being funny? You might pick up some
tips from this TV star—but remember, she's...*

Mary, Mary,
Quite Contrary

Profile by Charlotte Gray

Meet Marg Delahunty. She's
Canada's most fearless comic
character, lampooning politicians
and skewering the media weekly on
This Hour Has 22 Minutes.

Marg Delahunty isn't real, of course.
She's the delicious invention of Mary Walsh,
creator and co-star of CBC-TV's *This Hour
Has 22 Minutes*, a show that attracts nearly a
million viewers. Besides the feisty Delahunty
(named for a friend of her Auntie May), Walsh's
comic inventions include Dakey Dunn, a male
character based on her brother, Greg, and
Connie Bloor.

GOALS AT A GLANCE

■ Analyse the structure of magazine articles.
■ Create a comedy skit.

141

The show's knife-edged satire has catapulted Walsh to national fame, along with her co-stars, fellow Newfoundlanders Cathy Jones, Greg Thomey, and Rick Mercer. But while the brassy Marg would take such acclaim as her due, it seems that Walsh can't quite get used to success.

"Humour is a shield," Walsh admits. "It allows you to say the unsayable. I'm not in the least emotionally brave myself." Sitting in the sunny Toronto living room of writer Sandra Gwyn, a fellow Newfoundlander, Walsh hugs her knees to her chin. With a mix of teeth-gritting honesty and disarming chuckles, she talks about the self-doubt that has dogged her from childhood.

There were eight children in Walsh's family in St. John's, but she didn't grow up with her siblings. In 1952, aged eight months, she caught pneumonia and was sent next door to stay with her aunt because her parents' house was too damp for a sickly baby. She never went back, but she recalls the wicked attraction of her next-door family, always getting into trouble.

Auntie May is still a beloved figure in Walsh's life, regularly phoned and visited in her nursing home. But Walsh cracks her knuckles as she recalls how she used to wonder, Why me? Why did they give me away? "Being abandoned...it's one of those things that plays on you."

After finishing high school, Walsh made two mainland forays. The first was to Colorado, with an American boyfriend. It was a disaster. The second venture was to Toronto, at age twenty, to enroll in acting classes at Ryerson Polytechnical Institute. During a summer job at CBC Radio in St. John's, Walsh had decided she wanted to be a performer. But in Toronto, she was soon wooed away from school by a bunch of wickedly talented compatriots who were putting on a play at Theatre Passe Muraille. The group, which included Cathy Jones, Dyan Olsen, Greg Malone, and Tommy Sexton, would later become the comedy troupe CODCO.

The play, *Cod on a Stick*, was loosely based on the group's experiences as Newfoundlanders in Toronto. It was a success from the day it opened in 1973, and it was sweet revenge for a troupe sick and tired of Newfie jokes. Toronto audiences were so busy laughing that it didn't seem to matter that the jokes were on them! The play was also crucial to Walsh's own development: it took her back to the place where she didn't feel an outsider.

After touring the play through Newfoundland and Labrador, the CODCO members decided to stay home and use comedy to hold a mirror up to their own province. They wrote about Newfoundlanders leaving for Toronto, and the threat from greedy developers to St. John's historic downtown. It was in these skits that Walsh developed some of her finest comic creations, such as Mrs. Budgell, owner of a St. John's rooming house. Showing a prospective tenant around a broom closet, she says: "Don't let the size fool you, Mr. Macerelle. It is an efficiency apartment. You can stand in the middle of the apartment and touch everything..."

Walsh's characters succeed because she never patronizes them, says Jackie Maxwell, former artistic director of Toronto's Factory Theatre, who worked with Walsh on a 1986 show called *Hockey Wives*. "Her characters are too rich and human to be stereotypes, because she taps into their psyches. It's not a smart person play-acting someone stupid." Sandra Gwyn agrees that real emotion drives Walsh's comedy. "She feels passionately, and she's not afraid to break taboos."

By the early 1980s, Walsh was a well-established fixture in St. John's. Along with her CODCO work, she had taken on the administration of the Longshoremen's Protective Union Hall, a ramshackle building that housed an exuberant explosion of experimental theatre. As director, actress, and writer, she was involved with many of the hall's shows.

As an artist, Walsh flourished in this maelstrom of creative activity. But the small St. John's world also meant suffocating intimacy and competition, plus endless boozy post-performance binges. One dinner party ended with the dining chairs and wineglasses smashed, and Walsh last seen sitting on the top of a car.

Friends urged Walsh to do more theatre outside St. John's. Usually she ducked the challenge, but there were periodic glimpses of her in theatre on the mainland. Then all the CODCO players reached a national audience between 1987 and 1993, when the CBC ran seven seasons of half-hour comedy shows. The show allowed Walsh to learn how to shape her satire for TV. By the time CODCO went off the air, however, its members had had enough. "It was like a family, wonderful and horrible," says Walsh. "We'd been together too long."

Walsh was spreading her wings. She spent the summer of 1987 in a small Innu village in Labrador, organizing a community theatre project around the disruption caused by Armed Forces flights over Innu land. In 1992, she directed Ann-Marie MacDonald's *Goodnight Desdemona, Good Morning Juliet* at Montreal's Centaur Theatre. In 1993, her performance in Eugene O'Neill's *A Moon for the Misbegotten* in London, Ontario, received enthusiastic reviews.

By now, Walsh had a real family. In 1989, she had adopted a baby boy, Jessie. "Jessie changed everything," Walsh says. The most dramatic change was her gradual acknowledgment that alcohol was interfering with her life. "I'd always wanted to see myself as this romantic, wild, impassioned

The cast of *This Hour Has 22 Minutes.*

actress." But there was no room in this vision for a chubby baby and the demands of motherhood. So, in 1992, she quit drinking. In the process, she says, she grew up.

The success of *This Hour Has 22 Minutes* has reinforced Walsh's confidence. "You haven't got time to beat up on yourself when you've got to do the program every week. And I know that, even if by midweek I've still got nothing ready to record on Friday, somehow it all comes together." The format—a spoof newscast—allows Walsh to play to the best of her strengths, biting political commentary.

Walsh may have finally achieved a balance between life and work, but she still takes nothing for granted. As Marg Delahunty would say with a loud guffaw, "It's up with a rocket, down with the sticks, you know."

----

1. RESPONDING TO THE PROFILE

a. What, if anything, does the title of the article have to do with the nursery rhyme of the same name? Why do you think the author chose this title?

b. Mary Walsh says in this article, "Humour is a shield." What does she mean? Compare this humorist's definition of *humour* to the definition of *humour* you wrote for "Bad Driving."

c. Mary Walsh talks about the self-doubt that has plagued her since childhood, yet she's still able to perform in front of people. What feelings of self-doubt do you have? Do these feelings help you or prevent you from doing the things you want to do?

d. Not everyone is a performer. What type of personality do you think makes a good performer?

2. LITERATURE STUDIES MAGAZINE PROFILES

"Mary, Mary, Quite Contrary" is a *profile* (an article that is part biography and part "snapshot" of a well-known person). Reread this profile and note what it says in the introduction, the examples it uses, and how it concludes. Does it follow the model of an essay? Does it have a thesis that it develops and proves? Compare this profile to others you have read. Briefly explain what you have learned about the way profiles are written and organized.

3. MEDIA MAKER CREATE A COMEDY SKIT

Mary Walsh's comedy skits often use humour directed at TV shows, commercials, or famous people. Often, the humour grows from something she and her co-writers find ridiculous in the original. If possible, watch a few episodes of *This Hour Has 22 Minutes* and analyse how the group creates humour.

Work with a partner to write a five-minute comedy skit on something you find ridiculous (school lunches, a local politician, a commercial). Present your scene to a group of students or the class and ask for feedback.
PEER ASSESSMENT: What do others think of your scene? Do they find it as funny as you do? Do you agree with their comments? Explain.

4. LANGUAGE CONVENTIONS ADVERB CLAUSES

Adverbs can modify a verb or an adjective. A *clause* (a group of words that has a subject and a verb) can also act like an adverb and sometimes is used to introduce a sentence. Here is an example of an adverb clause:

> <u>After she finished high school</u>, Walsh made two mainland forays.

What does the clause add to the sentence? It gives you information about the verb, "made." It explains *when* Walsh made her "mainland forays." Notice, too, that at the end of the clause there is a comma. The comma separates the subordinate adverb clause from the main part of the sentence. If a clause comes at the end of a sentence, it has no comma. For example,

> Walsh made two mainland forays <u>after she finished high school</u>.

These words often begin adverb clauses: *after, although, as, before, if, once, since, until, when,* and *while.* How could you use adverb clauses to tighten your writing?

Notes for a Movie Script

Poem by M. Carl Holman

Fade in the sound of summer music,
Picture a hand plunging through her hair,
Next his socked feet and her scuffed dance slippers
Close, as they kiss on the rug-stripped stair.

Catch now the taxi from the station,
Capture her shoulders' sudden sag;
Switch to him silent in the barracks
While the room roars at the corporal's gag.

Let the drums dwindle in the distance,
Pile the green sea above the land;
While she prepares a single breakfast,
Reading the V mail in her hand.

Ride a cold moonbeam to the pillbox,*
Sidle the camera to his feet
Sprawled just outside in the gummy grasses,
Swollen like nightmare and not neat.

Now doorbell nudges the lazy morning:
She stills the sweeper for a while,
Twitches her dress, swings the screendoor open,
Cut—with no music—on her smile.

---

*pillbox: a small, low fortress with very thick walls and roof, having machine guns, antitank weapons, and so on.

1. Responding to the Poem

a. What story does the poem tell?

b. Why do you think the writer chose a movie **metaphor**? What other metaphor might be appropriate in telling this story? Explain your choice.

c. Locate the contrasting images the poet uses. What sense or picture do these pairs of images convey to you?

d. Why is there no music at the end?

> A **metaphor** is a comparison that describes one thing as something else, suggesting that they share a common quality.

2. Oral Language Present a Poem

Poems are meant to be heard as much as they are intended to be read. With a small group, read aloud "Notes for a Movie Script," and then listen as others read it. What different images do you imagine on hearing the poem? Discuss whether, when listening to a poem or song lyrics, you are more aware of the language of the words or the images the language creates in your mind.

3. Media Messages War Movie Review

With a small group, discuss a movie about war that you have all seen recently. In your notebook, briefly describe the events in the movie, and record answers to the following questions.

- Whose point of view was most of the movie told from?
- Whose point of view was not shown?
- Did the movie show all aspects of war? Explain.
- Did it glorify war in your opinion? Explain.
- How was music or sound effects used effectively or ineffectively?
- What shots or scenes were particularly effective? Why?
- What is your opinion of the acting? the script? the direction?
- Would you recommend this movie to others? Why or why not?

You could use these notes, and other points from your discussion, to develop a brief movie review. Write your review independently, and then compare it with the reviews of other group members.

Self-Assessment: Check that your review includes a brief synopsis of the movie without revealing the ending, your opinion on the acting, script, and direction, and a recommendation to others.

Before a movie gets filmed, an artist develops a storyboard—like this one.

To Build a Fire:

Bringing a Short Story to the Big Screen

Storyboard by Patrick Fitzgerald

Shooting a movie involves carefully planning each shot to get it right (on the first or second take, hopefully). A storyboard—a shot-by-shot visual of each scene in a script or story—can help the director, and the sound and special effects crew to foresee any problems. A detailed storyboard also helps them imagine what the finished movie will look like.

The following storyboard for the movie version of "To Build a Fire" shows the shot-by-shot planning for one of the story's most exciting scenes.

Scene:

A snowy, dark, winter day in the Far North. No clouds. Can tell from clothing that time period is early 19th century.

Characters:

Man, wearing mittens, hat with ear flaps, moccasins, warm socks, and a fur coat. Looks prepared for cold. Grey dog, wolfish, lean, hungry.

1. POV: FROM ABOVE/CUT TO
   LG SHOT, ESTABLISH ARCTIC SETTING/MOOD

GOALS AT A GLANCE

- Develop a treatment for a movie.
- Analyse the effect of movie techniques.

2. MED SHOT, CLOSE IN ON MAN AND DOG
   FILLING SCREEN
   SOUND FX: FIRE SIZZLES OUT

3. Man tries to grab dog with arms. Dog
   struggles.
   SOUND FX: WHINING OF DOG

4. Man now desperate.
   ZOOM IN ON MAN'S FACE/ZOOM IN ON EYES

5. Dog breaks away, backs up.
   CUT TO DOG'S FACE/CLOSE-UP
   SOUND FX: WHINE TURNS TO GROWL,
   SNARLING
   MAN'S PANICKED BREATHING

6. Dog has hackles raised, stance shows fear,
   anger.
   CAMERA FOLLOWS MOVEMENT OF DOG
   CUE MUSIC TO INCREASE VOLUME SLOWLY

7. Man looks despairingly at frozen hands.
   FADE TO MAN/CUT TO HANDS/TO CLOSE-UP
   OF DISMAYED FACE
   PULL BACK TO FULL SHOT INCLUDING
   THE DOG

8. Dog returns to unlit fire. Man tries to
   warm arms.
   MED SHOT OF MAN AND DOG
   CUT TO MAN'S ARMS FLAILING
   SOUND FX: BEAT OF ARMS DROWNS OUT
   MUSIC

9. In panic, man runs, stumbling through snow.
   SHOT OF MAN AND DOG, PANNING TO
   BLUE SKY
   CUT SOUND FX OF BEATING ARMS SHARPLY,
   TO SOUND OF RUNNING, HEAVY BREATHING

10. Man has vision of Mercury, Roman
    messenger of gods.
    MED SHOT OF MAN
    SUPERIMPOSE IMAGE, HIS VISION OF
    SELF AS MERCURY
    CLOSE-UP ON MERCURY'S WINGS
    SOUND FX: HOWLING OF DOG

11. Man stumbles and falls.
    MED SHOT OF MAN FALLING

12. Man rests. Looks peaceful.
    MED SHOT OF CRUMPLED BODY
    CLOSE-UP ON HANDS/CUT TO FACE
    CUE MUSIC, HAUNTING MELODY
    SUGGESTING COLD DEATH

13. Man forces himself to rise, begins to run
    again.
    POV: FROM ABOVE SEE MAN RISE
    PULL OUT TO A SHOT FROM GROUND
    LEVEL
    SOUND FX: LABOURED BREATHING,
    RUNNING

13. Man falls. Dog moves in, sits to watch
    alertly.
    POV: DOG'S EYE VIEW OF MAN
    PULL OUT TO MED SHOT INCLUDING DOG
    FADE TO CLOSE-UP ON MAN'S FACE

15. Man closes eyes, speaks, and after a while, dies. Dog sniffs warily.
    DIALOGUE: "YOU WERE RIGHT, OLD HOSS; YOU WERE RIGHT."
    CUT TO MED SHOT OF MAN AND DOG
    CUT TO DOG
    SOUND FX: DOG SNIFFING, WHINING

16. Dog moves off, the survivor. In distance, smoke indicates salvation is not that far away.
    POV: FROM GROUND SEE BACK OF DOG FOLLOW AS HE TROTS AWAY INTO DISTANCE
    CUT TO SHOT OF ARCTIC LANDSCAPE/AS IN OPENING OF SEQUENCE.

pov: point of view
med shot: medium shot
lg shot: long shot
sound fx: sound effects

1. RESPONDING TO THE STORYBOARD

a. Read the short story "To Build a Fire" on pages 99–113. How does the last scene of the short story compare to this storyboard?

b. Do you think you would like this movie? Why or why not? What elements of movies does it include that you usually enjoy?

c. Why do you think stories are often changed when they are made into movies?

d. Movies are a visual/auditory medium. Prose is meant to be read and sometimes heard. Both mediums, though, use some similar elements. Explain what you think they are and how they are used differently in each medium.

e. Music is suggested at various places in the storyboard. What music would you choose for these parts and why?

f. Add a "voice-over" narration to the storyboard sequence using the author's words. To add your narration, you should be able to answer these questions: What shots should have narration? How much should you add? Should it be in the first or third person?

2. MEDIA MAKER MOVIE TREATMENT

Scripts are rarely sold to a movie producer without someone first presenting a story synopsis called a *treatment*. This is a short narrative—without a lot of technical movie description—that gives a sense of what the movie will be about. Write a one-page treatment for the short story "To Build a Fire." Be sure to emphasize the dramatic elements that would make this movie interesting. Be aware that a movie is at least ninety minutes long. Short stories often don't have enough action to last this long on the screen. What other events will you have to add to make this story a feature-length film?

3. MEDIA MESSAGES ANALYSE TECHNIQUES

Filmmakers use a number of techniques to create a story: photography, sound effects, music, lighting, editing, and sometimes special visual effects. Select one of these elements (or one of your choosing) and, keeping it in mind, watch a movie. Write a one-page review explaining how the element you have chosen enhances or lessens the effect and enjoyment of the movie.

SELF-ASSESSMENT: How critical are you when you watch a movie or TV program? Do you notice techniques such as photography or sound effects? Are performances more important to you than technique? Explain.

*Unco-operative caribou and wolves that had
to be taught to be wild were only
some of the problems in making this hit movie.*

The Saga
of Filming
Never Cry Wolf

Article by Bruce Brown

E ven before he was fully awake, the man could feel the late summer
afternoon change course. He had dozed off after a solitary swim in an
arctic lake, and now he found himself in the path of a heavy-breath-
ing herd of caribou. Some of the animals seemed agitated. Scanning the
herd, the man saw why: they were being driven by a pack of wolves
hunting along their flank. Impulsively, the man began to run.

Zigzagging across the tundra, he was swept along with the chase. He
saw the way the wolves worked, testing the caribou with quick bursts that
were just as quickly abandoned if the deer seemed strong. Then the wolves
sensed one sick caribou and poured on the speed, isolating the animal from
the rest of the herd and running it hard. The fatigued buck turned to face
his attackers on a small rise, but in an instant 5 wolves flew at him like
blades from a knife thrower's hand. They knocked the buck down on the
first strike and killed him while other caribou hurried past, sniffing the air.

Those who see Carroll Ballard's *Never Cry Wolf** may find their own
nostrils flaring, for this hunting scene vividly conveys both the power of
the wolf pack and the misconceptions many have about *Canis lupus***.
Based on the 1963 Farley Mowat bestseller of the same name, the movie

---

* **Never Cry Wolf:** a movie based on a Farley Mowat novel of the same name, was released in theatres
in 1983. It was directed by Carroll Ballard and starred Charles Martin Smith and Brian Dennehy.
Canis lupus: wolf.

GOALS AT A GLANCE

■ Respond critically to the article.
■ Analyse the use of phrases and clauses.

tells of a bearded young biologist named Tyler who is studying arctic wolves for the Canadian Wildlife Service. He finds that wolves eat chiefly mice and rodents. When they do kill a sick or injured caribou, they confirm the Inuit saying, "The wolf keeps the caribou strong."

The tale that Ballard brings to the screen is about the loss of wildness in the world. The same directorial eye with which he made *The Black Stallion*, a landmark in animal photography, is evident in the handling of the wolves. The three wolves that Tyler comes to call George, Angeline, and Uncle Albert emerge as characters who watch Tyler when he doesn't realize it, but let him watch them only when they choose. Their habits structure Tyler's days, and in the end they propel the film to its dramatic climax.

To play Tyler, Ballard chose Charles Martin Smith, best known for his role as Terry in *American Graffiti*. Two Canadians play other major parts: Samson Jorah plays Mike, and Zachary Ittimangnaq plays the wolf shaman Ootek.

Ballard managed to coax exceptional performances from his animal stars—even though all the wolves in the film were raised in captivity and had to be taught to behave like wild wolves.

A scene from *Never Cry Wolf*.

Almost as remarkable as the animal scenes, are the difficulties the *Never Cry Wolf* crew encountered during what became a marathon filming in the North. In his planning in early 1980, Ballard discovered it would be impossible to use wild caribou in a critical sequence. Some Inuit near Nome, Alaska, agreed to rent him a herd of about 2500 domestic caribou as long as the filming ended on June 15, when they would round up the animals and cut off their velvety new antlers, prized in Asia as an aphrodisiac.

But the sequence called for no snow on the ground, and the snow didn't melt until the beginning of June, so Ballard and his crew had about two weeks to shoot. "It rained the first 10 days," he recalled. "On the 11th day, buyers arrived with briefcases full of money for the antlers." Then the animals disappeared in a storm, and it took helicopters and riders several days to find them. With Ballard's production manager negotiating to hold off the Inuit and the buyers, shooting began.

In one scene, after emerging nude from a lake, Smith was to mingle with the herd. "I was supposed to spring over an embankment, surprise the caribou, and run among them. When I went over the top, though, they were long gone. You can't just sneak up on caribou—they make their living *not* being sneaked up on."

Ballard did not finish shooting before the caribou had their antlers cut off, and he decided to push on to Skagway, Alaska, for the next sequence. The roving film crew, made up largely of technicians from Vancouver, came to resemble a sort of arctic commando outfit that had to learn to accommodate to Ballard's style. He was always willing to keep reshooting a scene until it was absolutely right, or to sit and wait for the weather he wanted. Thus, the filming of *Never Cry Wolf* stretched into more than 9 months over a period of a year and a half.

Probably the most dangerous stunt in the movie occurs when biologist Tyler falls through lake ice, sinks to the bottom under the weight of his gear, fights free to the surface, shatters the ice with his shotgun, and drags himself to the shore. In preparation, holes were cut in the half-metre-thick ice and allowed to refreeze a bit. Underneath the ice, ropes and platforms were rigged; after Smith fell through, divers would give him oxygen and help get him in position to break back up through the ice.

"Right away," recounts Ballard, "2 of the divers got into trouble— oxygen-regulator freeze-up—and had to be hauled out. Then a stunt person tried, and he got into trouble. So we were down to Charlie, and I asked him. 'You want to try it?'" Ballard laughed. "Charlie said, 'Sure'—he put on the gear, dropped into the lake, swam 15 m under the ice and did the scene. Not once, but twice." The second time was to satisfy Ballard's desire to get the segment just right.

To find the 2 Inuit actors, Ballard dispatched freelance consultant John Houston on a more than 16 000-km trek across the Canadian North. "It was a tremendously romantic journey," said Houston, a Canadian whose father, James, is the author of *The White Dawn* and other books about the Arctic. "We travelled by plane, snowmobile, and dogsled."

At each settlement, Houston—who later became Ballard's assistant—broadcast a radio invitation to local residents to audition for the movie. "I would say, 'Good morning, I am the son of the Left-Handed Man'—my father's name among the Inuit—'and I have come on behalf of the folks who bring you *Wonderful World*.'

"Because Walt Disney has provided a good deal of TV entertainment in the Arctic, scores would show up to audition on videotape. Many of the shows they put on for us were quite imaginative. One man demonstrated his expertise with an 11-m dog whip."

At Baker Lake, Nunavut, Houston found the Inuit who plays Mike. "At the end of our taping sessions," Houston said, "a man walked in who said his name was Samson Jorah and that he was an apprentice mechanic and had done some hunting." As Jorah opened up and delivered a monologue, he reminded Houston of the young Buster Keaton. "He had great comic ability, delivering deadpan lines with wonderful intuitive timing. When I screened the tape for the director, he said, 'I want to have a shot at this man.'"

Houston's next stop, Pelly Bay, provided the second Inuit character, the wolf shaman Ootek. "When we asked about an older man to appear in the movie, everyone said, 'Older man? Talk to Zachary Ittimangnaq. He's got a lot of movie experience.' It turned out that Zachary had appeared in a series of films made by the National Film Board about the old ways of the Inuit. Fifteen years later, he was living as a sort of retired movie star in Pelly Bay." Houston knew right away that Ballard would choose Ittimangnaq to play Ootek because he is a venerable man, "what the Japanese call a living national treasure."

The 30 wolves used in making *Never Cry Wolf* were accompanied 24 hours a day by trainers skilled at the judicious dispensation of chicken parts, wieners, and, sometimes, authority. Ballard once persuaded Kolchak, the wolf that plays George, to sniff for a close-up by having a live chicken in a cage sitting on top of his own head as he sat behind the whirring camera.

The wolves not only had to be coaxed and coached, they had to learn at least some lessons of the wild the hard way. The 5 used in the caribou attack-scene, for instance, had never hunted caribou. The leader of the pack, a large male

Tyler threatens poachers who have been capturing wolves.

named Avatar, tried to take on a healthy caribou buck with a broad span of antlers. Avatar ran the buck for nearly a kilometre and finally drove it out into the water. The wolf dove in pursuit, but as soon as his feet no longer touched the strand, the caribou (still touching bottom) wheeled, caught the wolf with its rack and hurled him high in the air. "I'll never forget the look in Avatar's eyes when he came down," says Debbie Coe, the wolf's trainer. Avatar survived the encounter, and thereafter the wolves concentrated on the weaker members of the herd.

When the *Never Cry Wolf* crew returned to Nome, Alaska, in June 1981 to have a second try at the caribou hunt sequence, wolves and people were better prepared, and the crucial scene was finished. But even with all filming completed, months of work remained.

"The problems in shooting were nothing compared to what we had in postproduction," says Ballard. The material was edited, re-edited, and eventually cut to 2900 m of film from an original 229 000 m. At last, 3$^{1/2}$ years after starting the project, Ballard was satisfied.

Some of the movie's happiest incidents just happened to be filmed in Ballard's eagerness to get it all. At the very end of *Never Cry Wolf*, while the credits roll, Tyler and Ootek sit together in the evening sunlight. Tyler makes 3 snowballs, juggles them, and then hands them to the old man. The grey-haired wolf shaman takes them with a laugh, tries unsuccessfully to match Tyler, and then performs a juggling pantomime. In this spontaneous moment fact and fiction meet, like hands pressed to the mirror, and become the image of 2 people having the time of their lives.

1. RESPONDING TO THE ARTICLE

a. What do you think the purpose of this article is?

b. Reread the first two paragraphs. What impression do they convey? Compare them to the last paragraph. How are they similar? What idea is the author trying to express in the introduction and the last paragraph?

c. How is the director of the movie portrayed? What do you imagine are the qualities that would make a good movie director?

d. Does the author have a personal point of view? Discuss why you think writers of information articles should or shouldn't have a point of view.

2. LANGUAGE CONVENTIONS PHRASES AND CLAUSES

Simple sentences are made up of a subject and a verb, for example, "She thinks" or "The dog is barking." Of course, most of what you read, as well as what you write, uses more involved sentence constructions. **Phrases** and **clauses** are elements of sentences that allow you to express more complex ideas. Look at the definitions at right and compare them to the following examples from the article.

> A **phrase** is a group of related words that does not have *both* a subject and a verb.
> A **clause** is a group of related words that has both a subject and a verb or verb phrase. A *main clause* is an independent sentence. A *subordinate clause* can't stand alone as a sentence; it supports the main clause.

Phrase   To play Tyler, Ballard chose Charles Martin Smith, best known for his role as Terry in *American Graffiti.*

Clause   As Jorah opened up and delivered a monologue, he reminded Houston of the young Buster Keaton.

Each phrase and clause modifies some part of the main sentence. What do the above underlined words modify? Reread "The Saga of Filming *Never Cry Wolf*" and list a few more phrase and clause examples, explaining what they modify.

SELF-ASSESSMENT: If you examine your own writing, you will see that you use both phrases and clauses. Do you know what they modify? Do they help make your writing clearer?

HOW TO WRITE A MOVIE REVIEW

Goals at a Glance

- Summarize and describe a movie. • Present an opinion with supporting evidence.

A movie critic's job is to let the audience know if a movie is worth seeing. To be a great critic, you should know your audience, be able to state your opinion clearly and concisely, and really love the movies.

Review Styles and Features

Take a look at the variety of movie reviews in newspapers, magazines, video and TV guides, and on Web sites. Take note of the different styles and approaches to reviewing. These are the common elements in movie reviews:

- basic information about the movie
- an opinion on the overall quality of the movie
- supporting evidence to back up the opinion
- a descriptive opening sentence
- the movie title and genre (romantic comedy, drama, documentary, horror, and so on)
- the names of the leading actors, producers, director, and sometimes the cinematographer or screenwriter
- a final rating

At the Movies

Choose a movie that you think your readers will want to see. Remember to bring a notebook when you view the movie so that you can make notes either during or immediately after the screening. Jot down the title, the director, the leading actors, and any other pertinent information.

After you've seen the movie, think about your initial reaction to it. You might want to focus on the following elements and record your responses to them.

- The **actors**: Were they well cast? Were they good actors or not?
- The **directing**: Did the director handle the actors and screenplay well?
- The **screenplay**: Was the script mediocre or superb?
- The **cinematography:** Was the camera work spectacular or boring?

PROCESS

Writing Your Review

Here are some strategies you can use to help you organize and write your review.

1. Decide on the one major element that made the movie good or bad. This might be the acting, direction, or screenplay.

2. Your opening paragraph should grab the reader's attention by setting the tone of the review. It needs to include a description of the movie as well as your opinion of it. Use vivid adjectives, such as *fast-paced, witty, disturbing, shocking,* or *action-packed.*

3. The synopsis, or summary, of the movie should be brief. It should describe the main action or conflict and characters without giving away the whole story or the ending. If what makes the movie so good is a surprise in the plot that you have to reveal, include a warning giving the reader a choice about whether or not to keep reading.

4. Give your opinion of the movie, offering evidence to support it. Examine why you have such strong feelings about the movie. Ask yourself the following questions:
   - Was the story well-developed?
   - Were the characters believable and multi-dimensional, or stereotypical? If they were stereotypical, was there a good reason?
   - Was the movie too long or too short?
   - Were you entertained throughout the movie or were there parts that dragged?
   - If you state that the movie was funny and well-written, give examples of humorous lines. If you claim that the acting was poor, offer reasons. If you have mixed feelings about the movie, sort out what you believe were the good and bad parts, and write about these separately.

5. End with a concluding statement explaining why you recommend or do not recommend the movie.

6. Give the movie a rating. You can use letters of the alphabet (A being the best, D being the worst) or stars (five stars, the top rating, one star, the lowest). Expressing your personal opinion here is vital, as many readers will determine whether or not to see a movie based on your review and rating.

Revising Your Review

At the revision stage, you have a chance to make sure your review has achieved the right tone and mood, and will be useful in helping your readers decide whether or not to see the movie.

Self-Assessment

Use the checklist below to assess your review.

- ❏ I researched various types of reviews.
- ❏ I selected a movie that was appropriate for my audience.
- ❏ I watched the movie with a critical eye, examining the writing, acting, cinematography, directing, music, and so on.
- ❏ I recorded my initial reactions to the movie.
- ❏ I informed the readers about the basics of the movie.
- ❏ I presented my opinions and supported them with examples.

Internet Is Hero's **Window**

When it comes to publishing magazines, the Internet has changed many things. Hero Joy Nightingale demonstrates how.

NEWSPAPER ARTICLE BY MARA BELLABY

CANTERBURY, England Hero Joy Nightingale lets the whole world know what's on her mind, though she's unable to speak or walk.

Nightingale puts together an Internet magazine that boasts readers in 77 countries and guest writers like U.N. Secretary-General Kofi Annan, Canadian author Margaret Atwood, and the leader of the Anglican Church, Archbishop George Carey.

Now on its 5th issue, *From the Window* began 2 years ago as a way for Nightingale to meet people beyond Canterbury, the fabled city where she lives.

It has evolved, however, into an acclaimed and award-winning project that led to a visit with Annan

Hero Joy Nightingale, who has a rare neurological condition, p[]
together an Internet magazine that boasts readers in 77 countri[]
and guest writers such as Margaret Atwood.

in his 38th-floor office at the United Nations headquarters in New York, a globetrotting journey to pick up a prize in Australia, and a rush of new friends.

"I can't find the superlative to describe it," says Wendy Clarke, head

GOALS AT A GLANCE

- Develop a form for evaluating Web sites.
- Analyse the structure and content of newspaper articles.

of occupational therapy for the East Kent Health Authority, who has worked with Nightingale since she was 2. "It has opened up the world to her."

Nightingale was born with what doctors call a "locked-in condition." It is marked by an inability to perform complex movements of any of her muscles, abnormally low muscle tone, and an unknown neurological disorder.

To communicate, Nightingale's arm must be supported while she scrawls letters into an assistant's palm. The "enabler," currently Nightingale's mother, must recognize the subtle movements of Nightingale's hand and transcribe her thoughts. It is a slow, arduous, word-by-word process.

"Writing is everything," says Nightingale. "Without writing I am nothing because everything I feel, think, and need must be conveyed through my spelling."

It is that love of writing—and meeting new people—that has made the Internet such a critical part of her life, she says.

Working with her mother in a cozy room overflowing with books, Nightingale spends all day in front of the computer screen. She hunts down potential essayists, sifts through contributions, and puts down her own thoughts.

It is nearly a full-time job—for Nightingale and her mother, who must type all of her dictation into the computer.

Nightingale, who also composes music and plans giant art installations, keeps a list of people she wants contributions from for the magazine. Successes so far: Annan, Atwood, and Helen Sharman, the first Briton in space. Among those on the wanted list: new British poet laureate Andrew Motion, writer John Mortimer, and tennis star Tim Henman.

"It's very difficult for me to explain or even understand why some small percentage of my targets respond and an even smaller percentage respond with an article," Nightingale says. "But it's very nice when it happens."

From the Window is graphically simple. But the heavy-hitting contributors who write first-person accounts of their experiences and Nightingale's blunt talk about being disabled—put the site in a category all its own.

"I don't dwell on what I might have been like if I were not disabled, because it's too ridiculously silly to do so," Nightingale says.

It is her straight-talking descriptions about herself and her disability that make *From the Window* come alive.

"I have a lot to do and I have to get on with it," she says.

From the Window can be found at <http://atschool.eduweb.co.uk/hojoy/>.

Web Tips:
The Equation

#1: Content (is King or Queen!)

No matter how flashy or impressive a Web site is, it will ultimately be judged by its content. Is the text well written? Is it succinct and communicative? Is it tailored to the target audience? These questions are paramount for the design of a successful Web site.

#2: Visual Appeal

Layout, image quality, and colour scheme each play an important role in the overall appearance of a Web site. The legibility of the text should be top priority—always try to have a high contrast between the text and the background.

#3: Creativity

Develop a theme or metaphor for the Web site. It is challenging, but well worth the effort. When the images and overall look of a site create "thematic glue," the site is an experience as opposed to a mere collection of information.

#4: Ease of Navigation

Is the information logically laid out? Would a novice user be able to navigate easily through the site? How deep into the site is the critical information? Always test the site with inexperienced Web users and use their feedback. Create a navigation scheme that makes sense for the novice but that doesn't annoy the expert. Use colour coding where possible and keep a consistent layout.

#5: Responsiveness

"If I don't see something in ten seconds, I leave!" Believe it or not, this is a very common statement among Web users. Sites that download quickly are sites that will be used at least once! Ensure that images appear quickly, but without compromising on image quality. Have the text download first and then let the images fill in.

#6: Multi-Platform Compatibility

Does the site perform properly on the major browsers? On different releases of the browsers? Does the site work well on low-end systems (640X480 resolution and 256 colour-depth)? What about high-end systems? Does the site look great on Apple systems as well as PCs? These questions are critical since you have no way of controlling the user's environment.

#7: Marketing

"Build it and they will come." This statement is a fallacy on the Web. The site must be easy to find from the commonly used search engines. All marketing materials, including print advertising, letterhead, and so on, should promote the site. Encourage repeat visits by ensuring that the site is not static. Keep it fresh by changing content regularly.

=

Result

An award-winning high traffic site!

1. RESPONDING TO THE SELECTION

a. Why is the Internet a particularly important tool for Hero Nightingale?

b. On the Internet, find an example of a personal Web site (or examine *From the Window*). Write a brief review of the site.

c. The Web tips are written to help explain how to create a successful Web site. Explain whether you think this information is helpful.

d. List the information on Web sites that you didn't understand. What resources could you use to find this information?

e. What did you learn from this article about creating e-zines and Web sites? What more do you want to learn?

2. MEDIA MESSAGES WEB SITE EVALUATION

Web sites on the Internet use both print and visual media to convey information. They are organized with sections and subsections. Not all sites, however, are interesting, easy to follow, or comprehensible.

Create a report form that you can use to evaluate Web sites. For example, your report form could contain the subject or purpose of the site, how it is organized, how easy it is to get around or navigate, its use of graphics, and whether it is easy or difficult to read and understand. Use this form to assess several Web sites. Share this information with your classmates.

3. MEDIA MESSAGES ANALYSE NEWSPAPER ARTICLES

If you examine newspaper articles, you'll find they have many elements in common. Choose several newspaper articles and answer these questions:

- What does the first paragraph tell you about the article?
- How is the heading related to the first paragraph?
- Does each article answer the 5 W's of journalism?
- What is the average length of each paragraph?
- How does each article use quotations?

Summarize what you have learned about how newspaper articles are written.

SELF-ASSESSMENT: Choose an article that you've written and shorten it by half its length. Does it still convey the same basic information? Does it read better in the shortened version?

SELF-ASSESSMENT: MEDIA

As you worked on the activities in this unit, what did you learn about

- films and film scripts?
- storyboards?
- movie reviews?
- news reporting?
- TV?
- Internet Web sites?
- advertising?

How did this unit help you learn more about what goes on behind the scenes in creating various media? Write a statement in your notebook explaining what you learned.

MEDIA MAKER MOVIES

With a partner, discuss what you learned about analysing and creating movies during this unit. Together, generate ideas that you think would make a good movie. Write a one-page film treatment proposing the best idea for the next blockbuster. Outline how you think the story should develop. Write a one-paragraph description for each of the main characters. Share your treatment with another group.

MEDIA MESSAGES ANALYSE ADS

Choose a print or TV ad that you think is effective. Show the ad to a number of people, and have each person write a sentence or two about what image or message the ad conveys to them. Summarize the results of your survey.

Now research the product the ad is selling. Look in consumer magazines and books for information or search the Internet for consumer opinions and information. Interview people who have used the product and ask for their recommendations.

Compare your findings with the summary of your survey. In an essay, explain whether or not the ad accurately described the product. Did the facts you discovered support the claims in the ad?

PERSONAL FOCUS

"First say to yourself
what you would be,
and then do what you
have to do."

—*Epictetus*

IDENTITY

*Have you ever
pulled a prank
and regretted
it later?*

I've Got
Gloria

Short Story by M. E. Kerr

"Hello? Mrs. Whitman?"

"Yes?"

"I've got Gloria."

"Oh, thank heaven! Is she all right?"

"She's fine, Mrs. Whitman."

"Where is she?"

"She's here with me."

"Who are you?"

"You can call me Bud."

"Bud who?"

"Never mind that, Mrs. Whitman. I've got your little dog and she's anxious to get back home."

"Oh, I know she is. She must miss me terribly. Where are you? I'll come and get her right away."

"Not so fast, Mrs. Whitman. First, there's a little something you must do."

"Anything. Just tell me where to find you."

"*I'll* find *you*, Mrs. Whitman, *after* you do as I say."

"What do you mean, Bud?"

"I mean that I'll need some money before I get Gloria home safely to you."

"Money?"

"She's a very valuable dog."

"Not really. I got her from the pound."

GOALS AT A GLANCE

■ Analyse how writers develop characters.
■ Write a story modelled on the selection.

"But she's valuable to you, isn't she?"

"She's everything to me."

"So you have to prove it, Mrs. Whitman."

"What is this?"

"A dognapping. I have your dog and you have to pay to have her returned safely to you."

There was a pause.

I could just imagine her face—that face I hated ever since she flunked me. That mean, freckled face, with the glasses over those hard little green eyes, the small, pursed lips, the mop of frizzy red hair topping it all…Well, top this, Mrs. Whitman: I do not even have that nutsy little bulldog of yours. She *is* lost, just as your countless signs nailed up everywhere announce that she is…All I have is this one chance to get revenge, and I'm grabbing it!

Now her voice came carefully. "How much do you want?"

"A thousand dollars, Mrs. Whitman. A thou, in one-hundred-dollar bills,

and Gloria will be back drooling on your lap."

"A *thousand* dollars?"

Got to you, didn't I? Did your stomach turn over the way mine did when I saw that F in math?

"You heard me, Mrs. Whitman."

"Are you one of my students?"

"Oh, like I'm going to tell you if I am."

"You must be."

"I could be, couldn't I? You're not everyone's dream teacher, are you?"

"Please, don't hurt my dog."

"I'm not cruel by nature."

I don't take after my old man. He said he was sorry that I flunked math because he knew how much I was counting on the hike through Yellowstone this summer. He said maybe the other guys would take some photos so I could see what I was missing while I went to summer school to get a passing grade. "Gee, Scott," he said, "what a shame, and now you won't get an allowance, either, or have TV in your bedroom, or the use of the computer. But never mind, sonny boy," he said, "there'll be lots to do around the house. I'll leave lists for you every day of things to be done before I get home."

Mrs. Whitman whined, "I just don't have a thousand dollars. I don't know where I'll get so much money, either."

Sometimes I whined that way, and my mom would say, "Scotty, we wouldn't be so hard on you if you'd only take responsibility for your actions. We tell you to be in at eleven p.m. and you claim the bus was late. We ask you to take the tapes back to Videoland and you say we never said to do it. You always have an excuse for everything! You never blame yourself!"

"Mrs. Whitman? I don't mean to be hard on you but that's the deal, see. A thou in hundreds."

"Just don't hurt Gloria."

"Gee, what a shame that you have to worry about such a thing. She's a sweet little dog, and I know she misses you because she's not eating."

"She doesn't eat dog food, Bud. I cook for her."

"That's why she doesn't eat, hmm? I don't know how to cook."

"You could just put a frozen dinner in the microwave. A turkey dinner, or a Swanson's pot roast. I'll pay you for it."

"A thousand dollars plus ten for frozen dinners? Is that what you're suggesting?"

"Let me think. Please. I have to think how I can get the money."

"Of course, you do. I'll call you back, Mrs. Whitman, and meanwhile I'll go to the store and get some Swanson's frozen dinners."

"When will you—"

I hung up.

I could hear Dad coming up the stairs.

"Scott?"

"Yes, sir?"

"I'm going to take the car in for an oil change. I want you to come with me."

"I have some homework, sir."

"I want you to come with me. *Now.*"

In the car, he said, "We need to talk."

"About what?" I said.

There was one of her Lost Dog signs tacked to the telephone pole at the end of our street.

"We need to talk about this summer," he said.

"What about it?"

"You *have* to make up the math grade. That you *have* to do. I'm sorry you can't go to Yellowstone."

"Yeah."

"There's no other way if you want to get into any kind of college. Your other grades are fine. But you need math...What's so hard about math, Scott?"

"I hate it!"

"I did, too, but I learned it. You have to study."

"Mrs. Whitman doesn't like me."

"Why doesn't she like you?"

"She doesn't like anyone but that bulldog."

"Who's lost, apparently."

"Yeah."

"The signs are everywhere."

"Yeah."

"But she wouldn't deliberately flunk you, would she?"

"Who knows?"

"Do you really think a teacher would flunk you because she doesn't like you?"

"Who knows?"

"Scott, you've got to admit when you're wrong. I'll give you an example. I was wrong when I said you couldn't have an allowance or TV or use of the computer, et cetera. I was angry and I just blew! That was wrong. It wouldn't have made it any easier for you while you're trying to get a passing grade in math. So I was wrong! I apologize and I take it back."

"How come?"

"How come? Because I'm sorry. I thought about it and it bothered me. I'm a hothead, and I don't like that about myself. Okay?"

"Yeah."

"Maybe that's what's wrong here."

"What's wrong where?"

"Between us."

"Is something wrong between us?"

"Scotty, I'm trying to talk with you. About us. I want to work things out so we get along better."

"Yeah."

"Sometimes I do or say rash things."

"Yeah."

"I always feel lousy after."

"Oh, yeah?"

"Do you understand? I shouldn't take things out on you. That's petty. Life is hard enough. We don't have to be mean and spiteful with each other. Agreed?"

"Yeah." I was thinking about the time our dog didn't come home one night. I couldn't sleep. I even prayed. When he got back all muddy the next morning, I broke into tears and told him, "Now you're making me blubber like a baby!"

Dad was still on my case.

"Scott, I want you to think about why Mrs. Whitman flunked you."

"I just told you: she doesn't like me."

"Are you really convinced that you're good at math but the reason you failed was because she doesn't like you?"

"Maybe."

"Is she a good teacher?"

"She never smiles. She's got these tight little lips and these ugly freckles."

"So she's not a good teacher?"

"I can't learn from her."

"Did you study hard?"

"I studied. Sure. I studied."

"How many others flunked math?"

"What?"

"How many others flunked math?"

"No one."

"Speak up."

"I said, I'm the only one."

"So others learn from her despite her tight little lips and ugly freckles?"

"I guess."

"Scott, who's to blame for your flunking math?"

"Okay," I said. "Okay."

"Who is to blame?"

"Me. Okay? I didn't study that hard."

He sighed and said, "There. Good. You've accepted the blame...How do you feel?"

"I feel okay." I really didn't, though. I was thinking about that dumb bulldog running loose somewhere, and about Mrs. Whitman worried sick now that she thought Gloria'd been dognapped.

Dad said, "I think we both feel a lot better."

We sat around in the waiting room at the service centre.

Dad read *Sports Illustrated*, but I couldn't concentrate on the magazines there or the ballgame on TV. I was down. I knew what Dad meant when he'd told me he felt bad after he "blew" and that he didn't like himself for it.

I kept glancing toward the pay phone. I stuck my hands in my pants pockets. I had a few quarters.

"I'm going to call Al and see what he's doing tonight," I said.

Dad said, "Wait until you get home. We'll be leaving here very shortly."

"I'm going to look around," I said.

I didn't know Mrs. Whitman's number. I'd copied it down from one of the Lost Dog signs and ripped it up after I'd called her. I hadn't planned to follow up the call, get money from her: nothing like that. I just wanted to give her a good scare.

I went over to the phone book and looked her up.

Then I ducked inside the phone booth, fed the slot a quarter, and dialled.

"Hello?"

"Mrs. Whitman? I don't have your dog. I was playing a joke."

"I know you don't have my dog. Gloria's home. The dog warden found her and brought her back right after you hung up on me."

I was relieved. At least she wouldn't have to go all night worrying about getting Gloria back.

"I was wrong," I said. "It was petty. I'm sorry."

"Do you know what you put me through, Scott Perkins?"

I just hung up.

I stood there with my face flaming.

"Scott?" My father was looking all over for me, calling me and calling me. "Scott! Are you here? The car's ready!"

All the way home, he lectured me on how contrary I was. Why couldn't I have waited to phone Al? What was it about me that made me just go ahead and do something I was expressly told I shouldn't do? "Just when I think we've gotten someplace," he said, "you turn around and go against my wishes.

"*Why?*" he shouted.

I said, "What?" I hadn't been concentrating on all that he was saying. I was thinking that now she knew my name—don't ask me how—and now what was she going to do about it?

"I asked you *why* you go against my wishes," Dad said. "Nothing I say seems to register with you."

"It registers with me," I said. "I just seem to screw up sometimes."

"I can hardly believe my ears." He was smiling. "You actually said sometimes you screw up. That's a new one."

"Yeah," I said. "That's a new one."

Then we both laughed, but I was still shaking, remembering Mrs. Whitman saying my name that way.

When we got in the house, Mom said, "The funniest thing happened while you were gone. The phone rang and this woman asked what number this was. I told her, and she asked whom she was speaking to. I told her and she said, 'Perkins...Perkins. Do you have a boy named Scott?' I said that we did, and she said, 'This is Martha Whitman. Tell him I'll see him this summer. I'm teaching remedial math.'"

I figured that right after I'd hung up from calling her about Gloria, she'd dialled *69. I'd heard you could do that. The phone would ring whoever called you last. That was why she'd asked my mother what number it was and who was speaking.

Dad said, "You see, Scott, Mrs. Whitman doesn't dislike you, or she wouldn't have called here to tell you she'd see you this summer."

"I was wrong," I said. "Wrong again."

Oh, was I ever!

----

1. RESPONDING TO THE STORY

a. Why do you think there is a battle of wills between Scott and his father?

b. What do you think will happen on Scott's first day of summer school?

c. In your journal, write about an experience in your life that made you feel embarrassed or uncomfortable. How was that experience resolved (or was it resolved)?

d. With a partner discuss how the reader sees Mrs. Whitman through Scott's eyes, and how a **protagonist's** views can help to shape how we view different characters.

> The **protagonist** is the main character in a story. An **antagonist** is the character who acts against the protagonist.

2. LITERATURE STUDIES CHARACTER DEVELOPMENT

Character development is a change in how a character in a story thinks or deals with life situations. It is an awareness that a character develops to become who she or he is. Ideally, this development comes out of what happens in the story. When you read "I've Got Gloria," what impression did you have of Scott? Did it change by the end of the story? Explain your impressions. How does Scott change during the story?

Choose a story you have read recently in which you think a character changes or develops. Outline the events or situations that have led to this development. Discuss how the author convinces the reader that the character has changed.

S T R A T E G I E S

3. WRITING A SHORT STORY

Imagine a character who is continually doing the wrong thing. Generate story ideas that get your character into trouble, for example, making a crank call, or forgetting to babysit a younger sister or brother. Use one of these situations as the basis for a short story. Be sure to include some kind of resolution. Consider, too, whether your story should be in the first or third person. As you develop your story, think about the following:

- Keep your audience and purpose in mind. Ask yourself questions such as: What details does the reader need to know? How can I hold my reader's interest?
- Think about your characters. Short stories usually deal with a small number of well-developed characters.
- Focus on the plot. A good one keeps the reader guessing about what will happen next.
- Your setting should be clear to the readers. They should be able to picture a specific place and time.
- Is the conflict believable? An interesting struggle or opposition is an important element to the plot.
- What are you trying to accomplish with your story? What theme or message do you want to convey?

SELF-ASSESSMENT: Reread your story, checking that your character is fully developed, that you've explored his/her emotions about the situation, and that the story is believable.

4. LANGUAGE CONVENTIONS
USING QUOTATIONS WITHIN QUOTATIONS

You probably know the rules of using quotations in stories:

- Quotation marks go around a character's direct speech.

  "Please sit down."

- Punctuation usually goes *inside* quotation marks.

  "Please sit down**.**"

- The person who is speaking is never included within the quotation marks.

  "Please sit down," **he said**.

But what happens when a character who is speaking quotes someone else? Look at this example from the story.

> "I told her and she said, 'Perkins...Perkins. Do you have a boy named Scott?' I said that we did, and she said, 'This is Martha Whitman. Tell him I'll see him this summer. I'm teaching remedial math.'"

What do you notice about the use of quotations in this example? Where do the punctuation marks go? Why are there two kinds of quotation marks at the end of the last sentence? What rule can you write about using quotes within quotation marks?

As a teen, John set
a few goals for himself.
One hundred and twenty-seven
to be exact!

The Adventurous Life of John Goddard

Profile by
Stuart McLean

When John Goddard was fifteen years old, he sat down one night with a red pencil, a blue pen, and a yellow legal pad and made a list of things he wanted to do before he died.

His list began just the way you might expect:
- Become an Eagle Scout.
- Broad jump five metres.
- Make a parachute jump.
- Dive in a submarine.
- Learn jujitsu.

The more the boy wrote, the more his imagination took hold. The list soon left the realm of idle daydreams and entered the world of serious adolescent fantasy:
- Milk a poisonous snake.
- Watch a fire-walking ceremony in Surinam.
- Watch a cremation ceremony in Bali.

And it didn't stop there. As young Goddard continued his list, his vision expanded and showed signs of the grand adventurer he was going to grow up to be:
- Explore the Amazon.
- Swim in Lake Tanganyika.
- Climb the Matterhorn.
- Retrace the travels of Marco Polo and Alexander the Great.
- Visit every country in the world.

GOALS AT A GLANCE

- Research the life of an adventurer.
- Compare print and radio forms.

179

The ideas poured onto the page and at some point took a sharp turn in tone. As Goddard added to his list, he displayed an academic sophistication well beyond his fifteen years:

• Read the works of Shakespeare, Plato, Aristotle, Dickens, Thoreau, Rousseau, Hemingway, Twain, Burroughs, Talmage, Tolstoy, Longfellow, Keats, Poe, Bacon, Whittier, and Emerson.

• Become familiar with the compositions of Bach, Beethoven, Debussy, Ibert, Mendelssohn, Lalo, Milhaud, Ravel, Rimsky-Korsakov, Respighi, Rachmaninoff, Paganini, Stravinsky, Toch, Tchaikovsky, and Verdi.

• Read the Bible from cover to cover.

• Play the flute and the violin.

When he put his pen down, there were one hundred and twenty-seven items on Goddard's list.

Well. Yes.

We have all taken a stab at this sort of thing at one time or another. The extraordinary difference between John Goddard and the rest of us, however, is the unsettling fact that Goddard didn't throw his list out. Nor did he chuck it into the bottom of a drawer. He kept his list in plain sight and set out to complete every item line by line. Today, Goddard has check marks beside one hundred and eight of his original one hundred and twenty-seven goals. And that includes all of the items mentioned above.

Well, that's not exactly true. There are still thirty odd countries that he hasn't visited. But he is working on that.

I first read about John Goddard in *Life* magazine when I was a teenager. It was in one of those articles at the back of the magazine in a section called "Parting Shots." The article stuck in my mind (How could I forget it?) and I always hoped I would get a chance to talk to him. Fifteen years later, I sat down with his phone number in front of me and called him at his home in La Cañada, California. I wanted to talk to him, I explained, about the list I had seen so long ago in *Life*. I wanted to know if he was still working on it. Yes, he was. Did he remember what had inspired him to write it? John Goddard chuckled.

"I think what motivated me to write the list was listening to some family friends who were visiting with my parents. They had been over for dinner and were helping to clear the dishes. I was doing my home-work in a little alcove, a sort of breakfast nook. Dr. Keller looked at me and said to my parents, 'I'd give anything to be John's age again. I really would do things differently. I would set out and accomplish more of the dreams of my youth.' That was the gist of his conversation—if only he could start over—and I thought, here's a man only forty-two years old, and he is feeling life has passed him by, and I thought, if I start planning now, and really work on my goals, I won't end up that way."

Almost fifty years have passed since John Goddard wrote out his life goals. He is now in his mid-sixties. But the day we spoke, he was busy preparing for a trip to the North Pole—one half of goal number fifty-four, which is to visit both the North and the South poles. Another check mark. I spoke to John Goddard for almost two hours, and we talked about many things. I asked him if he remembered the day he wrote the list.

"I remember it vividly because it was such a rite of passage for me. It was a rainy Sunday afternoon in 1941. Until that time, I really hadn't crystallized all my ambitions and hopes and dreams. Writing them down was the first act in achieving them. You know, when you write something down with the sincere intent of doing it, it's a commitment. A lot of us fail to do that. We don't set deadlines and say, for example, by June of 1990 I'm going to have checked out in scuba, taken a rock-climbing course, and learned how to play the piano. The moment of writing it down is vivid in my mind because that was my formal com-mitment to that life list. And I felt I would give myself a lifetime to fulfil everything on it."

One of Goddard's early challenges was an expedition by kayak down the longest river on earth—the six-thousand-four-hundred kilometre Nile. He was the first person in the world to travel the length of the river from the headwaters to the Mediterranean. He took a bank loan to finance the trip and then paid off the loan by writing a book about his adventures. He sold the book on the lecture circuit. And that's the way he has made his living ever since. Goddard supports himself through his lectures, his books, and the sale of his films and tapes. He is not a wealthy man.

I asked him if he had ever been in any physical danger. He told me of the time he was lost in a sandstorm in the Sudan, and couldn't put up a tent because the wind was blowing so hard. But he couldn't sit still because if he had stopped moving, he would have been buried alive. He told me about the time he had been shot at by river pirates in Egypt. Later, I read that he had also been bitten by a rattlesnake, charged by an elephant, trapped in quicksand, been in more than one plane crash, and caught in more than one earthquake.

Sometimes I go on and on about a hazardous drive my family and I had one winter between Montréal and Toronto. It was snowing more than usual, the driving was tough, and there were a lot of cars off the road. There was also a service centre every eighty-odd kilometres, lots of snowploughs, and plenty of people to help out if I had got in trouble. Nevertheless, when I tell the story of the drive I can make it sound pretty dramatic.

Imagine being able to start a story with, "Exploring the Congo was difficult…"

"Exploring the Congo was difficult. It took me six months and resulted in the loss of life of my partner, Jack Yowell from Kenya. Six hundred and forty kilometres downstream we had a disaster when we both capsized on a raging stretch of rapids. It was the one hundred and twenty-fifth set of rapids, and we were paddling fragile twenty-seven kilogram, five-metre kayaks. He got swept to the left and flipped over, and racing over to help him I got flipped over, too, and nearly drowned myself. I tried to fight to the surface and banged into the river bottom. The river was so turbulent I couldn't really tell which way the surface was, and I was drowning because I was under the water an interminable time. I think the thing that saved me was the fact that I could hold my breath for three minutes in an emergency. I was finally washed to calm water and ran along the banks desperately trying to find Jack. I couldn't see him anywhere. Then suddenly a box of matches came floating by, then his pipe, overturned kayak, and aluminum paddle, but no Jack. It was very difficult to go on and travel the remaining three thousand seven hundred kilometres to the Atlantic. But, we had promised one another if one of us did die on the upper river that the survivor would continue and finish the expedition for both of us. So I fulfilled that promise."

John Goddard still has a lot of things left on his list, but at age sixty-four he is in good shape and determined to keep at it. He does one hundred sit-ups every morning, works out on cables and weights, and rides a stationary bike at least ten kilometres a day.

1. RESPONDING TO THE PROFILE

a. John Goddard explains what motivated him to write his list. Why do you think he has spent his life trying to do everything on the list?

b. Imagine yourself at sixty-four. Describe what you think your life might be like.

c. List ten things you would like to do or accomplish before you're forty. Realistically, which ones do you think you will do?

d. If you had to choose between a life of far-off adventure by yourself or staying in one place with friends and family, which one would you choose? Explain your choice.

e. What do you think of the goals listed? Which would be the easiest to accomplish? the hardest? Why?

2. RESEARCHING ADVENTURERS

One of the first best-selling books was *The Travels of Marco Polo,* published at the end of the thirteenth century. It seems that people have always been fascinated by adventure stories. Research an adventurer who once captured people's imagination, for example, Amelia Earhart, Jacques Cousteau, or Harriet Tubman. Write a brief character description of your adventurer. In your description, suggest how the person's character might have influenced his or her life. Share your report with a group of classmates. What other adventurers do your classmates admire?

SELF-ASSESSMENT: As you researched, did you remember to check your information for bias, accuracy, and relevance?

3. MEDIA MESSAGES RADIO JOURNALISM

Stuart McLean is both a radio commentator and a print journalist. This piece was originally written to be read over the airwaves. Reread the profile and explain what makes it more a radio documentary than a magazine profile. Include examples to support your opinion. Read a section of the selection out loud as you think McLean intended.

Gifts

Poems by **Alden Nowlan**

Dry Spell

I stare at the yellow paper
in my typewriter until I find myself
contemplating its texture
and even the bruises
where the machines pressed too hard
become important to me
but, above all, the blankness
is more beautiful than any mark
I could put on it today,
so I write only:
there is nothing on this sheet,
and realize at once that it is impossible
for these words ever to be true.
That is one more of the many things
I can never tell you.

GOALS AT A GLANCE

■ Respond personally and critically to poetry.
■ Share personal viewpoints in oral discussions.

An Exchange of Gifts

As long as you read this poem
I will be writing it.
I am writing it here and now
before your eyes,
although you can't see me.
Perhaps you'll dismiss this
as a verbal trick,
the joke is you're wrong;
the real trick
is your pretending
this is something
fixed and solid,
external to us both.
I tell you better:
I will keep on
writing this poem for you
even after I'm dead.

---

1. RESPONDING TO THE POEMS

a. What is Alden Nowlan writing about in "Dry Spell"?

b. Who do you think the "you" refers to in "Dry Spell" and "An Exchange of Gifts"?

c. What is "An Exchange of Gifts" trying to say in the last three lines of the poem?

d. These poems are together in a section called "Gifts." What gifts are each of these poems describing?

2. ORAL LANGUAGE GROUP DISCUSSION

Do you view life as something "fixed and solid" and never changing, or as a blank sheet of paper waiting to be filled in and revised as you live? Share your ideas with a group or the class.

HOW TO

WRITE POETRY

Goals at a Glance
- Develop strategies for writing poetry.
- Experiment with language and sounds to create effects.

Poetry can express feelings, describe observations, recall experiences, explore ideas, tell a story, capture an image in words, and play with sound. There are many forms and types of poetry to choose from, such as free verse, haiku, sonnets, ballads, and so on. The form you choose depends on what effect you're trying to create. Below are some suggestions to help you write poetry with ease.

Developing Your Idea

Turn any of your ideas into a poem. The subject doesn't have to be profound or unusual; it just has to be something you care about. Use the following strategies to develop your ideas into poems.

1. Analyse a poem that you like. You could write your poem using the same pattern of lines, stanzas, and rhythms.
2. Write something in prose form first. Next, take out every word that is not necessary to express the meaning. Work with the words and phrases that are left.
3. You could also generate a list, develop a web, or make sketches to help you explore the emotions, images, places, or people connected to your idea.
4. Choose the *point of view* that will work best for your poem. Will you use first, second, or third person?

The Language of Poetry

Every word counts in a poem. Your job as a poet is to select the best words and put them in the most effective order. Nouns should be specific and verbs vivid. Sometimes poets even create words to describe an experience. Descriptions should be detailed enough for a reader to be able to experience the poem through the senses. Think about using the following types of language to create images or spark the imagination.

PROCESS

- **Simile**—use *like* or *as* to compare two different things. *fast as lightning*
- **Metaphor**—represent one thing as something else. *muscles of iron*
- **Personification**—give human qualities to a thing or idea. *The stream gurgled down the mountainside.*
- **Hyperbole**—use exaggeration for effect. *I died from laughter.*
- **Symbol**—use a person, place, thing, or event to represent something else. A white dove, for example, is often seen as a symbol of peace.

The Sound of Poetry

In poetry, the sound of words is just as important as the meaning. Read your poem aloud and adjust the language until it sounds right to your ear. Here are some sound devices you might try:

- **Alliteration**—repeat the same first sound in a group of words. *He clasped the crag with crooked hands.*
- **Onomatopoeia**—use words that imitate the sound they name. *zoom, patter, swish*
- **Repetition**—use the same words, phrases, or lines more than once. *Run straight / Run high / Run hard*
- **Rhyme**—place rhyming words at the ends, or in the middle, of lines.
- **Rhythm**—arrange the stresses, or beats, in a line. Certain types of poetry (sonnets and quatrains) have a set rhythm.

- **Consonants**—select soft consonants like *s, m, n, l,* and *r* to create a gentle sound; use hard consonants like *b, p, d, t,* and *k* to create a harsh sound.

Break the Rules

Experiment by breaking the rules. You can create a form that suits your own mood and purpose. Explore free verse, which has no rhyme or regular stanzas.

- **Punctuation**—play with the punctuation in your poem. Break some of the rules of grammar and see what effects this creates. You may even choose not to use punctuation at all.
- **Line arrangement**—use line breaks and spaces between words to show your reader where to pause. Try different lines breaks, and read each arrangement out loud. Choose the one that works best. Experiment with using more than one space between words.

Revising

Use the following checklist to help you revise your poem.

- ❑ I used different devices and techniques to improve my poem.
- ❑ I used original and interesting comparisons.
- ❑ I experimented with the sounds of words.
- ❑ I experimented with line breaks and punctuation.
- ❑ I revised specific words to make my poem more vivid.

PROCESS

The Way I Feel

12 Years Old

Song by Kim Stockwood, Peter Vettese, and Abenaa Frempong
from the CD *12 Years Old*

I just can't stand the way I feel
I just can't wait until tomorrow comes
So if you'd care to see my face again
You'll have to be the one to let me know

'Cause I feel like I'm 12 years old
And I feel like I'm in the cold
And I feel like I'm 12 years old
And my dog just died
And my bike's been stolen again

How can it be that you're so vain
And how can it be that I am such a pain
Or so you say
Why can't you see this time you've gone too far
Today I couldn't care less where you are

'Cause I feel like I'm 12 years old
And I feel like I'm in the cold
And I feel like I don't
No, No
know where I am
And I feel like I'm left behind
And I feel like I'm the last in line
And I feel like I'm 12 years old
And my dog just died
And my bike's been stolen

It seems so juvenile
Feeling like a little child
I guess it never goes away
So maybe I should play, ok

La La La La La (Repeat × 4)

And I feel like I'm 12 years old
And I feel like I'm in the cold
And I feel like I don't know where I am
No, No
And I feel like I'm left behind
And I feel like I'm last in line
And I feel like I'm 12 years old
And my dog just died
My bike's been stoled
I missed the ball
And I dropped my ice cream again

La La La La La (Repeat × 4)

yeah yeah yeah (Repeat × 4)

Feel like I'm 12 years old
Feel like I'm in the cold
Feel like I'm 12 years old

Feel like I'm 12 years old
Feel like I'm in the cold
Feel like I'm 12 years old
Feel like I'm all alone

Enlightenment and Muscular Dystrophy

Poem by Eli Coppola

The first miles were easy,
you've heard it before.
I took sixteen years in giant strides,
on impulse, in flight.
Breath-less, care-less
child.
And it was over about that quickly.

I was left with a string of small water planets,
a charmed circle I wear around my throat.
It's taken me these last fourteen years to learn that certain things
broken
stay broken.
And also to notice the space the breaking has made
that lets the whole world in.

Now wherever I go I always go slowly.
Gravity and I have long conversations through my legs.
I cooperate with the smallest pebble.
I study imperceptible inclines
I fall and I   get up   and I fall and   I get
up   and   I fall and   I   get up.
My miles are good long miles.

When I work hard I think better.
But I lose a little more each year,
a few degrees of motor control.
So far always
less than they predict,
and always more
than I can surrender.

This year, in a photograph, I did not recognize my hands.
It's a fierce thing, this enlightenment.

To James

Poem by Frank Horne

Do you remember
How you won
That last race...?
How you flung your body
At the start...
How your spikes
Ripped the cinders
In the stretch
How you catapulted
Through the tape...
Do you remember...?
Don't you think
I lurched with you
Out of those starting holes...?
Don't you think
My sinews tightened
At those first
Few strides...
And when you flew into the stretch
Was not all my thrill
Of a thousand races
In your blood...?
At your final drive
Through the finish line
Did not my shout
Tell of the
Triumphant ecstasy
Of victory...?
As I have taught you
To run, Boy—

It's a short dash
Dig your starting holes
Deep and firm
Lurch out of them
Into the straightaway
With all the power
That is in you
Look straight ahead
To the finish line
Think only of the goal
Run straight
Run high
Run hard
Save nothing
And finish
With an ecstatic burst
That carries you
Hurtling
Through the tape
To victory...

1. RESPONDING TO THE SELECTIONS

a. Choose an example from one of the poems or song that describes being young. In a sentence or two, describe what the poem says about being young.

b. Describe what *your* childhood was like. How does it compare to the views expressed in these selections?

c. In "Enlightenment and Muscular Dystrophy," the poet writes, "It's a fierce thing, this enlightenment." Explain why the writer sees enlightenment as a "fierce thing."

d. If the race in "To James" is taken as a metaphor, what do you think it stands for?

2. POET'S CRAFT UNDERSTANDING POETRY

The three selections represent very different ways of expressing poetic thoughts and language. Each is written in a different style and uses a different form or format. There is a rhyme scheme of sorts in "12 Years Old," and because it is a song, repetition of certain lines. In "Enlightenment and Muscular Dystrophy," none of the lines rhyme but, like "12 Years Old," it is divided into sections or stanzas. "To James" isn't divided into stanzas and uses very short lines.

What other elements do you notice in these three selections? How do they use repetition? What type of language do they use? How does what they are trying to express match the form they are written in and their use of language? Discuss the poems with a small group of classmates.

3. WRITING POETRY

Think back to your childhood and jot down some of your more vivid memories. What do you remember best: people, things you did, or places you visited? Choose one of your memories and, free-writing, jot down everything that comes to mind. Don't worry about the order of the words or whether they are in complete sentences or not. Then think about the words and images you have written. Use some or all of them in a poem about being young.

 Decide how you'd like to share your poem: by reading it to your classmates, or publishing it in a school newspaper or Web site.

SELF-ASSESSMENT: How did you decide what format to use for your poem? Do you notice *how* a poem is written as well as what it is trying to say?

A worried mother waits, and remembers.

Stains

Short Story by Sharon MacFarlane

Her wrists burn in the icy water. But the water must be cold if she is to get all the stains out. She folds the leg of the jeans, rubs the layers of heavy denim together. With the bar of harsh laundry soap she scrubs the spots over and over. The water darkens with blood. She twists the jeans, wringing out as much water as she can, sets them carefully beside the sink.

When she lifts the tee shirt a small piece of curled, white skin floats free of the jagged tear, rises to the surface. She swallows, takes a deep breath.

When the clothes—a pair of shorts, a pair of socks, the tee shirt, and the jeans—are all in the washer she sits down at the kitchen table. She's never been good at waiting. "Go home," they told her, "there's nothing you can do here. We'll call you." She stares at the clock, not sure if she wants the hands to move faster or slower. Should she call one of her friends to wait with her? She couldn't bear to make small talk, couldn't concentrate on anything but the pictures that fill her mind. The image of him—grey, unconscious, his dark blood seeping through the bandage, seeping into the white sheet of the hospital bed. No, she will wait now as she waited seventeen years ago for his birth. Alone. She sees the baby with snowy hair, the five year old in an over-sized hockey uniform, the fourth-grade wise man in the school pageant...thinks of all the hopes she had for him.

She goes to the washer as soon as it stops. There is a circle of red-tinged suds on the inside of the lid. She puts the clothes into the dryer, then with an old towel scrubs the enamel lid. She rinses the towel again and again; when it is clean, she hangs it over the tap to dry.

In the kitchen, she fills the kettle and sets it on the burner. She spoons tea leaves into a small brown pot and takes a china mug from the cupboard. When the tea is ready she sits for a moment holding the warm mug in both hands. She drinks two cups but in a few minutes she is thirsty again. Worry parches her mouth, it's always been that way.

She learned to keep a pitcher of water and a glass beside her, the nights she sat up with him when he was sick. With every illness he ran a high fever. When he was a baby and she held him in her arms in the rocking chair all night she wished that she could absorb the heat from his body into her own. Wished him cool—well again—sleeping in his crib with the white quilt tucked around him. When he was three or four, the fevers made him delirious, made him babble nonsense, reach to pluck imaginary balloons from the air. She thought then that when he was older, after he'd had all the childhood diseases, everything would be all right. If only this was as simple as a bout of croup or measles.

The fear has been with her for a long time. She realized that when the doorbell rang at 4 a.m. She awoke instantly, went to the door, saw the police officer standing there. "...Your son—there's been an accident..." She knew then that, somehow, she'd been waiting for those words.

Noon. He'd be getting up about now if this was an ordinary Saturday. He'd come into the kitchen, bleary-eyed, his hair rumpled, wearing only his wrinkled jeans. He'd go to the fridge, take a drink of milk straight from the carton. She'd say, "For Pete's sake, can't you get a glass?" He'd shrug, both of them knowing she wasn't upset about the milk but about his hangover, his boozing, his friends... A Saturday ritual that had been going on for a year now. Today—there is only the faint hum of the dryer and the ticking of the clock.

When she takes the clothes out of the dryer she spreads them on top of the machine, inspects them carefully, satisfies herself that there is no trace of stains. She folds them and puts them in his dresser. Except the shirt. She takes the shirt to the sewing machine. The gash is so long—from the shoulder almost to the hem—that it distorts the beer logo printed on the chest. Of course, he has other shirts—a red one, a soft silvery-grey one, a black one that makes him look even blonder than he is—lots of nice shirts; but he prefers this one. A stretched tee shirt that shows the world he is a beer drinker—a man.

Booze erases his shyness, gives him confidence. She should have praised him more when he was younger, criticized him less, helped him to have a better self-image. She knows that now. Maybe then he'd have excelled at something—school, sports, drama—wouldn't have needed to booze to make him feel important.

In the sewing room, she takes a cardboard box from the top shelf. She must find material to match the shirt. She turns the box upside down, spills hundreds of odd-shaped scraps onto the floor. She sifts through them carefully, picks up, then rejects, five or six. Finally, she finds a piece of soft cotton that matches exactly the faded blue of the shirt. She pins it carefully in place under the tear and starts sewing. The machine's zigzag stitches pull the edges neatly together. The mend will be almost invisible. But there is still three centimetres left to sew when the telephone rings.

1. RESPONDING TO THE STORY

a. How does the first paragraph set the mood and tone of the story?

b. In the last paragraph, the author describes common, mundane tasks that the mother performs. Why would the author end the story in this way?

c. What do you think happened to the son? What were the reasons behind what happened? Why does the author hold back some important information until later in the story?

d. Why does the mother feel guilty about her son? Explain whether or not you think this guilt is justified.

e. What do you think happens at the end of the story?

2. READING SUSPENSE

Read the definition of **suspense** at right. With a group of classmates, discuss this technique and how it adds to the plots of novels and short stories. Choose another short story you've read recently in which suspense is a key element and compare it with "Stains." Discuss how each author uses suspense to advance the plot. Does suspense help you understand the characters better or is it strictly part of the plot? Are the examples of suspense different for each story, or do they have common elements? Summarize your discussion in the form of a chart similar to the one below.

> **Suspense** is a feeling of tension, anxiety, or excitement resulting from uncertainty. An author creates suspense to keep the reader interested.

Story	Example of Suspense	Purpose in Story

3. WRITING HUNCHES

A *hunch* is a feeling or impression that something is about to happen. Authors sometimes use a character's hunches to create suspense or to tie together a group of events. For example, in "Stains," the mother has been afraid for her son "for a long time. She realized that when the doorbell rang at 4 a.m."

Write a story about a character's hunches. Try to use this hunch not only to create suspense, but to help explain the action that comes at the end of the story.

4. LANGUAGE CONVENTIONS THE DASH

Reread "Stains," paying attention to the **dashes** used in the story. Dashes are most often used to replace other types of punctuation, such as commas, semicolons, or parentheses. When used in this way, the dash creates a very strong pause. With a partner, discuss how Sharon MacFarlane uses dashes, and her purpose for doing so.

> A **dash** is a punctuation mark used to indicate a pause or break in a sentence.

Looking Back

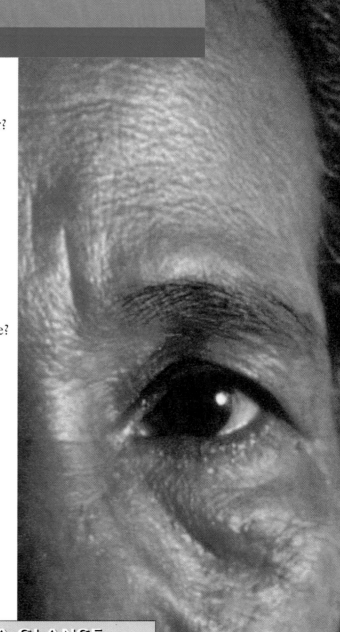

Now I See You

Poem by Maxine Tynes

(poem for my mother, Ada Maxwell Tynes)

When did I start looking at you, my mother?
I don't know;
but often, it's your hands I'll watch
all brown, and bumpy-smooth
those same hands that
held and cradled me,
in my new life.

I look at your nose,
so high and strong, for a Black woman;
the same nose of
some noble African tribe. But where? Where?

I look at your eyes.
They've seen so much. So much.
You'll never tell me.

The hardest look of all
was the one I took of you sleeping,
and, missing my dad, still;
you lie with pillows piled high
and nestled close beside you, in sleep.

GOALS AT A GLANCE

■ Respond personally and critically to poetry.
■ Analyse imagery in a poem.

197

Ancestors' Graves in Kurakawa

Poem by Joy Kogawa

Down down across the open sea to Shikoku
To story book island of mist and mystery
By train and bus through remote mountain villages
Following my father's boyhood backwards
Retracing the mountain path he crossed on rice husk slippers
With his dreams of countries beyond seas beyond seas
His dreams still intact, his flight perpetual
Back down the steep red mountain path
To the high hillside grave of my ancestors
Grey and green ferns hang down
Edging my faint beginnings with shades
Maintaining muteness in a wordless flickering
The hiddenness stretches beyond my reach
Strange dew drops through cedar incense
And I greet the dead who smile through trees
Accepting the pebbles that melt through my eyes.

- -

1. RESPONDING TO THE POEMS

a. In "Ancestors' Graves in Kurakawa," what journey is the writer taking? Joy Kogawa writes that "the hiddenness stretches beyond my reach." What do you think she means?

b. In "Now I See You," what picture do you have of the mother?

c. Choose an image from each poem and explain what picture you had when you read it.

d. Compare how each of the poets describes her parents.

e. In a paragraph, describe your parents or another adult.

*What do you do
when your mother
is positive that you're
a potential genius?*

TWO KINDS

Short Story by Amy Tan

My mother believed you could be anything you wanted to be in America. You could open a restaurant. You could work for the government and get good retirement. You could buy a house with almost no money down. You could become rich. You could become instantly famous.

"Of course you can be prodigy, too," my mother told me when I was nine. "You can be best anything. What does Auntie Lindo know? Her daughter, she is only best tricky."

America was where all my mother's hopes lay. She had come here in 1949 after losing everything in China: her mother and father, her family home, her first husband, and two daughters, twin baby girls. But she never looked back with regret. There were so many ways for things to get better.

GOALS AT A GLANCE

■ Write a letter of apology.
■ Analyse the use of conjunctions.

199

We didn't immediately pick the right kind of prodigy. At first my mother thought I could be a Chinese Shirley Temple. We'd watch Shirley's old movies on TV as though they were training films. My mother would poke my arm and say, "*Ni kan*"—You watch. And I would see Shirley tapping her feet, or singing a sailor song, or pursing her lips into a very round O while saying, "Oh my goodness."

"*Ni kan*," said my mother as Shirley's eyes flooded with tears. "You already know how. Don't need talent for crying!"

Soon after my mother got this idea about Shirley Temple, she took me to a beauty training school in the Mission district and put me in the hands of a student who could barely hold the scissors without shaking. Instead of getting big fat curls, I emerged with an uneven mass of crinkly black fuzz. My mother dragged me off to the bathroom and tried to wet down my hair.

"You look like a Negro Chinese," she lamented, as if I had done this on purpose.

The instructor of the beauty training school had to lop off these soggy clumps to make my hair even again. "Peter Pan is very popular these days," the instructor assured my mother. I now had hair the length of a boy's, with straight-across bangs that hung at a slant two inches above my eyebrows. I liked the haircut and it made me actually look forward to my future fame.

In fact, in the beginning, I was just as excited as my mother, maybe even more so. I pictured this prodigy part of me as many different images, trying each one on for size. I was a dainty ballerina girl standing by the curtains, waiting to hear the right music that would send me floating on my tiptoes. I was like the Christ child lifted out of the straw manger, crying with holy indignity. I was Cinderella stepping from her pumpkin carriage with sparkly cartoon music filling the air.

In all of my imaginings, I was filled with a sense that I would soon become *perfect*. My mother and father would adore me. I would be beyond reproach. I would never feel the need to sulk for anything.

But sometimes the prodigy in me became impatient. "If you don't hurry up and get me out of here, I'm disappearing for good," it warned. "And then you'll always be nothing."

Every night after dinner, my mother and I would sit at the Formica kitchen table. She would present new tests, taking her examples from stories of amazing children she had read in *Ripley's Believe It or Not*, or *Good Housekeeping*, *Reader's Digest*, and a dozen other magazines she kept in a pile in our bathroom. My mother got these magazines from people whose houses she cleaned. And since she cleaned many houses each week, we had a great assortment. She would look through them all, searching for stories about remarkable children.

The first night she brought out a story about a three-year-old boy who knew the capitals of all the states and even most of the European countries. A teacher was quoted as saying the little boy could also pronounce the names of the foreign cities correctly.

"What's the capital of Finland?" my mother asked me, looking at the magazine story.

All I knew was the capital of California, because Sacramento was the name of the street we lived on in Chinatown. "Nairobi!" I guessed, saying the most foreign word I could think of. She checked to see if that was possibly one way to pronounce "Helsinki" before showing me the answer.

The tests got harder—multiplying numbers in my head, finding the queen of hearts in a deck of cards, trying to stand on my head without using my hands, predicting the daily temperatures in Los Angeles, New York, and London.

One night I had to look at a page from the Bible for three minutes and then report everything I could remember. "Now Jehoshaphat had riches and honor in abundance and...that's all I remember, Ma." I said.

And after seeing my mother's disappointed face once again, something inside of me began to die. I hated the tests, the raised hopes and failed expectations. Before going to bed that night, I looked in the mirror above the bathroom sink and when I saw only my face staring back—and that it would always be this ordinary face—I began to cry. Such a sad, ugly girl! I made high-pitched noises like a crazed animal, trying to scratch out the face in the mirror.

And then I saw what seemed to be the prodigy side of me—because I had never seen that face before. I looked at my reflection, blinking so I could see more clearly. The girl staring back at me was angry, powerful. This girl and I were the same. I had new thoughts, willful thoughts, or rather thoughts filled with lots of won'ts. I won't let her change me, I promised myself. I won't be what I'm not.

So now on nights when my mother presented her tests, I performed listlessly, my head propped on one arm. I pretended to be bored. And I was. I got so bored I started counting the bellows of the foghorns out on the bay while my mother drilled me in other areas. The sound was comforting and reminded me of the cow jumping over the moon. And the next day, I played a game with myself, seeing if my mother would give up on me before eight bellows.

After a while, I usually counted only one, maybe two bellows at most. At last she was beginning to give up hope.

Two or three months had gone by without any mention of my being a prodigy again. And then one day my mother was watching *The Ed Sullivan Show* on TV. The TV was old and the sound kept shorting out. Every time my mother got halfway up from the sofa to adjust the set, the sound would go back on and Ed would be talking. As soon as she sat down, Ed would go silent again. She got up, the TV broke into loud piano music. She sat down. Silence. Up and down, back and forth, quiet and loud. It was like a stiff embraceless dance between her and the TV set. Finally she stood by the set with her hand on the sound dial.

She seemed entranced by the music, a little frenzied piano piece with this mesmerizing quality, sort of quick passages and then teasing lilting ones before it returned to the quick playful parts.

"*Ni kan,*" my mother said, calling me over with hurried hand gestures. "Look here."

I could see why my mother was fascinated by the music. It was being pounded out by a little Chinese girl, about nine years old, with a Peter Pan haircut. The girl had the sauciness of a Shirley Temple. She was proudly modest like a proper Chinese child. And she also did this fancy sweep of a curtsy, so that the fluffy skirt of her white dress cascaded slowly to the floor like the petals of a large carnation.

In spite of these warning signs, I wasn't worried. Our family had no piano and we couldn't afford to buy one, let alone reams of sheet music and piano lessons. So I could be generous in my comments when my mother bad-mouthed the little girl on TV.

"Play note right, but doesn't sound good! No singing sound," complained my mother.

"What are you picking on her for?" I said carelessly. "She's pretty good. Maybe she's not the best, but she's trying hard." I knew almost immediately I would be sorry I said that.

"Just like you," she said. "Not the best. Because you not trying." She gave a little huff as she let go of the sound dial and sat down on the sofa.

The little Chinese girl sat down also to play an encore of "Anitra's Dance" by Grieg. I remember the song, because later on I had to learn how to play it.

Three days after watching *The Ed Sullivan Show*, my mother told me what my schedule would be for piano lessons and piano practice. She had talked to Mr. Chong, who lived on the first floor of our apartment building. Mr. Chong was a retired piano teacher and my mother had traded housecleaning services for weekly lessons and a piano for me to practice on every day, two hours a day, from four until six.

When my mother told me this, I felt as though I had been sent to hell. I whined and then kicked my foot a little when I couldn't stand it anymore.

"Why don't you like me the way I am? I'm *not* a genius! I can't play the piano. And even if I could, I wouldn't go on TV if you paid me a million dollars!" I cried.

My mother slapped me. "Who ask you be genius?" she shouted. "Only ask you be your best. For you sake. You think I want you be genius? Hnnh! What for! Who ask you!"

"So ungrateful," I heard her mutter in Chinese. "If she had as much talent as she has temper, she would be famous now."

Mr. Chong, whom I secretly nicknamed Old Chong, was very strange, always tapping his fingers to the silent music of an invisible orchestra. He looked ancient in my eyes. He had lost most of the hair on top of his head and he wore thick glasses and had eyes that always looked tired and sleepy. But he must have been younger than I thought, since he lived with his mother and was not yet married.

I met Old Lady Chong once and that was enough. She had this peculiar smell like a baby that had done something in its pants. And her fingers felt like a dead person's, like an old peach I once found in the back of the refrigerator; the skin just slid off the meat when I picked it up.

I soon found out why Old Chong had retired from teaching piano. He was deaf. "Like Beethoven!" he shouted to me. "We're both listening only in our head!" And he would start to conduct his frantic silent sonatas.

Our lessons went like this. He would open the book and point to different things, explaining their purpose: "Key! Treble! Bass! No sharps or flats! So this is C major! Listen now and play after me!"

And then he would play the C scale a few times, a simple chord, and then, as if inspired by an old, unreachable itch, he gradually added more notes and running trills and a pounding bass until the music was really something quite grand.

I would play after him, the simple scale, the simple chord, and then I just played some nonsense that sounded like a cat running up and down on top of garbage cans. Old Chong smiled and applauded and then said, "Very good! But now you must learn to keep time!"

So that's how I discovered that Old Chong's eyes were too slow to keep up with the wrong notes I was playing. He went through the motions in half-time. To help me keep rhythm, he stood behind me, pushing down on my right shoulder for every beat. He balanced pennies on top of my wrists so I would keep them still as I slowly played scales and arpeggios. He had me curve my hand around an apple and keep that shape when playing chords. He marched stiffly to show how to make each finger dance up and down, staccato like an obedient little soldier.

He taught me all these things, and that was how I also learned I could be lazy and get away with mistakes, lots of mistakes. If I hit the wrong notes because I hadn't practiced enough, I never corrected myself. I just kept playing in rhythm. And Old Chong kept conducting his own private reverie.

So maybe I never really gave myself a fair chance. I did pick up the basics pretty quickly, and I might have become a good pianist at that young age. But I was so determined not to try, not to be anybody different that I learned to play only the most ear-splitting preludes, the most discordant hymns.

Over the next year, I practiced like this, dutifully in my own way. And then one day I heard my mother and her friend Lindo Jong both talking in a loud bragging tone of voice so others could hear. It was after church, and I was leaning against the brick wall wearing a dress with stiff white petticoats. Auntie Lindo's daughter, Waverly, who was about my age, was standing farther down the wall about five feet away. We had grown up together and shared all the closeness of two sisters squabbling over crayons and dolls. In other words, for the most part, we hated each other. I thought she was snotty. Waverly Jong had gained a certain amount of fame as "Chinatown's Littlest Chinese Chess Champion."

"She bring home too many trophy," lamented Auntie Lindo that Sunday. "All day she play chess. All day I have no time do nothing but dust off her winnings." She threw a scolding look at Waverly, who pretended not to see her.

"You lucky you don't have this problem," said Auntie Lindo with a sigh to my mother.

And my mother squared her shoulders and bragged: "Our problem worser than yours. If we ask Jing-Mei wash dish, she hear nothing but music. It's like you can't stop this natural talent."

And right then, I was determined to put a stop to her foolish pride.

A few weeks later, Old Chong and my mother conspired to have me play in a talent show which would be held in the church hall. By then, my parents had saved up enough to buy me a secondhand piano, a black Wurlitzer spinet with a scarred bench. It was the showpiece of our living room.

For the talent show, I was to play a piece called "Pleading Child" from Schumann's *Scenes from Childhood*. It was a simple, moody piece that sounded more difficult than it was. I was supposed to memorize the whole thing, playing the repeat parts twice to make the piece sound longer. But I dawdled over it, playing a few bars and then cheating, looking up to see what notes followed. I never really listened to what I was playing. I day-dreamed about being somewhere else, about being someone else.

The part I liked to practice best was the fancy curtsy: right foot out, touch the rose on the carpet with a pointed foot, sweep to the side, left leg bends, look up and smile.

My parents invited all the couples from the Joy Luck Club to witness my debut. Auntie Lindo and Uncle Tin were there. Waverly and her two older brothers had also come. The first two rows were filled with children both younger and older than I was. The littlest ones got to go first. They recited simple nursery rhymes, squawked out tunes on miniature violins, twirled Hula Hoops, pranced in pink ballet tutus, and when they bowed or curtsied, the audience would sigh in unison, "Awww," and then clap enthusiastically.

When my turn came, I was very confident. I remember my childish excitement. It was as if I knew, without a doubt, that the prodigy side of me really did exist. I had no fear whatsoever, no nervousness. I remember thinking to myself, This is it! This is it! I looked out over the audience, at my mother's blank face, my father's yawn, Auntie Lindo's stiff-lipped smile, Waverly's sulky expression. I had on a white dress layered with sheets of lace, and a pink bow in my Peter Pan haircut. As I sat down I envisioned people jumping to their feet and Ed Sullivan rushing up to introduce me to everyone on TV.

And I started to play. It was so beautiful. I was so caught up in how lovely I looked that at first I didn't worry how I would sound. So it was a surprise to me when I hit the first wrong note and I realized something didn't sound quite right. And then I hit another and another followed that. A chill started at the top of my head and began to trickle down. Yet I couldn't stop playing, as though my hands were bewitched. I kept thinking my fingers would adjust themselves back, like a train switching to the right track. I played this strange jumble through two repeats, the sour notes staying with me all the way to the end.

When I stood up, I discovered my legs were shaking. Maybe I had just been nervous and the audience, like Old Chong, had seen me go through the right motions and had not heard anything wrong at all. I swept my right foot out, went down on my knee, looked up and smiled. The room was

quiet, except for Old Chong, who was beaming and shouting, "Bravo! Bravo! Well done!" But then I saw my mother's face, her stricken face. The audience clapped weakly, and as I walked back to my chair, with my whole face quivering as I tried not to cry, I heard a little boy whisper loudly to his mother, "That was awful," and the mother whispered back, "Well, she certainly tried."

And now I realized how many people were in the audience, the whole world it seemed. I was aware of eyes burning into my back. I felt the shame of my mother and father as they sat stiffly throughout the rest of the show.

We could have escaped during intermission. Pride and some strange sense of honor must have anchored my parents to their chairs. And so we watched it all: the eighteen-year-old boy with a fake mustache who did a magic show and juggled flaming hoops while riding a unicycle. The breasted girl with white makeup who sang from *Madama Butterfly* and got honorable mention. And the eleven-year-old boy who won first prize playing a tricky violin song that sounded like a busy bee.

After the show, the Hsus, the Jongs, and the St. Clairs from the Joy Luck Club came up to my mother and father.

"Lots of talented kids," Auntie Lindo said vaguely, smiling broadly.

"That was somethin' else," said my father, and I wondered if he was referring to me in a humorous way, or whether he even remembered what I had done.

Waverly looked at me and shrugged her shoulders. "You aren't a genius like me," she said matter-of-factly. And if I hadn't felt so bad, I would have pulled her braids and punched her stomach.

But my mother's expression was what devastated me: a quiet, blank look that said she had lost everything. I felt the same way, and it seemed as if everybody were now coming up, like gawkers at the scene of an accident, to see what parts were actually missing. When we got on the bus to go home, my father was humming the busy-bee tune and my mother was silent. I kept thinking she wanted to wait until we got home before shouting at me. But when my father unlocked the door to our apartment, my mother walked in and then went to the back, into the bedroom. No accusations. No blame. And in a way, I felt disappointed. I had been waiting for her to start shouting, so I could shout back and cry and blame her for all my misery.

I assumed my talent-show fiasco meant I never had to play the piano again. But two days later, after school, my mother came out of the kitchen and saw me watching TV.

"Four clock," she reminded me as if it were any other day. I was stunned, as though she were asking me to go through the talent-show torture again. I wedged myself more tightly in front of the TV.

"Turn off TV," she called from the kitchen five minutes later.

I didn't budge. And then I decided. I didn't have to do what my mother said anymore. I wasn't her slave. This wasn't China. I had listened to her before and look what happened. She was the stupid one.

She came out from the kitchen and stood in the arched entryway of the living room. "Four clock," she said once again, louder.

"I'm not going to play anymore," I said nonchalantly. "Why should I? I'm not a genius."

She walked over and stood in front of the TV. I saw her chest was heaving up and down in an angry way.

"No!" I said, and now I felt stronger, as if my true self had finally emerged. So this was what had been inside me all along.

"No! I won't!" I screamed.

She yanked me by the arm, pulled me off the floor, snapped off the TV. She was frighteningly strong, half pulling, half carrying me toward the piano as I kicked the throw rugs under my feet. She lifted me up and onto the hard bench. I was sobbing by now, looking at her bitterly. Her chest was heaving even more and her mouth was open, smiling crazily as if she were pleased I was crying.

"You want me to be someone that I'm not!" I sobbed. "I'll never be the kind of daughter you want me to be!"

"Only two kinds of daughters," she shouted in Chinese. "Those who are obedient and those who follow their own mind! Only one kind of daughter can live in this house. Obedient daughter!"

"Then I wish I wasn't your daughter. I wish you weren't my mother," I shouted. As I said these things I got scared. I felt like worms and toads and slimy things were crawling out of my chest, but it also felt good, as if this awful side of me had surfaced, at last.

"Too late change this," said my mother shrilly.

And I could sense her anger rising to its breaking point. I wanted to see it spill over. And that's when I remembered the babies she had lost in China, the ones we never talked about. "Then I wish I'd never been born!" I shouted. "I wish I were dead! Like them."

It was as if I had said the magic words. Alakazam!—and her face went blank, her mouth closed, her arms went slack, and she backed out of the room, stunned, as if she were blowing away like a small brown leaf, thin, brittle, lifeless.

It was not the only disappointment my mother felt in me. In the years that followed, I failed her so many times, each time asserting my own will, my right to fall short of expectations. I didn't get straight As. I didn't become class president. I didn't get into Stanford. I dropped out of college.

For unlike my mother, I did not believe I could be anything I wanted to be. I could only be me.

And for all those years, we never talked about the disaster at the recital or my terrible accusations afterward at the piano bench. All that remained unchecked, like a betrayal that was now unspeakable. So I never found a way to ask her why she had hoped for something so large that failure was inevitable.

And even worse, I never asked her what frightened me the most: Why had she given up hope?

For after our struggle at the piano, she never mentioned my playing again. The lessons stopped. The lid to the piano was closed, shutting out the dust, my misery, and her dreams.

So she surprised me. A few years ago, she offered to give me the piano, for my thirtieth birthday. I had not played in all those years. I saw the offer as a sign of forgiveness, a tremendous burden removed.

"Are you sure?" I asked shyly. "I mean, won't you and Dad miss it?"

"No, this your piano," she said firmly. "Always your piano. You only one can play."

"Well, I probably can't play anymore," I said. "It's been years."

"You pick up fast," said my mother, as if she knew this was certain. "You have natural talent. You could been genius if you want to."

"No I couldn't."

"You just not trying," said my mother. And she was neither angry nor sad. She said it as if to announce a fact that could never be disproved. "Take it," she said.

But I didn't at first. It was enough that she had offered it to me. And after that, every time I saw it in my parents' living room, standing in front of the bay windows, it made me feel proud, as if it were a shiny trophy I had won back.

Last week I sent a tuner over to my parents' apartment and had the piano reconditioned, for purely sentimental reasons. My mother had died a few months before and I had been getting things in order for my father, a little bit at a time. I put the jewelry in special silk pouches. The sweaters she had knitted in yellow, pink, bright orange—all the colors I hated—I put those in moth-proof boxes. I found some old Chinese silk dresses, the kind with little slits up the sides. I rubbed the old silk against my skin, then wrapped them in tissue and decided to take them home with me.

After I had the piano tuned, I opened the lid and touched the keys. It sounded even richer than I remembered. Really, it was a very good piano. Inside the bench were the same exercise notes with handwritten scales, the same second-hand music books with their covers held together with yellow tape.

I opened up the Schumann book to the dark little piece I had played at the recital. It was on the left-hand side of the page, "Pleading Child." It looked more difficult than I remembered. I played a few bars, surprised at how easily the notes came back to me.

And for the first time, or so it seemed, I noticed the piece on the right-hand side. It was called "Perfectly Contented." I tried to play this one as well. It had a lighter melody but the same flowing rhythm and turned out to be quite easy. "Pleading Child" was shorter but slower; "Perfectly Contented" was longer but faster. And after I played them both a few times, I realized they were two halves of the same song. ◆

1. RESPONDING TO THE STORY

a. What two kinds does the title refer to?

b. Why is the mother so insistent on her daughter becoming a prodigy? Why is the daughter so intent on not doing what her mother wants? Explain with whom you agree more: the mother or the daughter.

c. Do you think parents have a right to dictate their children's interests or what their children should become as adults? Give reasons for your views.

d. The mother says of her daughter's lack of success, "You just not trying." Do you agree with the mother's opinion? Does the daughter ever achieve success?

2. ORAL LANGUAGE GROUP DISCUSSION

Discuss with a group or the class whether society in general (parents, friends, school, government, and so on) expects everyone to be "the best" at something. What pressures are there on people to be successful? What images does society use to stand for success? Do you think success is important? Does it develop character? Should everyone want to be successful? Can *everyone* be successful?

3. WRITING LETTER OF APOLOGY

Have you ever felt badly about something you once did, but you never apologized for doing it? Well, here's your chance! Write a letter to that person explaining what you did and why you feel you have to apologize. Will you send your letter? You decide.

4. LITERATURE STUDIES UNDERSTANDING CHARACTER

Amy Tan paints a very vivid picture of the daughter and mother. With a partner, discuss how both of these characters develop throughout the story. What was your initial reaction to the mother? How did you feel about her by the end of the story? What was your initial reaction to the daughter? How did you feel about her by the end of the story? How does Tan show character development? Try one of these ideas when your write your own short stories.

5. LANGUAGE CONVENTIONS USING CONJUNCTIONS

Conjunctions are used to connect words in sentences. Sometimes authors use them to begin sentences. Reread "Two Kinds" and discuss with a partner Amy Tan's use of conjunctions. Does she begin sentences with conjunctions? What effect does this create? What does it say about character? What examples in other selections use conjunctions to begin sentences? If you take the conjunction away in these examples, the sentences still make sense. Why do you think authors use this part of speech to begin some sentences? What would be the effect if they were overused?

> A **conjunction** is a part of speech used to connect and relate words or sentences. Common conjunctions are *and, but, for, or, so,* and *yet.*

SELF-ASSESSMENT: Do you use conjunctions in your writing to start sentences? If you do, what conjunctions do you use most often? Do you think about using these conjunctions or are they just part of your writing style?

Putting a Colourful Life on Canvas

Profile by Afrodite Balogh–Tyszko

Paintings by Jean Chin

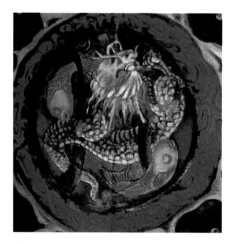

MANDALA

The paintings and sketches that clutter Jean Chin's small apartment are not her only works in progress. She, too, is a work in progress.

After studying at the Ontario College of Art and Design, the Jamaican-born Chin travelled to Italy, where she was to study print-making. She couldn't find a proper studio for print-making, so she began painting.

GOALS AT A GLANCE

- Write a profile using the selection as a model.
- Analyse an artist's work.

212

Chin displays her latest work in progress.

Eventually, this new interest led to the development of her current series on cultural displacement.

"It [the series] is really difficult to describe," she says, gesturing to a wooden easel that sits at the edge of her living room. "As an artist, a lot of thoughts come out as you work. It's only at the finish that you realize what you've done because the product is very different than what you start with."

The as yet untitled series keeps Chin busy, but it's not the only way the multi-talented twenty-three year old puts her skills to the test. She recently landed an apprenticing job with Toronto-based post-production company AXYZ and also works alongside veteran artist John Fraser.

Until a few months ago, she hadn't even heard of *matte painting* (a type of digital painting), which she's now beginning to master. "It's not as technical as some people might think. It's actually very creative and artistic because you create a mood with light and form."

As if she wasn't busy enough, Chin is also working on developing illustrations and, hopefully, a comic strip for a new women's magazine called *Shebang!*

Chin insists that as much as she wants her work to speak for itself, it cannot say everything. "What you create is a direct reflection of you," she says. "But there's also a lot more to you than what you create."

NUWA

ARTIST'S STATEMENT

The work is the creation of a visual language using personal symbols. It is the creation of contexts for myself—culturally and as a woman. It draws upon mythology, religious iconography, and pictorial/visual means of communication as inspiration. It is the exploration of all that I find magical, ethereal, and beautiful. It attempts to appeal to a sensitivity which I believe is innate in people. It defies the structure and specification of everyday language by not carrying "a message" or concise idea. Instead, I consider it to be an invitation of sorts. The symbols themselves are loaded with meanings and will summon different reactions from different people. It is a stimulus for the imagination, and welcomes projections and perception from the viewer.

1. Responding to the Profile

a. Jean Chin says, "there's...a lot more to you than what you create." What does she mean?

b. The artist puts on canvas images that express who she is. If you expressed yourself with images, what images would you choose? What would these images say about who you are?

c. What do you think Jean Chin means by *cultural displacement*?

d. Discuss the "Artist's Statement" in a small group. How does its message compare to the rest of the article?

e. The artist describes herself as a *work in progress*. In a paragraph explain whether you are a work in progress.

2. Writing A Profile

A profile is a short article about a person. It usually focusses on a few interesting aspects of the person's life and does not intend to be a complete biography. Reread the profile on Jean Chin and outline the way it was organized. Use this example of organization to write a profile of your own about someone you admire, for example, a person you know who has had an interesting life or who has something important to say about life.

3. Visual Communication Artists' Visions

In a small group, discuss the example of Jean Chin's work on the preceding pages. Does her artwork succeed in the way Chin hopes? Explain. Use art reference books to choose an artist who appeals to you. Select three examples of the artist's work (paintings, drawings, prints, or other visual media). Write a paragraph for each work, explaining what you think each means. Share your examples and your explanations with others. Do they see the same thing you do?

Janitor, neurosurgeon,
singer, or sleeper?
Robert Fulghum's
true occupation
is hard to pin down!

So, What Do You Do?

Essay by Robert Fulghum

"Well, so, what is it you do?" Your basic strangers-on-a-plane question. Comes up at the PTA potluck and the corporate cocktail party and just about any other stand-around-and-make-small-talk situation you get into. It's a politely veiled status inquiry to clarify social standing. The bureaucratic version of the question is terse: Fill in the blank marked "Occupation." The IRS wants it that way—and the police officer giving you a ticket, and the passport agency, and the bank. Say what you are paid to do, and we will know who you are and how to deal with you.

When I ask people what they do, I usually get a stiff little piece of 9 x 5-cm paper that summarizes their identity. Name, company name, title, address, lots of numbers—phone, fax, and e-mail. Business card. If you don't have a business card these days, you are not to be taken too seriously. Though I sometimes think the truth may be vice versa.

For example, a fellow traveller's card said he was vice-president for systems analysis of Unico. "Well, so, what is it you really DO?" And he pointed at his title as if I had overlooked it. I asked again. "I mean, if I followed you around all day long, what would I see you doing?" He talked for a long time. I still do not really know what he does. And I am not sure he knows, either.

When it was my turn, I had no business card. Can't seem to get me down on that little piece of paper. What I do is kind of complicated and takes such a long time to explain that I often avoid the question and just

GOALS AT A GLANCE

- Respond personally and critically.
- Analyse hyphenation.

pick something simple that's true but not the whole truth. Even this tactic has left me painted into difficult corners.

On an early-morning flight to San Francisco, I told my seatmate that I was a janitor, thinking that she might not want to pursue that and would leave me to read my book. *(When I think of how I have spent my life and how much of it involves cleaning and straightening and hauling trash—I don't get paid for it, but that's what I do a lot.)* Anyhow, she was fascinated. Turned out she wrote a housewives' column for a small newspaper and was glad to spend the rest of the flight sharing her tips for tidy housekeeping with me. Now, I know more about getting spots and stains out of rugs than I ever hoped to know.

Turned out, too, that she was a member of the church where I was to speak on Sunday. I didn't know that until I stood up in the pulpit and saw her there in the third row. And it further turned out that she knew who I was all along, but was creative enough to think that if I wanted to go around airplanes being a janitor, I probably had a reason.

Another time, I was bumped into first class on a flight to Thailand and was seated next to a very distinguished-looking Sikh gentleman. When he asked me the what-do-you-do question I replied off the top of my head that I was a neurosurgeon. "How wonderful," said he with delight. "So am I!" And he was. A real one. It took a while to unscramble things, and we had a wonderful conversation all the way to Bangkok.

Having learned my lesson, the next time I got on a plane and sat down next to someone who looked sympathetic, I told these stories and then suggested we play a game—just for the fun of it—and each make up our occupation and pretend all the way to Chicago. The guy went for it. So he declared he was a spy, and I decided I'd be a nun. We had a great time—one of the best conversations of my life. He said he couldn't wait until his wife asked him, "Well, dear, how was your flight?" "There was this nun dressed in a tweed suit..."

But it was the middle-aged couple from Green Bay who had occupied the seats behind us who were blown away. They had listened to the nun and the spy in stunned silence. They really had something to say when asked, "How was your flight?" As the man passed me in the concourse, he said, "Have a nice day, Sister."

Filling in forms has led to similar situations. At my bank, I wrote "prince" in the blank for "Occupation" on an income tax document. Just that morning, my wife had said to me, "Fulghum, sometimes you are a real prince." And sometimes, I am. So, since I was feeling princely, I put it in the blank. Clerk couldn't handle it. And we had a friendly argument right there that is at the heart of this matter of identity: Is my occupation what I get paid money for, or is it something larger and wider and richer—more a matter of what I am or how I think about myself?

Making a living and having a life are not the same thing. Making a living and making a life that's worthwhile are not the same thing. Living *the* good life and living *a* good life are not the same thing. A job title doesn't even come close to answering the question, "What do you do?"

Marcel Duchamp, whom most people think of as a fixture in the world of fine art during the period before 1940, was equally frustrated by the implications of the standard inquiry. He would answer, "I am a *respirateur*" *(a breather)*. He explained that he did more breathing than anything else, and was very, very good at it, too. After that, people were usually afraid to ask him what else he did.

I know, I know. We can't go around handing out two-hundred-page autobiographies every time someone asks for minimal information. But suppose that instead of answering that question with what we do to get money, we replied with what we do that gives us great pleasure or makes us feel useful to the human enterprise? *(If you happen to get paid to do what you love, feel fortunate, but a lot of people don't.)*

Shift the scale a bit and answer the what-do-you-do question in terms of how you spend a normal twenty-four-hour day. I might say that I am a *sleepeur* and a *napeur*—one who sleeps and is very good at it. If ever there is an Olympic event for napping, I will go for the gold. Eight hours in twenty-four I am asleep in my bed, and every afternoon I take a thirty-minute nap. That is more than one third of my life. If I live to be seventy-five years old, I will have spent more than twenty-five years asleep. No other activity commands so much of my time in one place. While asleep, I cause no one else any pain or trouble, and it is an ecologically sound activity. If I got paid for how well I do it, I would be a very rich man indeed. It would be a better world if more people got more sleep, or at least spent more time in bed. There are people I don't much like when they are awake, but they don't bother me at all while they are sleeping, drooling into their pillows.

Had you asked me the do-be-do question today, I would have said I am a singer. Not only do I not get paid to sing, but in some cases friends might offer to pay me *not* to sing. Nevertheless, I love to do it. In the shower, driving to work, while I'm working, walking to lunch, and along with whatever I recognize on the radio. I sing. It is what I do. God did not put my desire together with the necessary equipment. My voice is what you might politely call "uncertain." I can hear the music in my head, but I cannot reproduce what I have heard, though it sounds fine to me. Over a lifetime of trying out for leads in musicals, I have always been told that I would be best in the chorus. And then got eliminated from the chorus because there were too many of whatever it is I am. I liked being a parent to my children when they were young and had no musical standards and would uncritically sing with me. It didn't matter that we didn't always know all the words or have the tune just right—we made it up. We singers are not thrown by technicalities. Singers are those who sing. Period.

Sometimes, when asked the what-do-you-do question, it occurs to me to say that I work for the government. I have a government job, essential to national security. *I am a citizen*. Like the Supreme Court judges, my job is for life, and the well-being of my country depends on me. It seems fair to think that I should be accountable for my record in office in the same way I expect accountability from those who seek elected office. I would like to be able to say that I can stand on my record and am proud of it.

"What I do" is literally "how I spend my time." As of this writing, I figure in my life so far I have spent thirty-five thousand hours eating, thirty thousand hours in traffic getting from one place to another, two thousand five hundred and eight hours brushing my teeth, eight hundred and seventy thousand hours just coping with odds and ends—filling out forms, mending, repairing, paying bills, getting dressed and undressed, reading papers, attending committee meetings, being sick, and all that kind of stuff. And two hundred and seventeen thousand hours at work. There's not a whole lot left over when you get finished adding and subtracting. The good stuff has to be fitted in somewhere, or else the good stuff has to come at the very same time we do all the rest of the stuff.

Which is why I often say that I don't worry about the meaning *of* life—I can't handle that big stuff. What concerns me is the meaning *in* life—day by day, hour by hour, while I'm doing whatever it is that I do. What counts is not what I do, but how I think about myself while I'm doing it.

In truth, I have a business card now. Finally figured out what to put on it. One word. "Fulghum." That's my occupation. And when I give it away, it leads to fine conversations. What I do is to be the most Fulghum I can be. Which means being a son, father, husband, friend, singer, dancer, eater, breather, sleeper, janitor, dishwasher, bather, swimmer, runner, walker, artist, writer, painter, teacher, preacher, citizen, poet, counsellor, neighbour, dreamer, wisher, laugher, traveller, pilgrim, and on and on and on.

I and you—we are infinite, rich, large, contradictory, living, breathing miracles—free human beings, children of God and the everlasting universe. That's what we do. ◆

1. RESPONDING TO THE ESSAY

a. Why do you think the author doesn't want to be identified with one particular occupation?

b. Do you agree that people are classified by what they do for money instead of who they really are? Explain your view.

c. What do you most enjoy doing and why? What would you like to see on your business card in the future?

2. LITERATURE STUDIES ESSAYS

With a partner, reread Robert Fulghum's essay and discuss the *thesis* (the main argument in an essay). What is Fulghum's thesis? What supporting details does he outline to prove his argument? How does the essay end? Is the structure of the essay a traditional one? In what other ways can essays be structured?

Think about an issue that you care about. Develop an outline for an essay about this issue. Develop your thesis, and in point form outline the supporting evidence to back up your argument.

3. LANGUAGE CONVENTIONS HYPHENATED WORDS

You may have learned that a *hyphen* is a short dash used to break a word from one line to the next. It has other uses, however. A hyphen connects the written form of certain numbers between twenty and one hundred, such as *twenty-four* and *sixty-seven*. Another use is to join words together to create a new meaning, for example, *good-looking* or *self-discipline*.

Find examples of hyphens that Robert Fulghum uses in his essay and explain what each example means or stands for.

SELF-ASSESSMENT: Do you use hyphens in your writing? Do you notice them in stories and articles? Jot down a few rules for using hyphens in your notebook.

SELF-ASSESSMENT: WRITING

As you worked on activities in this unit, what did you learn about

- short stories?
- using quotations?
- monologues?
- poetry?
- letter of apology?
- using conjunctions?
- profiles?
- hyphenated words?

What else would you like to learn about writing?

WRITING COMPARE THEMES

Think about the selections you read in this unit. What themes and messages were explored? Write an essay comparing the theme or message of two selections.

ORAL LANGUAGE GROUP DISCUSSION

With a small group, choose one of the topics presented in this unit—like taking responsibility for your actions, or accepting who you are—and discuss it. Explore the reasons and opinions of the characters and your group members.

ESSAYS

"There is no room for the impurities of nature in an essay."

Virginia Woolf

In this speech, Harvey Locke presents his solution to the problem of "species selfishness."

Keep Faith
with Nature

Speech by Harvey Locke

We are here because we love the earth. We are gathered at dinner to celebrate our efforts to protect some of nature's bounty from despoliation. It is important that we do this together—that we laugh, celebrate, rejoice that some parts of this unbelievably wonderful country have been protected by law.

But when our party is over, most of us will leave here with a nagging sensation that we are not doing enough. That nature's fabric is unravelling all over the world and that we work valiantly, but in a doomed cause. How can it be that the Pacific is in danger of losing some species of wild salmon? How can the Atlantic be almost out of cod? How could industrial pollutants be embedded in the ice of Bow Glacier in Banff National Park and present in Arctic ecosystems?

We fear we labour for a doomed cause because we do not see a change in the way society deals with nature. We humans are now practising what has been described as "species selfishness" on a global scale, appropriating most of nature's bounty for ourselves. We environmentalists continue to try out our arguments to protect nature and are stymied by the response that the economy is more important.

Until humanity embraces nature as something more than an object of greed, we will inflict on this earth an extinction event equivalent to the death of the dinosaurs.

Many of us, in our hearts, fear this end. Is there a possible different end? The answer may lie in a return to the roots of the conservation movement and in embracing the spiritual community. We need to restore a sense of the sacred to creation if we are to save it.

GOALS AT A GLANCE

■ Compare formats.
■ Use oral skills to give a speech.

As a boy, I felt magic in nature. I did not know what to call it. I knew the Canadian Rockies were special to my parents. Places like Mt. Assiniboine and Lake O'Hara, Shadow Lake and Skoki were spoken of in reverent tones in my house. When my Dad finally took me to Skoki Lodge in the back country of Banff National Park, it was a rite of passage. I was now worthy of a mountain pilgrimage. It moved me deeply. Yet, it was not until I was an adult that I knew that other people felt the same deep resonance I did in the presence of natural beauty, whether it be the seashore, a grassland, or an ancient forest.

I came upon the writings of John Muir as a young adult. I was stunned to hear him state my feelings so profoundly—especially when I had never been any place Muir had been. He said, "Climb the mountains and get their good tidings," and I knew what he meant. Muir founded the Sierra Club, which was perhaps North America's first environmental activist group.

Let our hearts, who love her, not betray nature. Let us reach out to and embrace all others who believe that nature is sacred. Let us dream a world full of wild salmon and cod, a world full of cathedrals of old-growth forests, of grasslands carrying the music of the meadowlark and of streams of clear, cool water.

Let us dream of a world lit by the green fire in a wolf's eyes, where thousands of caribou thunder across the Arctic tundra, where the grizzly infuses the landscape with its power, and where the songbird sings forevermore.

Let us have the courage to be wild at heart, to keep faith with nature by joining hands with the spiritual community to work for the protection and restoration of nature's full glory. It is time for us to say this millennium is about the love of creation and to strive to make it so. ◆

1. RESPONDING TO THE SPEECH

a. Describe in a few sentences how Harvey Locke sees the natural world. What is Locke's message to his listeners? How do you view nature?

b. Locke speaks of going with his father to Skoki Lodge as "a rite of passage." What do you think he means by "rite of passage"? What "rite of passage" examples can you give from your own life?

c. In talking to his audience, to what does Locke appeal: emotions? intellect? a sense of nostalgia for something lost? some other human feeling? Explain your answer with supporting examples from the speech.

2. LITERATURE STUDIES COMPARE FORMATS

Find examples in the selection that indicate it is a speech rather than a formal essay. How is a speech like or unlike an essay? Reread this selection as well as Martin Luther King's speech on pages 259–263. List the elements in these speeches that make them different from essays and articles. Choose two or more non-fiction selections from any unit. In one or two paragraphs, compare the speeches to these non-fiction selections. Use the following questions to develop your comparison:

- What are the differences and similarities in the style of language and tone?
- Do speeches more often appeal to people's emotions or intellect?
- To what do the non-fiction examples appeal?
- What role, if any, does the audience play in speeches compared to the readers of non-fiction?

3. ORAL LANGUAGE GIVE A SPEECH

There are two methods of delivering a speech: to read from a prepared text, or to use notes and speak spontaneously. Both methods have advantages and disadvantages, depending on the subject of the speech and the nature of the speaker.

Think of a topic you could talk about for at least two minutes. Outline what you will say and, using your outline, record your speech on audio tape. Then write a speech based on your notes and record it. Which version is better and more interesting to hear?

SELF-ASSESSMENT: What did you learn about writing speeches? What did you learn about giving speeches? How could you improve your performance?

When her parents died, Brown Weasel
Woman became the head of her household,
but it was the warrior's life she wanted
and it was as one that she became…

RUNNING
EAGLE—

Woman Warrior of the Blackfeet

Expository Essay
by Beverly Hungry Wolf

R unning Eagle has become the most famous woman in the history of the Blackfoot Nation because she gave up the work of the household in exchange for the war trails usually followed by men. In fact, she became so successful on her war adventures that many men called her a chief and eagerly followed her whenever she would take them. She was finally killed during one of her war adventures.

Because this woman died sometime around 1850, the actual facts of her life are now hard to separate from the popular legends. My grandmothers of today still talk about her, and an old book about her life can be found on some library shelves. However, all the stories agree that this woman was very successful in all but her final efforts, and that she was well liked and respected by her people. It is generally believed that she was also a holy woman who put up Sun Dances, for which she qualified by never marrying or taking a lover in her life. It is said that she pledged herself to Sun, as the result of a vision of power.

GOALS AT A GLANCE

■ Respond personally and critically to the essay.
■ Participate in group discussions.

The popular story is that Running Eagle began life as an ordinary Blackfoot girl named Brown Weasel Woman. She had two brothers and two sisters, and her father was a well-known warrior. When she became of the age that boys begin to practise hunting, she asked her father to make a set of bow and arrows with which she could practise. He did so, though not without some argument from his wives. It is said that he even allowed her to go with him buffalo hunting, and that she learned to shoot well enough to bring some down.

It was during one of the buffalo hunts with her father that this unusual girl is said to have first shown her warrior's courage. There were only a few Blackfoot hunters in the party, and it was not far from the camps when an enemy war party attacked and chased it. As the people rode toward the camp at top speed, Brown Weasel Woman's father had his horse shot out from under him. One of the bravest deeds performed by warriors in the old days was to brave the enemy's fire while riding back to rescue a companion who was left on foot. This is what the daughter did for her father, both of them making their escape on her horse, after she stopped to unload the fresh meat that was tied on behind her. When word of the attack reached the rest of the tribe, a great crowd of warriors rode out after the enemy, killing many of them and chasing the rest away. The young woman's name was mentioned for days and nights after, as the people recounted what had taken place during this particular fight. It is said that some of the people complained, and feared that the young woman performing men's deeds would set a bad example which might lead other women to give up their household ways.

However, when her mother became helplessly ill sometime later, the future warrior woman decided on her own to take up household work. Since she was the eldest child in the family, there was no one to do the cooking and tanning while her mother slowly withered away. So she worked hard to learn what she had been avoiding, and she taught her younger brothers and sisters to help out wherever they could.

It is hard to say for how many years this young woman took the place of her mother in running the family household, but it is said that she did it very well. However, it is also said that she did it without receiving any pleasure from it, since she had probably already experienced too much excitement from the adventures of men's ways. At any rate, she had no boyfriends and she took no interest in the plans others her age were making for marriage.

The turning point in the young woman's life came when her father was killed while on the war trail. News of his death also killed his widow, in her weakened state. The young woman and her brothers and sisters suddenly were orphaned, and she decided at that point to devote herself to her dream power giving her directions to follow men's ways. She took a widow into the lodge to help with the household work, and she directed her brothers and sisters in doing their share. She even carried a rifle—inherited from her father—at a time when many men still relied mainly on their bows and arrows.

Her first war adventure came not long after she and her family had gotten over their initial mourning. A war party of men left the Blackfoot camps on the trail of Crow warriors who had come and stolen horses. When this party was well under way, one of its members noticed someone following behind, in the distance. It turned out to be the young woman, armed and dressed for battle. The leader of the party told her to go back, threatened her, and finally told her that he would take the whole party back home if she didn't leave them. She is said to have laughed and told him: "You can return if you want to; I will go on by myself."

One of the members of this party was a young man who was a cousin of the young woman—a brother, in Blackfoot relationships—and he offered to take her back himself. When she still refused to go, the leader of the party put the cousin in charge of her well-being, so that they could all continue on their way. She grew up with this cousin, and learned to hunt by his side, so the two got along well, in general.

The war party with the young woman spent several days on the trail before they reached the enemy camps of the Crows. They made a successful raid, going in and out of the camp many times, by cover of night, to bring out the choice horses that their owners kept in front of the lodges. It is said that the woman and her cousin went in together and that she, by herself, captured eleven of the valuable runners. Before daylight, they were mounted on their stolen horses and headed back toward their own homeland, driving ahead of them the rest of the captured herd. The Crows discovered their loss in the morning and chased the party for some way. But the raiders were able to change horses whenever the ones they were riding became worn out, and in that way they soon left the enemy followers way behind.

However, the most exciting part of this first war adventure of the young Blackfoot woman was yet to come, according to the legend that has survived her. While the rest of the party rested and cooked in a hidden location, she kept watch on the prairie country from the top of a nearby butte. From there, she saw the approach of two enemy riders, and before she could alert the rest of her party to the danger, the enemies were ready to round up the captured herd. It is said that she ran down the butte with her rifle and managed to grab the rope of the herd's lead horse, to keep the rest from running away. Then, as the enemies closed in on her, expecting no trouble from a woman, she shot the one who carried a rifle and forced the other one to turn and try an escape. Instead of reloading her own rifle, she ran and grabbed the rifle from the fallen enemy, and shot after the one getting away. She missed him, but others of the party went after him and shortly brought him down as well. Her companions were quite surprised and pleased at what she had done. Not only had she saved their whole herd from being captured, but she also killed an enemy and captured his gun. She even captured his horse.

Although the young woman's first war experience was quite successful, there were still many people who thought that the chiefs should make her stop following the ways of the men. However, the criticisms came to an end after she followed the advice of wise elders and went out to fast and seek a vision. She spent four days and nights alone and the Spirits rewarded her with a vision that gave her the power that men consider necessary for leading a successful warrior's life. Such visions were not always received by those seeking them, and very seldom have women received them at all. By tribal custom, no one questioned her about the vision, nor did they doubt her right to follow the directions which she was thus given. From then on, the people considered her as someone unusual, with special powers, whom only the Spirits could judge and guide.

The young woman's second war adventure took her west over the Rocky Mountains, to the camps of the Kalispell people. Among her companions were some of the same men who had been on her first war raid, including her cousin/brother, with whom she was spending a lot of her time. This time, instead of wearing her buckskin dress, she had on a new suit of warrior's clothing, including leggings, shirt, and breechcloth. She also carried a fine rawhide war shield, that had been given to her by the man who married the widow who had moved into the orphan household some time before.

The second raid was quite successful, although one member of the party was killed. They captured a herd of over six hundred horses, and killed a number of the enemy during a fight which followed their discovery during the raiding. The young woman was shot at, and would have been killed, but the two arrows both struck her shield, instead of her body.

The next time the tribe gathered for the annual medicine lodge ceremony, the young woman was asked to get up with the other warriors and tell the people about her war exploits. Other women had done so, but they had usually gone in the company of their husbands and had not accomplished such fearless deeds as she. When she finished her stories the people applauded with drum beats and war whoops, as was the custom. Then the head chief of the people, a man named Lone Walker, is said to have honoured her in a way never known to have been done for a woman. After a short talk and a prayer, he gave her a new name—

Running Eagle—an ancient name carried by several famous warriors in the tribe before her. In addition, the Braves Society of young warriors invited her to become a member, an honour she is said to have accepted as well.

From that point on, Running Eagle, the young woman warrior, was no longer a follower, but the leader of the war parties she went on. I cannot say how many such war raids existed, nor how many horses Running Eagle captured, nor how many enemies she killed. There are many different legends about them. There are also legends of the men who could not accept that this proud woman wanted no husband. They tried many different ways to try and make her change her mind about marriage. But the issue was settled when she explained that Sun had come in her vision and told her that she must belong only to him, and that she could not go on living if she broke such a commandment.

As Running Eagle lived by the war trail, so also she died. It happened when she led a large party of warriors against the Flathead people in revenge for their killing of some men and women who had gone from the Blackfoot camps one morning to hunt and butcher buffalo. The revenge party was a very large one, and she led it, during the night, right to the edge of the Flathead camp. In the early morning, after waiting for the camp to be cleared of the prize horses by their herders, she gave the cry to attack. There followed a long drawn-out battle in which many of the enemy were killed. After the initial shooting, the battle turned into a free-for-all in which clubs and knives were the main weapons. Running Eagle was attacked by a large enemy with a club, whom she killed, but another came up behind her and killed her with his club. One of Running Eagle's men in turn killed this man. When the battle was over, the members of her party found her, the large man in front, the other behind, and she dead in the middle. And so ended the career of the woman warrior whose life has become a legend among the Blackfeet.

---

1. RESPONDING TO THE EXPOSITORY ESSAY

a. What is the thesis of "Running Eagle: Woman Warrior of the Blackfeet"?

b. Why do you think Running Eagle rejected the traditional role of a Blackfoot woman?

c. What did Running Eagle do that made the Blackfoot warriors accept her?

d. Do you think men and women should be accepted for what they can do or for who they are? Explain your answer.

2. RESEARCHING WOMEN PROFESSIONALS

What situations today parallel Running Eagle's experience? For example, there are few woman who compete or are accepted in male-dominated sports. Discuss your views with a partner.

Use library resources, the Internet, teachers, family members, and friends to research stories about women who are successfully working in occupations once dominated by men. Work with a group to combine these profiles into a report or presentation. For example, you could profile women from a particular province, occupation, or age group. Your presentation might be in the form of a poster, a career booklet, or a live or videotaped TV-style news magazine.

3. ORAL LANGUAGE GROUP DISCUSSION

Men and women in some cultures have roles, patterns of behaviour, and occupations that are specific to their gender. With a group of classmates, or as a class, discuss whether you think this condition is true for you and your friends. Is it true for your parents' generation? How do you feel about the situation?

SELF-ASSESSMENT: Assess your participation in the group discussion. Did you listen to other opinions without first judging them? When explaining your views, did you use emotional arguments or did you present facts and examples?

I Am
Maxine Tynes

Personal Essay by Maxine Tynes

I am Maxine Tynes. I am a woman. I am Black. I am a poet. Four basic truths. None chosen. All joyful in my life.

As a writer, I know that this creative process was not "chosen" by me, consciously, as part of my life. The pursuit of The Muse; the passion of holding life and love and thought and feeling, and of handling them through words is not a consciously engineered selective process. It is not selected from a list of choices of being, perhaps, a clerk, a stonemason, a nurse or doctor, or a weaver.

It is, rather, an urge as strong, natural, and uncontrollable as an urge to laugh, to weep, to sleep, to hold one's beloved.

To write is powerful medicine, magic, weaponry, and love.

To write poetry is the ultimate in that power. It is a sweet and yielding power, as well as being an incisive and bludgeoning one.

Terrorist and oppressive regimes know this only too well. In Chile,[1] Nicaragua,[2] Northern Ireland,[3] in Johannesburg,[4] under Naziism or Fascism, the poets, the singers, the writers, the storytellers are among the first to be muzzled, silenced, and to disappear.

I write from a deep, eternal, and eclectic energy of my own making and that of all of those who have touched my life in my own time, as well as in the distant past before my own lifetime.

When I write, I feel the hand of my mother, Ada Maxwell Tynes; of my sisters; of my grandmothers on both and on all sides; of my father Joseph James Tynes; of my brothers; and of all the men and women in my life.

When I write, I feel the depth of my Blackness, and the spread of my Blackness through, and by, and beyond the poems and the stories of Black culture, Black life, and Black womanhood that I put on paper.

GOALS AT A GLANCE

- Respond personally to the essay.
- Write a character description.

My Blackness is as real to me in my poems as it is to me as I see my own Black hand move my pen and these words across the page.

My Blackness, my culture, and Black ethnicity becomes a shared thing then with those who are and are not Black like I am. I love that. To see the recognition of Black personhood in the eyes of others who share my history. To see the wonder, that curious mix of fear and wonder becoming awareness of same and different and the okayness of it all in those Caucasian or other eyes. I love that.

All of that from writing. All of that as a wonderful ethereal return for being a poet. That rare and wonderful state of being which I did not choose; yet, joyfully, I am.

I am Maxine Tynes. I am a woman. I am Black. I am a poet.

NOTES:

1. From 1973 to 1989, Chile was ruled by a military dictatorship.

2. In 1979, Nicaraguans revolted against a U.S.-backed dictator and established a popular government, which was then, during the 1980s, attacked by U.S.-backed "Contra" guerrillas.

3. Northern Ireland has been torn by Catholic-Protestant sectarian strife.

4. Johannesburg is a major city in South Africa, a state which has rigidly oppressed its Black majority population.

RESPONDING TO THE PERSONAL ESSAY

a. Describe Maxine Tynes to a partner. Write a character description after your discussion.

b. The author explains four basic truths about herself. What are they? What are four basic truths about *you*?

c. What does Tynes say about being a creative person? Do you agree with her? What do you think being creative means? Explain your opinion.

d. Tynes writes that she feels "the depth of [her] Blackness." When you express yourself in writing, in conversation, or creative activities, what are the elements in your life that most influence you?

David Blackwood's Newfoundland and Labrador

ART ESSAY

PAINTINGS BY DAVID BLACKWOOD • TEXT BY WILLIAM GOUGH

Canadian artist David Blackwood was born in Wesleyville, Newfoundland and Labrador, in 1941. He is the son and grandson of sea captains, and he grew up by the sea. So it isn't surprising that many of his paintings show the power of the waves. They tell how the sea can be calm or cruel. They tell about icebergs as big as islands and bleak ice fields that can crush a wooden boat to splinters. They also tell how people take their livelihood from the sea, and how sometimes they meet death, buried by the waves.

The paintings that follow are taken from *The Art of David Blackwood*. The accompanying text was written by William Gough, and is taken from the same book.

GOALS AT A GLANCE

- Analyse paintings.
- Create an image.

THE FAMILY

Wesleyville, as David Blackwood has mentioned, is flat rock next to ocean, and the light is frequently seen to glow at the horizon, appearing to spread in a circular manner. But that doesn't explain it fully. He adds, "In many cases the light is coming from within. People, naturally, because it is normal, ask, 'Where is the light coming from? Sunshine? Where?' Well, in many cases the light is, for example, inside the iceberg coming out, and the light is inside the person; coming from the person..."

THE *FLORA S. NICKERSON* DOWN ON THE LABRADOR

David Blackwood's own father is Captain Edward. When the artist
was a little boy, his father would take him for voyages on the schooner,
Flora S. Nickerson. He'd lean over the gunwales and stare at water, angling
in a driftwood bleach over the bow, watch gulls pointing the water, smell
the mix of salt and canvas.

PASSAGE

NORTH ATLANTIC

MARCH ICE RAFT

A place of startling storms, of bare light—sun rays staggering across a raging sky, and then the peace of a winter's night. Blackwood says, "The region is very flat and barren, the dominating features are the sea and the sky. In winter you feel this even more, all shades of grey, and black and white. That's the big influence."

MOLLY GLOVER LEAVING BRAGG'S ISLAND

Then one night, says Blackwood, Gram Glover had a dream. "I can remember her coming down to the kitchen one morning. 'Well, well, well,' she said. 'I had a funny dream last night, that we all had to pack up and leave this place. That we had to pack up and everything was torn to pieces, like there was another war coming. The whole place was in a shambles.' "

S<small>ICK</small> <small>CAPTAIN LEAVING</small>

ISLAND FUNERAL

This was a place that seemed to be forever. Men lived on the sea, and when they died, were buried by the sea, salt mixing tombstones with the ocean.

FIRE DOWN ON THE LABRADOR

Sitting perched on a rock, leaning against the earth, Blackwood would watch the boat, crisp against the day, and dream of the time when he'd head to the Labrador.

And so he did, past fire on ship, flames on water, with etching plate and paper, binding by the four elements and turning them into lines that edge a canvas, that hold a page—an artist, down on the Labrador.

1. RESPONDING TO THE ART ESSAY

a. What is the thesis of this art essay? What makes you think so?

b. In a paragraph, describe your impressions of David Blackwood's art.

c. In describing the light that is present in many of his paintings, Blackwood says that it "is coming from within." What do you think he means by this statement?

d. Which painting do you like the best? the least? Explain your choices.

2. VISUAL COMMUNICATION VIEWING THE ART ESSAY

Examine David Blackwood's paintings and discuss them with a partner. In what ways are they similar? What elements are repeated? What do you think these elements symbolize or represent? What are the main colours used and what are their effects? Which details in the paintings are most striking? What is your personal opinion of the images? Write three or four paragraphs explaining your reaction.

S T R A T E G I E S

3. MEDIA MAKER CREATE AN IMAGE

Newfoundland and Labrador has made an unforgettable impression on David Blackwood. Think of a place that has had an impact on you, and create an image representing this place. You could try one of the following ideas:

- If you like to paint, use water colours or oils. You can also draw using pastels, charcoal, or pencil.
- You could create a digital image and manipulate it. Scan a photo of your special place; then manipulate it on screen. Experiment with using different colours and background images.
- Take a series of photos. Experiment with ways to make the photos different. You could, for example, take photos at different times of the day.

Accompany the art with a caption or longer text explaining the significance of this special place.

SELF-ASSESSMENT: Examine your image. Does it present the mood or feeling you are trying to convey? How could you improve it?

SEVEN WONDERS

PERSONAL ESSAY
BY LEWIS THOMAS

A while ago, I received a letter from a magazine editor inviting me to join six other people at dinner to make a list of the Seven Wonders of the Modern World, to replace the seven old, out-of-date Wonders. I replied that I couldn't manage it, not on short order anyway, but still the question keeps hanging around in the lobby of my mind. I had to look up the old biodegradable Wonders, the Hanging Gardens of Babylon and all the rest, and then I had to look up that word *wonder* to make sure I understood what it meant. It occurred to me that if the magazine could get any seven people to agree on a list of any such seven things you'd have the modern Seven Wonders right there at the dinner table.

Wonder is a word to wonder about. It contains a mixture of messages: something marvellous and miraculous, surprising, raising unanswerable questions about itself, making the observer wonder, even raising skeptical questions like, "I *wonder* about that." *Miraculous* and *marvellous* are clues; both words come from an ancient Indo-European root meaning simply *to smile or to laugh.* Anything wonderful is something to smile in the presence of, in *admiration* (which, by the way, comes from the same root, along with, of all telling words, *mirror*).

I decided to try making a list, not for the magazine's dinner party, but for this occasion: seven things I wonder about the most.

I shall hold the first for the last, and move along.

GOALS AT A GLANCE

- Analyse essay structure.
- Use oral communication skills to debate.

My Number Two Wonder is a bacterial species never seen on the face of the earth until 1982, creatures never dreamed of before, living violation of what we used to regard as the laws of nature, things literally straight out of Hell. Or anyway what we used to think of as Hell, the hot unlivable interior of the earth. Such regions have recently come into scientific view from the research submarines designed to descend twenty-five hundred metres or more to the edge of deep holes in the sea bottom, where open vents spew superheated seawater in plumes from chimneys in the earth's crust, known to oceanographic scientists as "black smokers." This is not just hot water, or steam, or steam under pressure as exists in a laboratory autoclave (which we have relied upon for decades as the surest way to destroy all microbial life). This is extremely hot water under extremely high pressure, with temperatures in excess of three hundred degrees centigrade. At such heat, the existence of life as we know it would be simply inconceivable. Proteins and DNA would fall apart, enzymes would melt away, anything alive would die instantaneously. We have long since ruled out the possibility of life on Venus because of that planet's comparable temperature; we have ruled out the possibility of life in the earliest years of this planet, four billion or so years ago, on the same grounds.

Wonder Number Three.

B.J.A. Baross and J.W. Deming have recently discovered the presence of thriving colonies of bacteria in water fished directly from these deep-sea vents. Moreover, when brought to the surface, encased in titanium syringes and sealed in pressurized chambers heated to two hundred and fifty degrees centigrade, the bacteria not only survive, but reproduce themselves enthusiastically. They can be killed only by chilling them down in boiling water.

And yet they look just like ordinary bacteria. Under the electron microscope they have the same essential structure—cell walls, ribosomes, and all. If they were, as is now being suggested, the original archebacteria, ancestors of us all, how did they or their progeny ever learn to cool down? I cannot think of a more wonderful trick.

My Number Three Wonder is *oncideres*, a species of beetle encountered by a pathologist friend of mine who lives in Houston and has a lot of mimosa trees in his backyard. This beetle is not new, but it qualifies as a Modern Wonder because of the exceedingly modern questions raised for evolutionary biologists about the three consecutive things on the mind of the female of the species. Her first thought is for a mimosa tree, which she finds and climbs, ignoring all other kinds of trees in the vicinity. Her second thought is for the laying of eggs, which she does by crawling out on a limb, cutting a longitudinal slit with her mandible and depositing her eggs beneath the slit. Her third and last thought concerns the welfare of her offspring; beetle larvae cannot survive in live wood, so she backs up about a half a metre or so and cuts a neat circular girdle all around the limb, through the bark and down into the cambium. It takes her eight hours to finish this cabinetwork. Then she leaves and where she goes I do not know. The limb dies from the girdling, falls to the ground in the next breeze, the larvae feed and grow into the next generation, and the questions lie there unanswered. How on earth did these three linked thoughts in her mind evolve together in evolution? How could any one of the three become fixed as beetle behaviour by itself, without the other two? What are the odds favouring three totally separate bits of behaviour—liking a particular tree, cutting a slit for eggs, and then girdling the limb—happening together by random chance among a beetle's genes? Does this smart beetle know what she is doing? And how did the mimosa tree enter the picture in its evolution? Left to themselves, unpruned, mimosa trees have a life expectancy of twenty-five to thirty years. Pruned each year, which is what the beetle's girdling labour accomplishes, the tree can flourish for a century. The mimosa-beetle relationship is an elegant example of symbiotic partnership, a phenomenon now recognized as pervasive in nature. It is good for us to have around on our intellectual mantelpiece such creatures as this insect and its friend the tree, for they keep reminding us how little we know about nature.

The Fourth Wonder on my list is an infectious agent known as the scrapie virus, which causes a fatal disease of the brain in sheep, goats, and several laboratory animals. A close cousin of scrapie is the C-J virus, the cause of some cases of senile dementia in human beings. These are called "slow viruses," for the excellent reason that an animal exposed to infection today will not become ill until a year and a half or two years from today. The agent, whatever it is, can propagate itself in abundance from a few infectious units today to more than a billion next year. I use the phrase "whatever it is" advisedly. Nobody has yet been able to find any DNA or RNA in the scrapie or C-J viruses. It may be there, but if so it exists in amounts too small to detect. Meanwhile, there is plenty of protein, leading to a serious proposal that the virus may indeed be *all* protein. But protein, so far as we know, does not replicate itself all by itself, not on this planet anyway. Looked at this way, the scrapie agent seems the strangest thing in all biology and, until someone in some laboratory figures out what it is, a candidate for Modern Wonder.

My Fifth Wonder is the olfactory receptor cell, located in the epithelial tissue high in the nose, sniffing the air for clues to the environment, the fragrance of friends, the smell of leaf smoke, breakfast, nighttime and bedtime, and a rose, even, it is said, the odour of sanctity. The cell that does all these things, firing off urgent messages into the deepest parts of the brain, switching on one strange unaccountable memory after another, is itself a proper brain cell, a certified neuron belonging to the brain but kilometres away out in the open air, nosing around the world. How it manages to make sense of what it senses, discriminating between jasmine and anything else non-jasmine with infallibility, is one of the deep secrets of neurobiology. This would be wonder enough, but there is more. This population of brain cells, unlike any other neurons of the vertebrate central nervous system, turns itself over every few weeks; cells wear out, die, and are replaced by brand-new cells rewired to the same deep centres kilometres back in the brain, sensing and remembering the same wonderful smells. If and when we reach an understanding of these cells and their functions, including the moods and whims under their governance, we will know a lot more about the mind than we do now, a world away.

Sixth on my list is, I hesitate to say, another insect, the termite. This time, though, it is not the single insect that is the Wonder, it is the collectivity. There is nothing at all wonderful about a single, solitary termite, indeed there is really no such creature, functionally speaking, as a lone termite, any more than we can imagine a genuinely solitary human being; no such thing. Two or three termites gathered together on a dish are not much better; they may move about and touch each other nervously, but nothing happens. But keep adding more termites until they reach a critical mass, and then the miracle begins. As though they had suddenly received a piece of extraordinary news, they organize in platoons and begin stacking up pellets to precisely the right height, then turning the arches to connect the columns, constructing the cathedral and its chambers in which the colony will live out its life for the decades ahead, air-conditioned and humidity-controlled, following the chemical blueprint coded in their genes, flawlessly, stoneblind. They are not the dense mass of individual insects they appear to be, they are an organism, a thoughtful, meditative brain on a million legs. All we really know about this new thing is that it does its architecture and engineering by a complex system of chemical signals.

The Seventh Wonder of the modern world is a human child, any child. I used to wonder about childhood and the evolution of our species. It seemed to me unparsimonious to keep expending all that energy on such a long period of vulnerability and defenselessness, with nothing to show for it, in biological terms, beyond the feckless, irresponsible pleasure of childhood. After all, I used to think, it is one sixth of a whole human life span! Why didn't our evolution take care of that, allowing us to jump catlike from our juvenile to our adult (and, as I thought) productive stage of life? I had forgotten about language, the single human trait that marks us out as specifically human, the property that enables our survival as the most compulsively, biologically, obsessively social of all creatures on earth, more interdependent and interconnected even than the famous social insects. I had forgotten that, and forgotten that children *do* that in childhood. Language is what childhood is for.

There is another related but different creature, nothing like so wonderful as a human child, nothing like so hopeful, something to worry about all day and all night. It is *us*, aggregated together in our collective, critical masses. So far, we have learned how to be useful to each other only when we collect in small groups—families, circles of friends, once in a while (although still rarely) committees. The drive to be useful is encoded in our genes. But when we gather in very large numbers, as in the modern nation-state, we seem capable of levels of folly and self-destruction to be found nowhere else in all of Nature.

As a species, taking all in all, we are still too young, too juvenile, to be trusted. We have spread across the face of the earth in just a few thousand years, no time at all as evolution clocks time, covering all livable parts of the planet, endangering other forms of life, and now threatening ourselves. As a species, we have everything in the world to learn about living, but we may be running out of time. Provisionally, but only provisionally, we are a Wonder.

And now the first on my list, the one I put off at the beginning of making a list, the first of all Wonders of the modern world. To name this one, you have to redefine the world as it has indeed been redefined in this most scientific of all centuries. We named the place we live in the *world* long ago, from the Indo-European root *wiros*, which meant *man*. We now live in the whole universe, that stupefying piece of expanding geometry. Our suburbs are the local solar system, into which, sooner or later, we will spread life, and then, likely, beyond into the galaxy. Of all celestial bodies within reach or view, as far as we can see, out to the edge, the most wonderful and marvellous and mysterious is turning out to be our planet Earth. There is nothing to match it anywhere, not yet anyway.

It is a living system, an immense organism, still developing, regulating itself, making its own oxygen, maintaining its own temperature, keeping all its infinite living parts connected and interdependent, including us. It is the strangest of all places, and there is everything in the world to learn about it. It can keep us awake and jubilant with questions for millennia ahead, if we can learn not to meddle and not to destroy. Our great hope is in being such a young species, thinking in language only a short while, still learning, still growing up.

We are not like the social insects. They have only the one way of doing things and they will do it forever, coded for that way. We are coded differently, not just for binary choices, *go* or *no-go*. We can go four ways at once, depending on how the air feels: *go, no-go*, but also *maybe*, plus *why not give it a try*? We are in for one surprise after another if we keep at it and keep alive. We can build structures for human society never seen before, thoughts never thought before, music never heard before.

Provided we do not kill ourselves off, and provided we can connect ourselves by the affection and respect for which I believe our genes are also coded, there is no end to what we might do on or off this planet.

At this early stage in our evolution, now through our infancy and into our childhood and then, with luck, our growing up, what our species needs most of all, right now, is simply a future. ◆

1. Responding to the Personal Essay

a. The Seven Wonders of the Ancient World were all structures, either buildings or statues that inspired awe in everyone who saw them. Do you think this sense of awe is what inspired Lewis Thomas to make his choices? Explain your answer and include supporting examples from the essay. How are Thomas's Seven Wonders different from the Seven Wonders of the Ancient World?

b. What idea or thesis does Thomas develop in this essay? Discuss whether you agree or disagree with him.

c. In a sentence, give your definition of *wonder*.

d. Why do you think the author leaves his First Wonder for the end of the essay?

e. Reread the essay and, with a partner, discuss the features of a personal essay.

f. List, in order of importance, your Seven Wonders of the World.

2. Oral Language Informal Debate

With a group, debate this statement by Lewis Thomas: "As a species, taking all in all, we are still too young, too juvenile, to be trusted." Divide your group in half, each side taking a different point of view. Debate in front of other students and ask the audience to vote on which side's arguments are the most convincing.

3. Language Conventions Root Words

Thomas explains the origin or root of several words in his essay. Choose one or two of the scientific terms used in the essay and research their origins or root. Where do the words *pathologist* or *onicideres* come from, for example? You could use a specialized science dictionary or a regular dictionary to help you.

4. ESSAY CRAFT ESSAY STRUCTURE

Thomas uses a simple structure for his essay. He directly states in his thesis how many examples he will discuss. It is a structure well suited to many of the writing assignments you'll do in school. For example:

- First, he indicates his thesis and the number of examples he will use: "I decided to try making a list...[of] seven things I wonder about the most."

- Then, with one exception, he proceeds to explain each example on his list. His exception gives the essay a "twist," because it ties together his other Six Wonders.

- His conclusion not only summarizes these examples, but also gives his thesis a sense of purpose: "There is no end to what we [humans] might do on or off the planet."

Think of a subject for an essay that could be developed with a certain number of examples. Here are some suggestions: "Three ways to achieve success," "Five ways to keep awake when watching a boring movie," or "Four factors that led to World War II."

As you write your essay, work with a partner or group to develop a good thesis sentence, as well as to edit and revise your first draft.

SELF-ASSESSMENT: Does your introduction state your thesis clearly? Does each paragraph develop one of your points? Have you included facts and opinions to support the argument? Does your conclusion summarize the important points of your essay?

HOW TO WRITE A
PERSUASIVE ESSAY

Goals at a Glance
● Analyse organizational patterns. ● Write a persuasive essay.

A *persuasive essay* offers and defends an opinion, persuading someone to agree with your opinion. How do you persuade someone of something? You decide on an answer, solution, or point of view, then defend your opinion by citing facts and examples. Your role as a writer is to build your case with the strongest possible arguments, arranged in the best possible way.

What Is a Persuasive Essay?

A persuasive essay has three parts.

1. In the **introduction** you identify the issue, its importance, your opinion, and the arguments that support your position (thesis).

2. The **body** develops your supporting arguments, and supports your statements with facts.

3. The **conclusion** summarizes the main points, restates your position (thesis) in view of the supporting arguments, and may call on the reader to take action.

What Do You Want to Say?

Consider the topic for your essay. For example, you might write about your opinion on the issue of recycling. It should not be vague or general, or so broad that it can't be covered in a few paragraphs. State the central theme of your essay in one or two sentences. Brainstorm your ideas, using an organizer such as a web or cluster chart. Select three to five of your strongest points. These are the points you will research, then defend in the body of your essay.

Support Your Opinion with Facts

How do you convince your reader that your position is valid? Support every one of your points with facts. You may need to conduct research to support your opinion sufficiently.

● **Keep track of your sources**. Record information about the sources of all your facts, examples, and quotations. You will need them

PROCESS

for your bibliography. These sources can help establish the strength of your position. If you are inaccurate or unable to support a claim, your reader might disbelieve all of your facts.

- **Imagine the questions your reader might have.** Your reader might ask "How do you know that?" or "What about the opposite point of view?" or "So what?" Predict the reader's questions and research the answers.

Organization Patterns

Each of the paragraphs in the body of your essay should defend one of your main points, and deal with possible arguments against it. Consider using any of these strategies:

- **Compare and Contrast:** State your arguments and those of the opposing point of view, and demonstrate why yours are stronger.
- **Question and Answer:** Ask a question about the issue, then answer it from several points of view, showing why your position is strongest.
- **Climatic Order:** Begin with your weakest arguments and build up to your strongest arguments.
- **Problem and Solution:** State each of your main points as a problem to be solved, then demonstrate how your position solves each problem.
- **Facts and Details:** State a fact or quotation about the theme, then show how the details strengthen your position.

Read it, Review It, and Revise It

Draft your introduction, body, and conclusion, then read the essay aloud. Does it flow logically from one idea to the next? Does it use transitions, such as *most importantly, based on the evidence, although, however,* and *on the other hand?* Do the paragraphs discuss the main points in the same order as they were given in the introduction? If not, change the order. Are the tone and mood of the essay consistent throughout? Ask someone else to read it aloud to you. He or she can provide feedback and suggestions.

Develop an appropriate title for your essay. Tip: Think about the titles of other essays in this unit.

Self-Assessment

Ask yourself these questions about your essay:

- ❏ Is my position stated clearly in my introductory paragraph?
- ❏ Do I grab my reader's attention with my opening sentence?
- ❏ Are each of my arguments supported by facts, examples, or quotations?
- ❏ Have I dealt with opposing arguments?
- ❏ Are my facts accurate and attributed to my sources?
- ❏ Would I be persuaded by my arguments?

No Room for Compromise

OPINION ESSAY BY ELLEN GOODMAN

The car in front of me bears this year's bumper sticker: Fur is dead. This news does not come as a surprise. Nor does the bumper sticker.

The photograph in the magazine on my desk shows a trapper with his foot on the throat of an animal. The copy talks about "the practice of peeling the skins from tormented animals to feed human vanity." It is one of many I've seen.

The pickets on the fanciest street in town are equally blunt. No one can enter the store unaware that the coats inside are made of dead animals.

These are just a few of the messages in the concerted effort to strip glamour off the backs of the two-footed, fur-bearing species called humans. The anti-fur folk are determined to enlighten or intimidate or at least embarrass consumers out of their skins.

The furriers in turn are equally determined to trap these opponents in their own logic. The counter-ads warn that the anti-fur advocates are not merely after lynx and minks but leather and steaks.

On one of the televised talk shows, I watched such zealots make their points recently and had trouble deciding which was the more appalling advocate. One raged about the frivolous cruelty to animals, and the consumer as accomplice to murder. The other cited the Bible as proof that humans had dominion over all the species.

But there is little moral distinction to be made between wearing a mink coat and wearing a goose-down coat; between killing an animal to wear it and killing one to eat it. There is even less distinction from the viewpoint of the animal.

Environmental purity, the ability to live a life without a single cruel act against nature, is impossible. So people make compromises.

GOALS AT A GLANCE

- Use oral communication skills in a panel discussion.
- Write a personal essay.

But they are rarely as dogmatic as those set down by the anti-fur brigade.

Is it wrong to wear wild creatures, to eat wild birds? Is it morally superior to kill what is raised to that end? Is a modern mink ranch more cruel than a modern chicken farm? Is it acceptable to wear fur for warmth, but unacceptable to wear it for fashion? Should we only wear what we would eat? Are animals that kill each other immoral?

The list of questions expands to an absurd exponential. The only pure answer is to avoid the use—or exploitation—of any other species. To neither walk on, nor sit on, nor devour any other creature. And, even then, who can say what toll the alternatives—from cotton fields to chemicals to farmlands— would take on human lives and the environment we share.

People make choices in these matters from the first time they knowingly eat a hamburger or catch a fish. We acknowledge ourselves as creatures of nature. Not many believe that animals were put on earth solely for human use. But most see our lives in a plan that isn't always benign.

The furriers may use delicate euphemisms to deny the harsh reality. They call rabbit *lapin,* and raccoon *tanuki.* But the anti-fur extremists prefer to win by intimidation. They have staked out a moral position that leaves no room for the way we live. It is, in its own peculiar way, unnatural.

---

1. RESPONDING TO THE OPINION ESSAY

a. Summarize the two sides of the argument presented in this essay. Explain in a paragraph which viewpoint you most agree with.

b. The essay asks, but does not answer, a number of questions. Choose one question to answer, and include in your response an example to support your view.

c. Do you think there is a difference between eating animals and using their skins for clothing? Explain your answer.

d. What is the thesis or main point of this essay? Do you agree with it? Explain.

2. RESEARCHING FOOD PRODUCTION

Animals consumed for food require much more energy to bring to slaughter than the equivalent amount of plant protein. This fact is one argument used in favour of eating less meat or becoming vegetarian. Supporters of this argument also point out that the extra energy needed to produce animal protein puts extra stress on our planet.

Research the facts on both sides of the food production issue. In a page, briefly summarize what you've learned and the opinion you've formed.

3. WRITING AN OPINION ESSAY

Using the information you researched in the activity above, write an opinion essay in which you comment on the two opposing viewpoints. Present both sides of the issue and draw a conclusion at the end. Take your essay through the writing process. As you develop the essay, use the process page "How to Write a Persuasive Essay" on pages 254–255 to help you.

SELF-ASSESSMENT: At the revision stage, consider the following questions: Have you written a clear thesis sentence? Do the following paragraphs develop the thesis or do they wander off topic? Are your arguments logical and clear? Does your conclusion summarize your main arguments?

4. ORAL LANGUAGE EXPRESS AN OPINION

The selection is an essay with no clear point of view. The author presents two views of an argument without taking sides. With a group of three classmates, conduct a panel discussion expressing your own viewpoint about the issue presented in the essay. Which side of the issue do you agree with? Why?

This is one of the most famous and most frequently reprinted speeches of the 20th century. It was delivered on August 28, 1963 at the Lincoln Memorial in Washington, D.C.

I Have a Dream

SPEECH BY MARTIN LUTHER KING JR.

I am happy to join with you today in what will go down in history as the greatest demonstration for freedom in the history of our nation.

Fivescore years ago, a great American, in whose symbolic shadow we stand today, signed the Emancipation Proclamation. This momentous decree came as a great beacon light of hope to millions of Negro slaves who had been seared in the flames of withering injustice. It came as a joyous daybreak to end the long night of their captivity.

But one hundred years later, the Negro still is not free; one hundred years later, the life of the Negro is still sadly crippled by the manacles of segregation and the chains of discrimination; one hundred years later, the Negro lives on a lonely island of poverty in the midst of a vast ocean of material prosperity; one hundred years later, the Negro is still languished in the corners of American society and finds himself in exile in his own land.

So we've come here today to dramatize a shameful condition. In a sense we've come to our nation's capital to cash a check. When the architects of our republic wrote the magnificent words of the Constitution and Declaration of Independence, they were signing a promissory note to which every American was to fall heir. This note was the promise that all men, yes, black men as well as white men, would be guaranteed the unalienable rights of life, liberty, and the pursuit of happiness.

It is obvious today that America has defaulted on this promissory note in so far as her citizens of color are concerned. Instead of honoring this sacred obligation, America has given the Negro people a bad check; a check which has come back marked "insufficient funds." We refuse to believe that there are insufficient funds in the great vaults of opportunity of this nation. And so we've come to cash this check, a check that will give us upon demand, the riches of freedom and the security of justice.

We have also come to this hallowed spot to remind America of the fierce urgency of now. This is no time to engage in the luxury of cooling off or to take the tranquilizing drug of gradualism. Now is the time to make real the promises of democracy; now is the time to rise from the dark and desolate valley of segregation to the sunlit path of racial justice; now is the time to lift our nation from the quicksands of racial injustice to the solid rock of brotherhood; now is the time to make justice a reality for all God's children. It would be fatal for the nation to overlook the urgency of the moment. This sweltering summer of the Negro's legitimate discontent will not pass until there is an invigorating autumn of freedom and equality.

Nineteen sixty-three is not an end, but a beginning. And those who hope that the Negro needed to blow off steam and will now be content, will have a rude awakening if the nation returns to business as usual.

There will be neither rest nor tranquillity in America until the Negro is granted his citizenship rights. The whirlwinds of revolt will continue to shake the foundations of our nation until the bright day of justice emerges.

But there is something that I must say to my people who stand on the warm threshold which leads into the palace of justice. In the process of gaining our rightful place we must not be guilty of wrongful deeds.

Let us not seek to satisfy our thirst for freedom by drinking from the cup of bitterness and hatred. We must forever conduct our struggle on the high plane of dignity and discipline. We must not allow our creative protest to degenerate into physical violence. Again and again we must rise to the majestic heights of meeting physical force with soul force.

The marvelous new militancy which has engulfed the Negro community must not lead us to a distrust of all white people, for many of our white

I've been to the mountaintop

brothers, as evidenced by their presence here today, have come to realize that their destiny is tied up with our destiny and they have come to realize that their freedom is inextricably bound to our freedom. This offense we share mounted to storm the battlements of injustice must be carried forth by a biracial army. We cannot walk alone.

And as we walk, we must make the pledge that we shall always march ahead. We cannot turn back. There are those who are asking the devotees of civil rights, "When will you be satisfied?" We can never be satisfied as long as the Negro is the victim of the unspeakable horrors of police brutality.

We can never be satisfied as long as our bodies, heavy with fatigue of travel, cannot gain lodging in the motels of the highways and the hotels of the cities. We cannot be satisfied as long as the Negro's basic mobility is from a smaller ghetto to a larger one.

We can never be satisfied as long as our children are stripped of their selfhood and robbed of their dignity by signs stating "for whites only." We cannot be satisfied as long as a Negro in Mississippi cannot vote and a Negro in New York believes he has nothing for which to vote. No, we are not satisfied, and we will not be satisfied until justice rolls down like waters and righteousness like a mighty stream.

I am not unmindful that some of you have come here out of excessive trials and tribulation. Some of you have come fresh from narrow jail cells. Some of you have come from areas where your quest for freedom left you battered by the storms of persecution and staggered by the winds of police brutality. You have been the veterans of creative suffering. Continue to work with the faith that unearned suffering is redemptive.

Go back to Mississippi; go back to Alabama; go back to South Carolina; go back to Georgia; go back to Louisiana; go back to the slums and ghettos of the northern cities, knowing that somehow this situation can, and will be changed. Let us not wallow in the valley of despair.

So I say to you, my friends, that even though we must face the difficulties of today and tomorrow, I still have a dream. It is a dream deeply rooted in the American dream that one day this nation will rise up and live out the true meaning of its creed—we hold these truths to be self-evident, that all men are created equal.

I have a dream that one day on the red hills of Georgia, sons of former slaves and sons of former slave-owners will be able to sit down together at the table of brotherhood.

I have a dream that one day, even the state of Mississippi, a state sweltering with the heat of injustice, sweltering with the heat of oppression, will be transformed into an oasis of freedom and justice.

I have a dream my four little children will one day live in a nation where they will not be judged by the color of their skin but by the content of their character. I have a dream today!

I have a dream that one day, down in Alabama, with its vicious racists, with its governor having his lips dripping with the words of interposition and nullification, that one day, right there in Alabama, little black boys and black girls will be able to join hands with little white boys and white girls as sisters and brothers. I have a dream today!

I have a dream that one day every valley shall be exalted, every hill and mountain shall be made low, the rough places shall be made plain, and the crooked places shall be made straight and the glory of the Lord will be revealed and all flesh shall see it together.

This is our hope. This is the faith that I go back to the South with.

With this faith we will be able to hew out of the mountain of despair a stone of hope. With this faith we will be able to transform the jangling discords of our nation into a beautiful symphony of brotherhood.

With this faith we will be able to work together, to pray together, to struggle together, to go to jail together, to stand up for freedom together, knowing that we will be free one day. This will be the day when all of

God's children will be able to sing with new meaning—"my country 'tis of thee; sweet land of liberty; of thee I sing; land where my fathers died, land of pilgrim's pride; from every mountain side, let freedom ring"—and if America is to be a great nation, this must become true.

So let freedom ring from the prodigious hilltops of New Hampshire.

Let freedom ring from the mighty mountains of New York.

Let freedom ring from the heightening Alleghenies of Pennsylvania.

Let freedom ring from the snow-capped Rockies of Colorado.

Let freedom ring from the curvaceous slopes of California.

But not only that.

Let freedom ring from Stone Mountain of Georgia.

Let freedom ring from Lookout Mountain of Tennessee.

Let freedom ring from every hill and molehill of Mississippi, from every mountainside, let freedom ring.

And when we allow freedom to ring, when we let it ring from every village and hamlet, from every state and city, we will be able to speed up that day when all of God's children—black men and white men, Jews and Gentiles, Catholics and Protestants—will be able to join hands and to sing in the words of the old Negro spiritual, "Free at last, free at last; thank God Almighty, we are free at last."

- -

1. RESPONDING TO THE SPEECH

a. In this speech, Martin Luther King Jr. paints a grim picture of the plight of African Americans in U.S. communities, especially the South, circa 1963. Briefly describe this picture, using examples from his speech.

b. What is the point or message of his speech?

c. King uses numerous metaphors. Choose three and explain what you think they suggest. Why do you think he would use this literary device to develop his ideas?

d. King was a Baptist minister as well as a civil rights activist. What parts of his speech demonstrate this fact?

e. While he is calling for change, King expresses a note of caution. What is he warning his audience *not* to do? Research the events that followed this speech, and decide if he was successful.

2. RESEARCHING DEVELOP QUESTIONS

Use at least three print resources and three electronic resources to research the civil rights movement in North America. With a partner, brainstorm a list of questions you would like to answer about the movement. You might also consider the following questions: What sparked the civil rights movement? What brought the issue of civil rights to the world's attention? What role did TV and the media play? Who were the important players?

Summarize your research in the form of notes. Work with a partner or group to develop your notes into a report or oral presentation. End your presentation or report with an assessment of the success of the movement. Were its goals achieved? What would King think of the world today? **SELF-ASSESSMENT:** Assess the benefits of developing research questions. Did they help you to focus your inquiry?

3. WRITING A QUESTION-AND-ANSWER ESSAY

King describes a society in which a group of people do not enjoy the privileges and freedoms that the majority take for granted. What types of social injustices existed in Canadian society around the same time period? Research the issue, and then write a question-and-answer essay comparing what it was like then to what the situation is like now. How far have we come? What does society still need to do? Or has the issue been resolved? You may also choose to compare and contrast the facts that King describes to the situation in Canada at that time.

4. ESSAY CRAFT PARALLEL STRUCTURE

To emphasize ideas and action, writers and speakers often repeat sentences or grammatical patterns. King uses this form of repetition very effectively in his speech, for example, in the seven sentences near the end of the speech that begin with "Let freedom ring." These are examples of what is called *parallel structure*. Reread King's speech and find another example of parallel structure. Why do you think this method is particularly effective in speeches? What effect would overusing this technique have?

*For some immigrants,
life in a new land is harder
than they ever expected.*

A Hard Life
But a Better One

PERSONAL ESSAY BY CHUI-LING TAM

My aunt married her sweetheart of twelve years last week. It was a simple wedding at home, with a justice of the peace who intoned the marriage vows in words they didn't understand.

That didn't matter. She knew when it was time to say "Yes," and she said it—emphatically—in a tight, hard voice that suppressed twelve long years of waiting to start her new life in Canada with her husband and family. Beside her, my new uncle grinned foolishly in relief a scant three days before his ninety-day grace period with immigration expired. It was the first time I'd seen him smile since he arrived from China.

It may seem strange for two people to wait twelve years to marry, but it was the price my aunt paid to leave her homeland, where she met her husband on a state farm in their late teens. She would not have been allowed to leave if they had married in China.

My aunt was the last member of my mother's family to come to Canada, by grace of the reunification program introduced in 1988. She came in search of a better life, and in the modest home she shares with her two younger sisters, her brother-in-law, and her father, she has found it.

Many Southeast-Asian immigrants arrived in the 1970s. My family was part of that group. We had little worldly wealth to lose. When we landed in Ottawa in 1972, we had about one hundred dollars in cash, and all we left behind, besides a rather extensive family and numerous friends, was a little two-room shack that passed for our home.

265

My mother has worked at the same restaurant for the past eighteen years, and my father has hopped along a string of jobs in other people's restaurants. They did not take a vacation until two years ago, and they did not go anywhere when they did. They couldn't afford it.

But they don't mind. My older brother and I are working—not in kitchens—and my younger brother and sister are in university. My parents now live in a red-brick bungalow surrounded by trees in a quiet suburb in Ottawa. They have running water, a 28-inch colour TV, and a car.

It's a far cry from the two-room home we left in Hong Kong, which had no running water. As a child of five, I recall trooping off to the big black outhouses down the street and the hordes of women and children who washed and bathed in the common watering area near our house.

When a thunderstorm knocked out the roof in the front room, the whole neighbourhood pitched in to attach a new corrugated-iron roof, and the air reeked with the smell of tar.

Not speaking English and with only a high school education, my parents never expected to find comfortable jobs. Some days, my mother doubts whether her life would have been any harder in Hong Kong, where she worked for a time at a laundromat. She knew the life of riches was long behind her, ever since the Chinese Communists forced her family to give up their mansion and servants in Canton.

Often, before my grandparents and aunts arrived in 1985, my mother would talk wistfully of them, never expecting to find the money to make the trip back. The last time I gave her roses, she told me that the blooms were more fragrant in China.

But I don't think my parents ever regretted their choice. They have friends and family in Canada, and their children will never know the life they had.

Canada hasn't been wonderful. The winters are hard, the work is hard, and the range of services is bewildering to a Chinese-speaking couple. In leaving Hong Kong, my parents gave up some of their independence. They rely on their children to help them with finances and visits to the doctor, or choosing paint and wallpaper at hardware stores.

My mother often stares at her knotted hands and murmurs that when she was a young woman, she had long, beautiful hands. Two decades of dish-washing and cooking eight hours a day, six days a week, have left brown spots from splashing grease.

Today, she and my father are both worried about how long their aging bodies can continue such work.

For all that, they have a good life. They have a comfortable home and enough to eat. They can brag about their children to friends. Their son, the pilot, their daughter, the journalist, their younger son and daughter, the university students. Very probably, my aunt and her husband will have a similar life. She works as a seamstress and he at a laundromat. They expect, and ask, for little more. It is enough that they can choose their lives, that their children will have an education and perhaps work in offices rather than endure the hard labour of state farms in China, or the hot kitchens and dirty hotel toilets in Canada.

I expect that they will brag about their children in twenty-five years, as do my parents. And they will quite likely have their own home and be grateful that after twelve long years, they were finally able to start the family they wanted for so long in a country where they could decide their future.

Their life will be hard, but I doubt that they will ever regret the loss of their homeland. While Canada is not the land of milk and honey, it offers them a lot more worldly wealth and freedom than China ever could. ◆

1. RESPONDING TO THE PERSONAL ESSAY

a. What are some of the difficulties Chui-Ling's family faced in Canada? What sacrifices did her family make? Do you think these experiences are typical of what other immigrants experience? Why or why not?

b. From the title, what did you expect this essay to be about? After reading the first paragraph, what did you expect? With a partner, discuss how this essay did or didn't meet your expectations.

c. What is the thesis of this essay? How does the author support the thesis?

d. How is this personal essay similar to or different from the personal essay "Seven Wonders"?

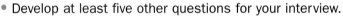

S T R A T E G I E S

2. RESEARCHING CONDUCT AN INTERVIEW

Research the stories and histories of immigrants who have come to Canada by interviewing a friend, family member, or neighbour about his or her experiences. What was it like for this person when he or she first arrived? What led him or her to leave home? What does he or she miss most? Use the following tips to help you as you conduct your interview:

- Develop at least five other questions for your interview.
- Ask open-ended questions to elicit information.
- Remember to make your guest feel comfortable. People sometimes find it difficult to talk about their personal experiences.
- Use the process page "How to Conduct an Interview" on pages 36–37 to help you conduct a successful interview.

Develop your interview into a report about this person's experience. You could obtain photos and other personal items to bring the report alive for your audience. Share your report with others in small groups. Are there common experiences?

SELF-ASSESSMENT: Assess the interview process. Did you ask the right questions? At the end of the interview, did you have a complete picture of what this person's life was like? Jot down a list of improvements you'd like to make the next time you conduct an interview.

You might say that the following essay really opens up a can of worms.

A Little Salad with Your Night Crawlers, Sir?

HUMOROUS ESSAY BY ARTHUR BLACK

So the story, as I understand it, goes like this. A teacher in Ottawa is in hot water because he feeds worms to his class. He didn't force or trick them to eat worms. The parents were informed by letter. The kids were allowed to make up their own minds whether to chow down or not. The worms were clean and chemical-free and tastefully presented—boiled for just a few minutes and served with lemon wedges.

So what's the fuss? It's not the first time wiggly squigglys have passed human lips. Ask Rusty Rice of Rialto College, California. Rusty holds the world title for worm eating, having forked up twenty-eight of the critters at a sitting a few years back. Not the first time worms have figured in *haute cuisine*, either. The top prize winner in a cooking competition, not too long ago, was a recipe for Earthworm Applesauce Surprise Cake. I don't think it entirely spoils the story to know that the competition was sponsored by the North American Bait Company.

Listen—strip worms of their stereotype and they're kind of attractive foodwise. They're boneless. You don't have to pluck them. Or scale or de-talon or flense, fillet, or stuff them. And before you wrinkle your nose and go GAAAAAH!, take a look at North America's *Menu du Jour*.

We belong to a culture that thinks nothing of taking great ugly under-water behemoths that look like leftovers from a space horror movie—lobsters, I'm talking about—plopping them on a plate, then dismantling them right there on the dinner table. We are a people that boil up and

---

GOALS AT A GLANCE

■ Write a humorous essay.
■ Examine sentence fragments.

nibble at the artichoke, a treacherous, mind-numbing foodstuff, the eating of which is about as much fun as licking eleven hundred stamps in a row. We eat parsley, which Ogden Nash pronounced *gharsley*. Rightly, I think.

And broccoli. Which is perhaps the one subject on which George Bush and I agree. Me, George, and Roy Blount Junior, actually. Mister Blount wrote a broccoli song once, the lyrics of which go: "The neighbourhood stores are all out of broccoli. Loccoli."

And what about oysters? What can you say about an assemblage of tastebuds that would lever a homely old oyster out of the seabed wrack and muck, winkle its barnacle-crusted shell open, and crow, "Hot dog! A brand new taste sensation!" When it comes to oysters, I'm with Miss Piggy, who once sniffed: "I simply cannot imagine why anyone would eat something slimy served on an ashtray."

Oh, I know there are a lot of oyster lovers out there, and that's fine. A lot of folks, believe it or not, find my favourite sandwich—peanut butter, marmalade, sliced Spanish onion with a light sprinkling of Worcestershire sauce—unpalatable. That's fine, too. There's no accounting for human taste. We just have to be careful about turning up our noses when new food ideas like, well, worms, come along. After all, the food fad of the eighties was sushi. Uncooked fish.

A Mexican comedian once told his English-speaking audience. "Down in Mexico we have a word for sushi. Bait."

Which, when you think about the kids eating worms in Ottawa, kind of brings us full circle, doesn't it?

----

1. RESPONDING TO THE HUMOROUS ESSAY

a. What is the essay's thesis?

b. Arthur Black uses many examples to support his viewpoint. Choose three and explain how they help develop the thesis.

c. What is the tone of the essay? Is it serious, comic, formal, or informal? Give examples to support your view.

d. Find one or two examples of Black's use of humour and explain what effects this technique creates.

e. What is the word play in the broccoli song: "The neighbourhood stores are all out of broccoli. Loccoli"?

2. LANGUAGE CONVENTIONS SENTENCE FRAGMENTS

Arthur Black uses *sentence fragments* (incomplete sentences), which can pose a problem for readers. Because sentence fragments are missing either a subject or a verb (and sometimes both), they can be more difficult to understand. Writers use them to reflect normal speech and, sometimes, to create special effects. Why do you think Black chose to use these "errors" in his essay? In a paragraph, discuss what you believe are his reasons.

SELF-ASSESSMENT: Choose a piece from your writing portfolio that you would like to revise and examine your use of sentences. Do you use sentence fragments in your writing? If so, what are your reasons, or are they simply grammar errors?

S T R A T E G I E S

3. WRITING A HUMOROUS ESSAY

With a partner, discuss the structure of Black's essay. How does he begin the essay? Where is the thesis? How does he develop the supporting arguments? What techniques does he use?

Using Black's piece as a model, develop your own humorous essay.

- Think of an interesting or amusing incident. Could you expand on the situation and turn it into an essay?
- You could try focussing on something that you strongly dislike or disagree with.
- Don't just give an opinion. Include supporting evidence that proves your arguments.
- Include funny examples to add humour.
- Conclude by summing up the main points.
- Exchange your essay with a partner. Does he or she find it amusing? Ask for suggestions to help you improve the essay.

Gotcha!

Persuasive Essay by Robert Fulford

In the course of a Shakespearean production in Toronto in 1987, there was a moment that briefly illustrated why contemporary society desperately needs literature and the literary imagination. The moment came just after the scene in *Henry V* in which some soldiers, about to leave for war, tearfully said goodbye to their wives. As soon as the women were safely out of sight, martial music poured from loudspeakers, the men shouted with joy, and patriotic signs were paraded across the stage. One sign held a single word: "Gotcha!"

What was remarkable about that little piece of modernized Shakespeare was that it placed, in the middle of a work from the greatest literary imagination of the ages, a graphic reminder of the twentieth-century imagination at its meanest and most degraded.

Not everyone in the Canadian audience understood why "Gotcha!" was there. This was the English Shakespeare Company, and the reference was to something that happened in England five years earlier. On the afternoon of May 3, 1982, west of the Falkland Islands, torpedoes from a British submarine hit the *General Belgrano*, an Argentine cruiser. Almost immediately, the ship began to sink. When the news of this victory reached London, the *Sun*, a hugely successful tabloid, put a one-word headline on the next morning's front page: Gotcha!

This quickly became famous as a symbol of blind jingoism, but it was also a spectacular instance of failed imagination. The people who put that headline on their newspaper were victims of the peculiar callousness that afflicts all of us to some degree. What they did was hideously inappropriate, but it was also in a sense consistent with their training, and consistent with the atmosphere of this period in history.

GOALS AT A GLANCE

- Examine vocabulary.
- Conduct research.

During the sinking, about three hundred sailors, many of them teenage conscripts, choked to death on smoke, burned to death in oil or boiling water, or sank to the bottom of the sea. The rest of the crew, eight hundred or so, spent thirty-six hours floating on rafts in icy water, praying for rescue. The appropriate response to any such event is pity and terror, but the response of the people at the *Sun* was childish glee. The *Sun* had already been treating the Falklands War as a kind of video game, a clash of abstract forces with no human meaning. The ships, the submarines, the helicopters, and the people on them were no more consequential than flickers of electric light on a screen.

Flickers of light are the problem—perhaps the greatest mass emotional problem of our era. Flickers of light on the TV screen, or the movie screen, have become our principal means of receiving information about distant reality. Television brings us close to certain forms of reality, such as war in the Persian Gulf, but it also separates us emotionally from whatever it shows us. The more we see, the less we feel. Television instructs us that one war looks much like another, one plane crash much like another; we lose our sense of the human meaning of disaster. Mass communication deadens, rather than enlivens us.

In the movies, too, we learn that the death of others is unimportant. For a quarter-century, the movies have been teaching us that people who die by gunfire are usually only extras, or deserve to die.

Those who defend violence in entertainment are quick to point out that it has always been part of drama and literature—there's violence in the Bible, in the Greek tragedies, and, of course, in Shakespeare. But until our time, violence in drama and literature was given meaning. It was given weight. It was set in a context that made the appropriate response—pity and terror—possible. In Shakespeare, no one dies without a purpose. One moral of the Shakespeare history plays is that those who kill their kings will live to rue it. Certainly those plays tell us, again and again, that the results of killing are never negligible—and that they will be felt for generations.

On the other hand, the editor who wrote: "Gotcha!" later said, "I agree that headline was a shame. But it wasn't meant in a blood-curdling way. We just felt excited and euphoric. Only when we began to hear reports of how many men died did we begin to have second thoughts." There speaks a sadly crippled imagination, desperately in need of literature.

The future of literature is in question. The novel is no longer, for most people, the central means of expressing a culture. Poetry is read by only a few. Literary studies no longer stand at the centre of the university curriculum. Some of literature's tasks, such as social observation, are often accomplished better by movies and TV programs. Even in the bookstores, literature is often pushed aside by journalism, how-to manuals, and cookbooks.

But literature remains the core of civilized life precisely because it is the only reliable antidote to everything in our existence that diminishes us. Only the literary imagination can save us from the deadening influence of visual news and visual entertainment. When it works as it should, literature takes us beyond our parochialism into other minds and other cultures. It makes us know that even our enemies are as humanly diverse as we are.

If we let it, literature can also save us from the narrowing effect of politics. Politics teaches us to see the world in functional terms, defined by power blocs and national borders and pressure groups. Pretending to offer freedom, politics asks us to identify ourselves by ethnicity or gender or class or nationality. Literature, on the other hand, dares us to feel our way across all boundaries of thought and feeling.

One of the more beautiful stories I've read in recent years was written by an Asian-Trinidadian-Canadian man, speaking in the voice of a Japanese woman: the writer, and his grateful readers, simply refused to be contained by the limits the world regards as normal. This is the immense power that literature puts in the hands of all of us.

In the same way, literature offers us the opportunity to escape the two most pressing forms of bondage in our normal existence: time and ego. Emotionally and intellectually, literature dissolves the rules of time and beckons us toward Periclean Athens, Czarist Russia, Elizabethan England, and a thousand other moments in the past. By lengthening our sense of time, it saves us from the maddening urgencies of the present. And when it succeeds on the highest level, it breaks the shell of our intense and tiresome self-consciousness. It forces itself inside the egotism fostered by the pressures of our lives and links us with human history and the vast ocean of humanity now on Earth. By taking us into other lives, it deepens our own.

Our clear task, if we hope to realize ourselves as a civilization, is to cherish the writers who have done their work and nourish the writers who are still doing it. The literary imagination is not a grace of life or a diversion: it is the best way we have found of reaching for the meaning of existence. ◆

1. Responding to the Persuasive Essay

a. To what does the title, "Gotcha!" refer?

b. How do you think violent acts, such as wars and riots, should be reported in the media?

c. What is Robert Fulford's thesis? In a paragraph, explain whether you agree or disagree.

d. Do you agree or disagree with Fulford when he maintains that "flickers of light are the problem"? Discuss your view with a partner.

e. Is there too much violence portrayed in the news media and on TV shows? Explain your views, as well as giving supporting examples.

2. Word Craft   Examine Vocabulary

Reread the essay and list all the words and phrases whose meaning you're not familiar with. Use the context of the surrounding sentences to guess at their meaning. Then use a dictionary or encyclopedia to find out what each word means. Were your guesses correct? Add these words to your Personal Word List. The next time you write an essay, report, or story, consult your word list.

Self-Assessment: As you read texts, do you make note of words whose meaning you don't know? Do you look these words up in a dictionary? Do you try to use some of the words in your Personal Word List when you write?

3. Writing   Opinion

Fulford says in his essay that "even in the bookstores, literature is often pushed aside by journalism, how-to manuals, and cookbooks." Write an essay explaining how you feel about this statement. Is reading for information somehow inferior or less worthy than reading fiction and poetry? Which do you enjoy reading more, fiction or non-fiction? How should a piece of writing be judged or should it be judged at all? To develop your essay, you could begin by brainstorming a list of the pros and cons of both fiction and non-fiction.

4. Researching   Canadian Authors

Use the library and Internet resources to find out more about Robert Fulford. What are his interests? What does he do for a living? How does knowing his background help you to understand the essay? Discuss your findings with a partner.

REFLECTING ON THE UNIT

SELF-ASSESSMENT: ESSAY CRAFT

As you worked on the activities in this unit, what did you learn about
• opinion essays?
• personal essays?
• speeches?
• art essays?
• researching?
• developing a thesis?
• supporting arguments?
• parallel structure?

What else would you like to learn about developing and writing essays?

LITERATURE STUDIES ANALYSE ESSAYS

Choose a selection in this unit that you think is effectively written and interesting to read. In a page or more, describe what elements in the essay make it effective. For example, you might consider the following:
• the clarity of its thesis
• thesis development
• its use of language (grammar, vocabulary, paragraphing, and so on)
• its tone
• reasons why it is interesting

WRITING AN ESSAY

A research essay is organized similarly to other types of essays except that it uses verifiable facts and expert opinion to support its thesis. Choose one of the research topics you have worked on in this unit. Work independently or with a partner to develop a thesis statement that's based on your research and write an essay. Remember that, in a research essay, the thesis states something that is provable. Try to narrow your thesis so that the subject you choose can be developed in about one thousand words. Include your bibliography at the end of the essay.

"We do not see nature with our eyes, but with our understandings and our hearts."

William Hazlitt

ENVIRONMENT

ENVIRONMENT

ENCOUNTERS WITH NATURE

The Shark

Poem by **E.J. Pratt**

He seemed to know the harbour,
So leisurely he swam;
His fin,
Like a piece of sheet-iron,
Three-cornered,
And with knife-edge,
Stirred not a bubble
As it moved
With its base-line on the water.

His body was tubular
And tapered,
And smoke-blue,
And as he passed the wharf
He turned,
And snapped at a flat-fish
That was dead and floating.
And I saw the flash of a white throat,
And a double row of white teeth,
And eyes of metallic grey,
Hard and narrow and slit.

Then out of the harbour,
With that three-cornered fin
Shearing without a bubble the water
Lithely,
Leisurely,
He swam—
That strange fish,
Tubular, tapered, smoke-blue,
Part vulture, part wolf,
Part neither—for his blood was cold.

GOALS AT A GLANCE

- Analyse the use of literary devices.
- Conduct research.

1. RESPONDING TO THE POEM

a. If you didn't know the title of the poem, what words and phrases allow you to identify the fish as a shark?

b. What literary devices does E.J. Pratt use in the poem? What colours does Pratt use to describe the shark? What impression do they convey about the shark's nature?

c. The poem says of the shark that "his blood is cold." There are two meanings for this description. One is scientific, the other expresses a human emotion. Briefly explain how each meaning adds to the poem's effect on the reader.

d. The last stanza repeats words and phrases from the first and second stanzas in the poem. What effect does the repetition create?

e. Why is this poem an appropriate piece to begin a unit called "Environment: Encounters with Nature"? What encounter is described?

2. LITERATURE STUDIES LITERARY DEVICES

Some *literary devices*, such as alliteration, **assonance**, **consonance**, rhyme, and repetition are used by writers to appeal to the reader's sense of hearing. With a partner, identify two examples of these literary devices in the poem. What sound effects do they create?

Jot down an example of alliteration, rhyme, or repetition in your notebook and explain the effect it creates.

> **Assonance** is the repetition of similar vowel sounds in neighbouring words. An example is *sweet dreams*.
> **Consonance** is the repetition of similar consonants in words. An example is *wonder/wander*.

3. RESEARCHING ANIMALS

Find out more about sharks or other animals that many people fear or dislike, for example, rats, bats, and snakes. Include information from at least two of the following sources: reference books, periodicals, non-fiction books, the Internet, video, and other non-print media. In your report you could:

- give basic information about the animal
- discuss fears, myths, or superstitions
- reveal little-known facts

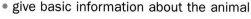

Be sure to include a visual and to list your sources.

SELF-ASSESSMENT: What was your best source of information? What are the benefits or drawbacks to the type of sources that you used?

In the wilderness of British Columbia, a hike becomes a waking nightmare.

Attacked by a Mountain Grizzly!

MAGAZINE ARTICLE BY KATHY COOK

Veering off the Trans-Canada Highway, Ann Quaterman took her 4-wheel drive Ford Ranger onto a bumpy logging road into the mountains near Revelstoke in southeastern British Columbia. She followed the road for 12 km before reaching the wilderness trail where she and friend Christine Bialkowski planned to hike.

Ann, at 28, an outdoor enthusiast and expert skier, had applied for a cook's job at a lodge high in the Selkirk Mountains. Wanting to get to know the area, she had decided to hike to her interview on that rainy morning of October 1, 1994, rather than take the usual helicopter ride in. Christine, 25, had come along for the adventure.

It was 9 a.m. when the two women grabbed their packs from the back of the truck for the 6-hour hike. Ann, a robust 175 cm tall, with shoulder-length brown hair and a bright smile, took a look at the hand-drawn map of the trail. It was 15 km to the Selkirk Mountain Experience lodge, located on the other side of a glacier at an altitude of 2000 m.

Ann pulled a can of bear repellent out of her pack and strapped it to a holster on her hip. She often carried it with her, especially when venturing into areas where bears were known to feed. "Just in case," she said, smiling at Christine. The two had met the year before when Ann worked as a cook

GOALS AT A GLANCE

- Locate, organize, and summarize information.
- Write a story in response to the selection.

and Christine as a waitress at a hotel in the mountain town of Rossland. Christine, a small, fair-skinned woman with long blond hair, had recently arrived from Toronto and was looking for great skiing. Ann had moved to Rossland from Québec a few years earlier and was happy to find a new ski partner in Christine. They became fast friends.

The hike began casually as a slow, uphill stroll through the coniferous mountain forest. The two women appeared to be the only people on the trail, but Christine, spotting an unsightly plastic grocery bag hanging from a tree, knew others had been around. "I wish people would show more respect for nature," she thought disgustedly.

Soon the trail narrowed into a thin, overgrown path that led the two women into steep and rocky terrain. They crawled over large rocks and jumped across shallow creeks, taking particular care to keep constant the pace of conversation, warning any bears of their presence.

Three hours into the gruelling hike, at an altitude just above 1800 m, they climbed over a ridge and came out above the tree line into an alpine meadow. Ann gazed at the valley below, which, despite a low-lying fog, glowed with the colours of autumn.

The trail curved around, descended towards the meadow and then continued up the mountain. Ann and Christine sauntered along the path for a few moments, still appreciating the view. Then Ann looked down into the meadow again and suddenly stopped. "Look, Christine! Three bears." Below them, about 300 m away, they saw a female grizzly with two cubs.

Neither woman was frightened. Both had seen bears many times. They knew that if they didn't startle them, they should be safe. Then they realized the bears were running towards them. Christine glanced nervously at Ann.

"They're so far away, they have to be running after something else," Ann thought. But the mother, leaving her cubs behind, kept moving in their direction. Still not sure they were in any real danger, Ann thought, "This has got to be a false charge."

Simultaneously, Christine and Ann began yelling, trying to intimidate the bear. But the mother grizzly kept coming. With no trees to climb, panic welled up inside Christine, and she turned and started running. "Christine, don't run!" Ann yelled, thinking this would make the bear even more inclined to attack.

Christine slowed down to a walk and, with racing hearts, both women walked down a bank out of sight of the grizzly.

"The bear mace," Ann remembered. She unlatched it from its holster and pulled the safety clip out. She still didn't believe the bear would attack. She knew from living in an area with a dense bear population that they often make charges to scare intruders. She looked up and waited to see if the bear would appear.

"Oh, please be gone," she thought desperately. Just then the head of the grizzly popped up over the ridge, 5 m away. Ann aimed the can at the approaching animal. "I have just one chance to do this right."

Two metres from her, the grizzly rose up on its hind legs, towering over her. Their eyes locked and for a moment Ann froze, mesmerized by the fierce black stare. Then she pressed the trigger, unleashing the burning red spray into the bear's face. Reeling in pain, the grizzly dropped to the ground and ran past her. Ann was relieved, but then she remembered Christine wasn't carrying any spray, and she turned around to see what had befallen her friend.

Gripped by fear, Christine watched as the bear now ran towards her. Before she could react, it clenched her left arm and began savagely thrashing her back and forth. While the 225-kg beast dragged her along the ground,

Christine's only thoughts were of her family and how upsetting the news of her death would be.

Despite the violence of the attack on her friend, Ann sprang into action, running over to mace the bear a second time. In a rage, the bear now threw Christine into some bushes and lunged at Ann. She tried the spray again, but the can was empty. Ann dropped it and turned away in horror, her right arm still outstretched. "I must be dreaming," she thought.

Biting into her arm, the grizzly knocked Ann over, and together they rolled down the embankment. She screamed as she felt her arm being ripped open. Her only thought was: "Please kill me quickly."

But then her mind cleared. Everything she had read about bears came flooding back. It was useless to try to defend herself. "I have to play dead."

Pulling her ravaged arm free from the grizzly's mouth, Ann rolled onto her stomach. In response, the grizzly bit into her side and flipped her back over so that her stomach was again exposed. Summoning all her strength, Ann again flipped herself onto her stomach. She put her hands behind her neck and lay still.

The grizzly bit and clawed into the backpack Ann was still wearing. Then it moved to her head. Although she had a baseball

Doing the only thing she could think of, she gave the bear's head a kick, then fell backward. Almost immediately the grizzly was on top of her, trying to bite her neck. Christine fought back, legs flailing, and she managed to land a solid kick on the animal's nose.

The grizzly recoiled and moved to Christine's side, sinking its teeth deep into her hip, just missing the femoral artery. But then, all of a sudden, it released its grip and, with a final huff, ran behind some shrubs and downhill out of sight.

With adrenaline still pumping, Christine got up and approached Ann. Her friend lay still and silent, her clothing torn and soaked in blood.

"Is it gone?" Ann asked, lifting her head slowly. Christine winced as she watched a chunk of Ann's scalp flap up and fall back into place on her blood-soaked head.

"Let's get out of here before she comes back," Christine said.

"No," said Ann, "we need to bandage ourselves up first." Painfully, she reached into her pack, grabbed a shirt and tried to wrap it around her head. "I can't

cap and hood on, the bear managed to peel a large chunk of flesh away from her head. Curiously, Ann felt no pain as she was scalped in one quick swipe.

Crouched in the bushes, Christine watched and knew she would be next. She looked helplessly around at the meadow. "This is where I'm going to die."

Suddenly, she was jerked back to reality. "I can't stand by and watch Ann be mauled to death." Freeing herself from her backpack, Christine strode towards her friend and the grizzly. "If I'm going to die, I'll put up a fight."

"I'm coming, Ann!" she yelled.

use my right arm," she said. "Can you help me?" Using one arm each, the two women managed to wrap Ann's head and tie other clothing around their injured arms.

It was drizzling and, with the temperature just above freezing, the rain would likely turn to snow later in the day. Wet already, badly injured and losing blood, the two women had to make the 3-hour trek back to their vehicle before the afternoon light faded. A night in the wilderness could prove to be fatal.

Their slow descent from the mountain drained what little energy they had. On one hill, Ann lost her footing and slipped down over the rocky terrain. Her head bandage fell off. But, she got back on her feet and, with Christine's help, retied her bandages. They kept chatting and singing so as not to surprise the bear again.

Ann continued to weaken step by step, and her spirits sank after every turn when the truck was still not in sight. "I don't think I can make it," she said faintly. "You've been a great friend, Chris. If I don't make it, tell my sister and her family in Rossland that I love them."

"Keep going," urged Christine. She had no idea where they were, but she said: "We're almost there. The truck's just a couple more bends ahead. I recognize this place."

As they trudged over the next few kilometres, Ann's pace got even slower. Christine still had no idea how far they had to go. Then, at last, she saw the plastic bag hanging from a tree that had so disgusted her at the beginning of their hike that morning. They really were almost there! They had one last hill to climb.

Her body well past exhaustion, Ann's heart pounded as she struggled to force one foot in front of the other. Finally, their truck was in sight.

As Ann bent over to unlock the door, a large pool of blood that had collected in her raincoat splashed to the ground. Seeing that, she passed her keys to Christine.

Christine pulled herself slowly into the driver's seat, put the key in the ignition—and froze. In shock, she couldn't remember how to drive. So Ann, using her good left arm, changed the gears while Christine steered the truck down the mountain road's dangerous switchbacks with her good right arm.

Just before the highway junction, they came upon a man cutting wood. "We've just been attacked by a grizzly bear," Christine called out. "Could you take us to the hospital?"

The man's face turned ashen as he looked at the blood-soaked women. "There's a road crew working just up ahead," he said.

"They're sure to have a radio. I'll lead you to them."

Sandy Patterson was directing traffic when a logger ran up the road towards her followed by a truck. "You've got to help," he yelled. "I've got two women here who've been attacked by a grizzly!"

Grabbing a co-worker who had first-aid training, Patterson approached the two shaking women. But upon seeing them, she feared they might die from shock, and she ran back to her radio and called for an ambulance. In 20 minutes, Ann and Christine were on their way to Queen Victoria Hospital in Revelstoke. They each required some 50 stitches.

While in hospital, Ann and Christine were interviewed by a wildlife control officer. They agreed that the mother bear should not be put down. "She was just doing what she should naturally do," said Christine. "We were intruders."

Except for a 5-cm scar beside her left eye, most of Ann's scars are hidden under her hairline. Physiotherapy has helped to restore the use of her left arm, although she did lose some muscle tissue. Christine has fully recovered, except for scars on her arms, hips, and legs.

More than a year after their near-fatal ordeal, Ann and Christine reunited for another outdoor adventure: a week-long ski holiday in B.C.'s Kokanee Glacier Provincial Park. "This time there was no hiking," says Ann with a smile.

- -

1. RESPONDING TO THE ARTICLE

a. What did you know about grizzly bears before reading the article? What did you learn about them from reading the article?

b. How does the title create a sense of suspense when you begin reading the article?

c. Both women demonstrate tremendous courage. Give two examples of their courage. What would you have done in their place?

d. Do you agree with Christine's statement that the mother bear "was just doing what she should naturally do. We were the intruders"? Explain your opinion.

e. In your notebook, write a description of what you've observed of a wild animal in its natural setting, be it a wilderness park, the country, or a city park.

2. RESEARCHING SURVIVING BEAR ENCOUNTERS

There are a number of provoked and unprovoked bear attacks in Canada each year. With a small group, research examples of bear attacks and the advice animal experts give on avoiding these attacks. Write a help manual on the topic. You could develop your manual in a question-and-answer format or post it on your school Web site.

Each member in the group could be responsible for a different task, such as researching, writing, editing, or publishing. Evaluate the credibility of each source. Is the information coming from an expert on the topic? Do different sources give the same information? Consider using word processing or publishing software to produce your manual.

SELF-ASSESSMENT: Did you indicate in your manual the sources you used for your information? Are your instructions or tips clear and helpful?

3. WRITING A SHORT STORY

A common response of people who suddenly find themselves in a dangerous situation is, "This can't be happening to me." With a partner, brainstorm a list of dangerous situations. Choose one that could be developed into an exciting story. Using "This can't be happening to me" as a story starter, write a story about how you might react to the situation. See "How to Develop a Plot Line" on pages 68–69 for help in developing your story.

Prairie Images

Cree Ponies

Poem by **R.A. Kawalikak**

Silhouettes, they lean against a ringed moon,
their heads down against the threat of snow.
Below, in the distance
a diesel moans runs along the tracks
where dead coal cinders gather
and play out towards Calgary.

No movement. They hump against the night.
Only quivering patches of skin crack the air,
memories of summer fly off.

Mane and tail hanging vertical as ice,
they sleep dead centuries,
or if ponies dream they dream.

Below on the flat where light strikes water,
a last ember sparks out. A dog complains.

The diesel warns again, begins its roar, passes.
They raise their heads, blink,
then drop back once more into centuries or dreams.

Road Between Saskatoon and Edmonton

Poem by **Elizabeth Brewster**

Yes—there are hills on the prairie,
trees, even; the road sometimes winds.
It is not
home on the range
with perpetually sunny skies,
for up there in that sky
wider and higher than the one I grew up with
clouds shift and reshift,
drop sudden showers,
vanish again in sunlight.

I name over the foreign words and objects:
those almost lakes are sloughs;
that is a windbreak of poplars,
geometrically planted before the square farmhouse.
The chief difference in the land
is that there is more of it.

The little towns are prairie clichés,
each with its grain elevator
onion-domed church
and Chinese restaurant.

But there are hints of Celtic landscape
near Kitscoty and Innisfree
lake water set in valleys
Irish and wet,
with new green grass,
and I can even imagine
the nine bean-rows
and a homesick immigrant
almost finding himself at home.

Will I ever be at home in this country?
Will I ever be at home again away from it?

1. RESPONDING TO THE POEMS

a. In "Cree Ponies," what image symbolizes humans? How is it different from the image of the ponies themselves? Given these different images, how do you think the poet feels about ponies?

b. What does the diesel warn against in "Cree Ponies"? What do you think the Cree ponies are thinking when they hear the train?

c. What event in Canadian history is the poet alluding to?

d. What is the strongest image in "Road Between Saskatoon and Edmonton"?

e. The speaker in "Road Between Saskatoon and Edmonton" says: "there are hints of Celtic landscape." What is she referring to?

f. In a paragraph, summarize the view of the prairies each poem expresses. How do they differ?

2. WRITING FREE-WRITE A DESCRIPTION

Think of a place that you've visited, for example, a cottage lake, a city park, or a wilderness reserve. In your notebook, free-write the impressions of this environment that come to mind. Don't worry about using complete sentences. Allow your pen to flow across the page without worrying about spelling or grammar.

Once you've finished writing, reread your list of impressions. What overall image do they suggest to you? Try to describe this image in one or two stanzas of a poem. Work with a partner to edit and revise your first draft. Give your poem a title.

SELF-ASSESSMENT: Did free-writing help you generate ideas? Is it an effective writing technique? Were you able to turn your free-writing into a poem that satisfied you?

Canada has some of the most beautiful scenery Mother Nature has to offer. This article features two that provide the nature enthusiast with a challenge.

GREAT CANADIAN
Escapes

Magazine Article by Tom Cruickshank and Julia Asselstine

WEST COAST TRAIL:
PACIFIC RIM NATIONAL
PARK RESERVE
You might start feeling sorry for yourself a few hours into a hike along the West Coast Trail. Although blessed with more than its share of spectacular vistas over the Pacific Ocean, this is no stroll in the park. Tree roots threaten to trip you at every turn, a little rain can turn the trail into a quagmire, and after one tough uphill comes yet another. For the ill-prepared, the trip can be a disaster. Even for the expert, it can be a real endurance test.

But that's nothing compared with the experience of the first people to use the path in the early 1900s. They were shipwreck survivors, and the trail, blazed along the southwestern shore of Vancouver Island from Bamfield in

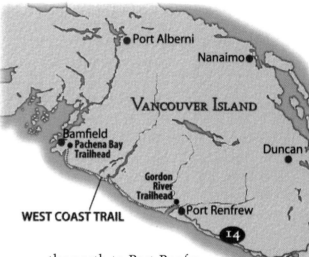

the north to Port Renfrew in the south, was designed to lead them to safety. Since those early days, some of the more demanding sections have been tamed with boardwalks, log bridges, and stair ladders. Even so, the West Coast Trail still ranks among the most challenging walks in Canada. Hikers can expect to wade through creeks and cross ravines in hand-

GOALS AT A GLANCE

■ Examine photos to write captions.
■ Use parenthetical phrases and clauses.

292

operated cable cars. Even where the going seems easy, some of those stair ladders are a long way up.

There are ample rewards for anyone who perseveres, however. The southern section meanders through primeval rain forests where the Sitka spruce tower 70 m high, while the shoreline passes some magnificent sand and gravel beaches. A highlight, near the Bamfield end of the trail, is Tsusiat Falls, which cascades over a 12-m cliff. It's a romantic idyll, but you probably won't be alone, since it is also one of the most popular camping areas.

So renowned is its scenic beauty that the West Coast Trail almost became a victim of its own success. By the early 1990s, it was host to more than 10 000 hikers a

year and the fragile ecosystem around it was showing signs of serious wear. So in 1992, Parks Canada decreed an annual quota of 8000 users, or about 52 people a day. Today admission can be obtained only by making reservations through Super Natural BC, or hikers may go on a waiting system at the trailheads.

It's hard to imagine that such a pristine wilderness, let alone one so diverse, still exists. The temperate rain forest is the dominant ecosystem, but the beaches and intertidal environment are equally fascinating. At low tide, it's fun to scan the tidal pools for starfish and anemones.

In early spring, you may glimpse migrating whales and sea lions. Bald eagles are common, but for newcomers, the star of the show is probably the lowly banana slug, which can be found sticking to every leaf and twig.

◆ ◆ ◆

EAST COAST TRAIL: ST. JOHN'S

By its very name, the East Coast Trail, which hugs the eastern shores of the Avalon Peninsula, invites comparisons with its better-known cousin, the West Coast Trail. Although they lie at opposite ends of the country, there are remarkable similarities. The latter is about as far west as you can go, and correspondingly, the East Coast Trail passes Cape Spear, the easternmost point in all of North America. Both traverse pristine wilderness on the outer edges of our nation, and the ocean is the calling card that lures hikers to venture forth.

But east is east and west is west, and the East Coast Trail has a character all its own. Unlike the temperate Pacific rain forest of the West Coast Trail, the eastern trail meanders through boreal forest and along rocky cliffs. More rugged than lush, the landscape is undeniably severe, and the winds are strong. During spring and summer, whales can be spotted breaching in the surf, while icebergs are another clue that this could only be Newfoundland. The going can be tough, especially the 25-km up-and-down-and-up trek to the Spout, a shoreside geyser near Bay Bulls, but overall, the East Coast Trail is easier and not as remote. No need to truck in a week's worth of supplies, because every few kilometres the path passes through a village where you can replenish your backpack, or even put it aside in favour of the luxury of a bed and breakfast.

The trail follows existing paths along the shore that have been used for centuries by fishers, hunters, and berry pickers. With shifts in settlement and the decline in hunting, many of these paths had fallen into disuse until a committee of local volunteers revived the route for recreational hikers in 1994. Currently, 125 km have been upgraded and marked. The ultimate goal is to open 380 km, from Topsail on Conception Bay to Trepassey near Cape Race. You can hop on or off the trail at dozens of entry points along the way, so you

lands, and even barren tundra, where large herds of caribou roam. There are also ancient coastal trees, called *tuckamores*, that are shaped by the wind and can range from "toe-high to double head-high," and *witchy wood*, which gets its name from its strange, twisted trunks and boils. Amid all of this are sheltered valleys and "old-beard" forests, where moss dangles from treetops, creating an almost eerie environment. Beyond the trail, you can feast your eyes on the awe-inspiring beauty of whales—humpbacks, fins, minkes, pilots, and the occasional orca—from July to August and icebergs from May to early July. Porpoises, dolphins, and harbour and grey seals can also be seen on nearby shores, and sea-birds, including common puffins, murres, terns, razorbills, and kittiwakes are always abundant, so don't forget your binoculars.

don't have to commit yourself for the long haul unless you want to.

The improved stretch from St. John's south to Cape Broyle is the most heavily travelled, but "heavy" is a relative term. The East Coast Trail is too new to be very well known, and you can walk for kilometres without seeing a soul. This brings to mind another comparison with the other trail out West, which is so popular that access is restricted. You will never have to line up for the East Coast Trail or make reservations to use it. You don't even have to pay for it.

The East Coast Trail wanders through boreal forest, rugged cliffs, coastal meadows, wet-

As you travel along the path, you'll have the opportunity to see abandoned villages, graveyards, old forts, and lighthouses. The trail currently links up with 12 communities where you can visit historic sites and museums or simply enjoy the local culture. ◆

1. RESPONDING TO THE ARTICLE

a. List the differences between the West Coast and the East Coast Trails. What are two reasons the West Coast Trail is more difficult to travel?

b. What did you learn about Canada's natural environment by reading this article?

c. "East is east and west is west" is a sentence borrowed from a poem by the English poet Rudyard Kipling (1865–1936): "Oh, East is East, and West is West, and never the twain shall meet." How does Kipling's line reflect these two wilderness areas?

d. Why do you think people use wilderness trails? With a partner, discuss the benefits of wilderness trails. Why is it important to preserve them?

2. MEDIA MAKER WRITE CAPTIONS

Often photos and illustrations in magazine articles include brief descriptions called *captions*. They explain something about the visual that would break up the flow of the article if included as part of the main text. Examine the photos in "Great Canadian Escapes" and write a caption for each one. Try to limit your captions to one or two sentences each.

3. ORAL LANGUAGE GROUP DISCUSSION

In a small group, brainstorm some rules of behaviour you think people should follow when travelling and camping in wilderness areas. Rank your list of rules from least to most important. Discuss ways that your list could be made available to wilderness travellers.

4. ORAL LANGUAGE PANEL DISCUSSION

With a group of three classmates, prepare and conduct a panel discussion about the loss of wilderness areas, and how this loss contributes to the increasing number of encounters between humans and wild animals. You could choose from the following roles: one classmate could act as the moderator and two could discuss the issue. In the discussion, suggest ideas for ensuring that animals, such as grizzly bears, will stay in their natural environment.

To prepare for the panel discussion, conduct some background research about wild animals and how their natural habitats are being diminished. The moderator could develop a list of questions for the panelists and create an opening statement outlining the context of the discussion for the audience.

GROUP ASSESSMENT: After the panel discussion, assess the group's presentation. Did group members try to engage the audience's interest by using gestures and intonation and making eye contact? Were opinions clearly presented and backed up with supporting evidence and examples?

5. LANGUAGE CONVENTIONS
PARENTHETICAL CLAUSES AND PHRASES

Magazine articles and essays often deal with complex ideas and information. Sometimes it's difficult for the writer to fit these ideas into simple sentence constructions. Therefore, the writer often uses parenthetical clauses and phrases to add non-essential information to sentences. Parenthetical information may be set off from the main sentence in a number of ways: with commas, dashes, or parentheses. Here are some examples from "Great Canadian Escapes":

- It's hard to imagine that such pristine wilderness, <u>let alone one so diverse</u>, still exists.
- Beyond the trail, you can feast your eyes on the awe-inspiring beauty of whales—<u>humpbacks, fins, minkes, pilots, and the occasional orca</u>—from July to August…"

Reread the article and find other examples, and then try writing some examples of your own.

SELF-ASSESSMENT: Do you use parenthetical clauses and phrases in your writing? If so, what kind do you use? Do they make your sentences easier or harder to understand?

HOW TO WRITE A MAGAZINE ARTICLE

Goals at a Glance

● Formulate questions to guide research. ● Write a magazine article.

What piques your interest in a particular magazine article, such as "Attacked by a Mountain Grizzly" or "Great Canadian Escapes"? Does the opening sentence draw you in to find out more? Does the writing make you feel as though you are in the middle of the action? Do the pictures and captions help you understand more about the subject?

Your job as a writer is to make your subject compelling. How do you do that? Use the following suggestions to craft an engaging magazine article.

Plan the Article

1. Think about your purpose. Are you writing to inform, to entertain, to persuade, or to express your ideas?
2. Consider your readers. What do you want them to learn from the article? What impressions do you want them to have about the subject? What do you want them to remember?

3. Narrow your topic. Find some part of it that interests you. In a few sentences, summarize the information you know about the topic.
4. Formulate a list of questions that you or your readers might wonder about, and use them to guide your research. Decide what information you need to gather to answer the questions.

Research for Information

1. If possible, interview a teacher in your school, or a local expert, about your topic. Use quotations from your interview to add interest and authenticity to the article.
2. As you read books and magazines and explore the Internet, be alert for details that will help your writing come alive. Watch for sensory descriptions that tell you about the sights, sounds, smells, taste, or feel of your subject.

PROCESS

Draft the Article

1. Where do you want to place your most important information—at the end of the article, so it will stay in the reader's mind afterward, or at the beginning where it will catch your reader's attention? At the beginning is the traditional approach, but you could try something innovative.

   How will you order the other information—from least to most important, most important to least, first step to last step, or the general to the specific?

2. Make it easy for your reader to understand your points.
   - Include diagrams, charts, graphs, or photos.
   - Define difficult terms.
   - Use a sub-heading for each section of the article.

3. Make it interesting for your reader.
   - Include action as well as description.
   - Consider using flashbacks or foreshadowing if it suits your subject.
   - Select an interesting or exciting sentence from the body of the text and turn it into a large-type "pull quote."

4. You don't have to start at the beginning of the article and write in order. Do whatever works for you. You might leave the opening and closing for later, after the main body of the article is written.

5. As you write, don't worry about spelling or whether a sentence "sounds" right. Those refinements will come later when you edit your writing. Writing requires enthusiasm; editing requires judgment. Don't try to do both at once.

Hook Your Reader

Once you have a draft of your article completed, revise it.

1. Take a closer look at the opening. Have you hooked the reader? Consider using a question or quotation. You might try starting with action and a very brief summary. What about using a shocking opener, with a dangerous or life-threatening situation?

2. Consider your subject, reader, and purpose. What would work best for all three? You might wish to try several *leads* (opening sentence or paragraph) and ask a classmate for feedback on which is most effective.

Self-Assessment

Ask yourself these questions as you revise your article:

❑ Is the focus of my topic a manageable size?
❑ Is my information organized and presented in a logical way?
❑ Is my main idea clear?
❑ Do I make it easy for my reader to understand my meaning?
❑ Have I missed anything my reader might like to learn?
❑ Would I be drawn to read this article?

PROCESS

Having spent a lifetime observing a chimpanzee community in Africa,
Jane Goodall has some fascinating stories to tell.

Jane Goodall
and the
Chimps

Interview with Vicki Gabereau

Sometimes you have to wonder what it is that scientists do, research scientists especially. Often their fields are beyond comprehension. Not so with Jane Goodall, says Vicki Gabereau. It doesn't matter if we don't understand all the implications and intricate details of a primatologist's work, because we all love stories about chimpanzees.

Here Gabereau speaks with Jane Goodall about her life's work with the chimpanzees of Gombe Stream National Park in the East African nation of Tanzania.

VICKI GABEREAU: Your last *National Geographic* special had an outrageous number of people viewing it.

JANE GOODALL: It was 17.9 million. Isn't that staggering?

VG: People don't seem to be able to get enough of it.

JG: It is interesting, isn't it? I sometimes wonder why it is. I think it's partly because chimps are so like us and I also think that there is a strange myth around me because I was the first person to do this sort of thing.

GOALS AT A GLANCE

- Conduct research.
- Conduct a radio interview.

VG: At a time when it was odd for a young woman to do such a thing. Did you have this life in mind from childhood, that you would eventually rush off to the jungle?

JG: Apparently, when I was two I began watching animals and when I was four I disappeared. I was staying with my mother's family in the English countryside and I was gone so long that my mother called the police. After four and a half hours I appeared and I was so happy. I can still remember the moment. I'd been hiding in a hot, stuffy, little, dark henhouse because I could not understand where there was a hole big enough in the chicken for the egg to come out. So I waited. I waited for the chicken to come in and settle down in her nest and I can still see that egg coming out.

VG: Well, there's the basis of all your research—great patience.

JG: Exactly.

VG: The patience has been the key. You actually sat in that jungle for nearly two years before you could really get next to those chimps.

JG: That's right, it did take patience. But as I loved the life and I loved the forest—and I just loved being there—it didn't require as much patience as you might think. I didn't have to rush out and get a Ph.D. and earn my living, you know.

VG: But how did you keep up your enthusiasm and interest when there appeared to be no breakthroughs?

JG: Well, there were, because all the time I was sitting there I could see those chimps from a distance and little pieces of the puzzle began to fit together. But I've always liked being alone. It doesn't mean I'm antisocial; I'm not. I love being with people, too.

VG: How alone were you?

JG: All day, from the time I got up to the time I got back to the camp in the evening, when the authorities said I had to be with somebody. But even then I would climb up to some point and say, "You wait here, and I'll go over there."

VG: You are a rare breed, aren't you? Not too many do this kind of thing.

JG: There are far more now, let me tell you. I get so many letters from children and young people saying, "What do I do to get to do what you do?" This is a big responsibility, because these days it's getting very difficult to do what I did. The economic situation has changed and the political situation, too. More and more field stations are being closed down.

VG: You said that the Tanzanian officials didn't want you to be alone out there. Were they scratching their heads about you?

JG: They surely thought it was peculiar. Louis Leakey, who got the money for me to start off, was accused of being amoral. Sending a young woman off into the bush like that, it just wasn't done in those days.

VG: How did you get to Leakey in the first place? You didn't just march up to him, a legendary anthropologist and all.

JG: It wasn't quite that easy. I think when I was about eighteen my desire to be with animals really crystallized and I wanted to go to Africa. Eventually, I began to save enough money; in fact, I worked as a waitress to save up my fare. I had to get a return fare, you see. Finally, I got to Africa. I had a temporary job, so I wasn't dependent on anyone. And I had heard about Dr. Leakey. People told me, "If you are interested in animals, you should go to see him." So I did.

VG: Was he thrilled to meet you or did he think you a bit odd?

JG: Oh, no. Almost immediately, he offered me a job as his assistant. While I was working with him at the Olduvai Gorge where Zinjanthropus [the ancient human skeleton] was found, he started to talk to me about this little group of chimps on a wild lakeshore. I thought he was teasing, but one day he said, "Why do you think I'm talking to you about this? This is what I want you to do, to study those chimps there." It really was fantastic. But then he had to wait a whole year before he could find any money for me to go. Because it was so unique, nobody wanted to give any money, and I had no qualifications. At least no academic qualifications.

VG: Did he want you to have or get a degree?

JG: No, he didn't want me to. He wanted me to have an unbiassed mind. He wanted me to go because I wanted to find out.

VG: Do you remember the arrival at your camp in the bush?

JG: I certainly remember the moment I arrived and looked up at that rugged country, thinking, "It is going to be difficult, but how exciting. And I'm jolly well going to do it."

VG: Who was with you?

JG: My mother. This was the amazing thing. She is fantastic and an adventuress and she wanted to come. She lives in England, but when I was working with Dr. Leakey in Nairobi she came for a visit. When it came time for me to go in, and I told you I had to be with somebody, I chose her. She stayed for three months and she set up this clinic with the local fishers, which put me in such a good position with them.

VG: Is she a doctor or nurse?

JG: No, neither, but we have a medical family and my uncle was a surgeon. He gave us masses of medicine and instructions as to how to use it. Do you know it is nearly a quarter of a century ago?

VG: And I suppose some of the chimps that you encountered originally are still alive?

JG: Oh, sure they are, they live till they are fifty. And I am still working, and now I have ten Tanzanian field assistants and they are there all the time collecting data, even as I talk to you.

VG: Throughout your studies there, it seems to me that the only encroachment you made upon them was the institution of the banana station. Apart from that, you introduced nothing into the chimps' lives that would be foreign to them.

JG: That's right. But we did it very badly at one time, right at the beginning before I had any idea that this research could carry on in the way it has been. I wanted to find out as much as I could. I kept thinking, "Golly, this is the end, I have to go back and write my thesis and write my degree." So we gave bananas every day and this had the most dramatic effect on the social structure, on the levels of aggression. When I realized that I could continue the study and have students, then we had to change the feeding altogether.

VG: From bananas to what?

JG: We still feed bananas, but, say, six every ten days, whereas a chimp can eat fifty at one sitting. So six is a very tiny amount. We only give bananas if a chimp comes by himself or in a small group.

VG: So as to not create a party atmosphere?

JG: Just enough so that if they're in the neighbourhood, they'll drop by to see if there's anything going.

VG: At the local pub?

JG: That's right.

VG: Are they gluttonous? Will they eat till they burst?

JG: They'll eat till they really can't eat any more. They will stuff themselves. They do enjoy their food, and they make these lovely *oo-oo-ah* chimp noises. They're happy when they get food.

VG: It must be a temptation to try and communicate, but you don't?

JG: Oh, I don't. It is very important not to try and interact. One could. You could be right in there, part of the group. But we specifically don't.

VG: What is your reaction to people who do the reverse to what you do— make attempts to communicate through sign language or whatever?

JG: It certainly doesn't upset me. It's not so much another world as it is the other side of the coin. It is an attempt to find out about the chimp intellect in a way that I can't do in the wild. It could make for a very good collaborative attempt to understand this very complex creature. In fact, I was just visiting the original chimp who learned sign language. That chimp has now adopted a baby and she's teaching the baby sign language, in the lab.

VG: Isn't that a remarkable thing, that what she learned, she is now teaching?

JG: In the wild, although a young one learns from the mother by observing and imitating and practising, we now find that if a chimp is taught by humans, then she is capable of teaching. That is fascinating.

VG: Has any one of them ever become aggressive with you?

JG: Yes. The worst are the adolescent males, because they are out to intimidate the females of the community...Those adolescent males will treat me rather as they treat the females of the community. In other words, I must be intimidated. I don't think they'd ever really hurt one, but they jump up and they pound on you and hit you, and it does hurt. But once they've intimidated all the females, they work their way through the male hierarchy. Then they finally sort of grow up, as it were. They don't bother the females any more, and they don't bother with me.

VG: In your opinion, do you think that they think about you in any way?

JG: I don't think I could ever answer that. They basically pay very little attention to us, which is nice. It is the young ones who watch more carefully, though. The most intelligent female there today once watched me drink a cup of coffee, and then I set it down. I didn't even know what she was doing, but she came over and picked up that cup and tried to drink it as we would. But of course it was hot, and she didn't put her lip touching the cup, but she poured it just as we would. That is pretty incredible for a wild animal. And that is the only example I have ever seen of a chimp trying to imitate something we've done. They imitate each other, but not us, fortunately. Otherwise, we would really have trouble.

VG: Do the chimps rejoice in any way when you visit?

JG: No, thank goodness. But sometimes you feel a bit hurt. After all, I am so pleased to see them. Fifi, let's say, doesn't even look at me. But that is what I have been striving for, that is what I wanted, and that's what I've got.

◆ ◆ ◆

These days, Goodall spends only a few weeks a year in Gombe with the chimpanzees. Most of her time is spent travelling around the world, lecturing at schools and universities (where she does a haunting rendition of a chimp's call!). She has founded Jane Goodall Institutes in Africa, North America, and Europe. As well, she carries on a passionate campaign for chimpanzee conservation and research. Goodall is particularly concerned about the non-essential use of chimps, who are genetically very similar to humans, in medical research.

Goodall's two books, *In the Shadow of Man* and *Through the Window*, tell the dramatic tale of her thirty years spent with the chimpanzees of Gombe. As exciting to read as novels, they offer essential insights into animal behaviour—and human behaviour as well.

Goodall's closeness to the chimpanzee community has made her very aware of environmental problems. In her view, "humans are arrogantly spoiling the natural world, causing deserts and pollution." But she finds reasons for hope. People are beginning to face up to the problems that threaten the survival of many species on Earth. Young people especially, all around the world, are acting on their enthusiasm and commitment. Her message is inspiring: "Let's move into the next millennium with hope, respect for all living things, understanding, compassion, and love."

----

1. RESPONDING TO THE INTERVIEW

a. What impressions do you have about Jane Goodall after reading the interview?

b. According to Goodall, what qualities are needed to become a good animal observer? Why do you think she was able to study chimpanzees without having studied in university?

c. Goodall seemed to know at a very young age that she wanted to study animals. What did you want to become when you were younger? Do you still feel the same way or have your interests changed?

d. If you could study any animal in the wild, which one would it be? Explain why you made your choice.

e. From reading this interview, do you think that Goodall looks at the chimps she studies in an anthropomorphic way? (That is, does she give them humanlike qualities?) Use examples from the interview to explain your answers.

2. RESEARCHING BIOGRAPHIES

Research other people who have studied animals in the wild, for example, Diane Fossey, Birute Galdikas, or Amanda Vincent. What is it about their characters that makes them want to spend great periods of their lives away from people? Why do they want to observe and study wild animals? As you conduct your research, be sure to assess the reliability of the information.

- What is the copyright date of the resource? If you're checking a Web site on the Internet, the home page should say when the site was last updated.
- Consider whether the resource is biassed. Ask yourself whether the information comes from an individual or a group that may be trying to persuade people to hold a certain point of view.
- Be sure to select relevant information. What information is necessary or unnecessary?

Write a brief report profiling some of the people you researched. Share your report with a classmate.

SELF-ASSESSMENT: Did you use more than one source for your research? How do you know if a source is true or accurate, biassed or unbiassed? If you used Internet resources, how do you know they are accurate and not made up?

3. ORAL LANGUAGE RADIO INTERVIEW

Reread the interview and note the types of questions Vicki Gabereau asks. Which questions were probably planned? Which questions were based on reactions to Jane Goodall's answers? Since this interview was originally conducted for radio, it still reflects the spontaneity of spoken conversation. How much editing do you think the interview underwent between the tape-recorded version and the final printed version?

Conduct a radio interview in which you talk to a classmate about an area of his or her interest or expertise. Prepare questions that will draw out the interviewee, but also be ready to ask follow-up questions about information you hadn't expected. Tape-record your interview and play it for the class.

What would you do if an earthquake hit your home town? Read on to find out how the earthquake of '46 became a community legend.

EARTHQUAKE

D o you remember the earthquake of '46? Do you remember how the chimney fell through the roof of the elementary school and down through both storeys of classrooms and would have killed us all if this had not been a Sunday morning? (Would have killed Miss Gordon, too, lying out flat on her bench and fanning herself, in the midst of one of her spells.) Do you remember how the post office, which was the only brick building in the entire valley, collapsed in a heap of rubble where it had stood for twenty-three years, and how we were thrilled to think afterwards that it looked exactly as if it might have been bombed from the air? And how the bells on the little Anglican church went chiming, and the electric poles whipped back and forth like fly-fishermen's rods, and electric wires trooped low like skipping ropes and snapped tight and clearly *sang*, and how the earth came rolling up in waves and sent Cornelius Baxter's car out of control and up onto Millie Weston's porch?

Then you may also remember my uncle. Neddie Desmond? Lived just down the road a ways from us on that little farm with the buttercup-yellow house? Well my Uncle Neddie was the first one in our part of the valley to install an electric fence. Power had come as far as Waterville just the year before and none of us had become accustomed to its magic yet, nor learned to trust it. Neddie went out that morning to pull the inaugural switch, and to prepare himself to have a good laugh at the first cow to find out what it

---

GOALS AT A GLANCE

- Follow instructions to write a short story.
- Conduct research.

would mean from now on to stick her nose into a field where she wasn't wanted. Well Neddie pulled his switch and immediately the air began to hum, the world began to heave and roll, the trees began to dance and flop about and try to fly. Two guernseys dropped directly to their knees and started to bawl, a third went staggering sideways down the sloping earth and slammed into the cedar-shake wall of his barn. Chickens exploded out of their pen in a flurry of squawking feathers as if the jolt of electricity had somehow jumped a connection and zapped them. Naturally he thought that he and his fence were to blame for this upheaval but he could not make it stop by turning off his switch. Poor old Neddie had never been so frightened, he started to curse and blubber, he hollered for Gracie to get out and give him a hand. Never much of a man for religion, he promised God at the top of his lungs that he would abandon his lifelong fascination with modern inventions immediately. But God took far too long to think this offer over; by the time the earth's convulsions had settled, all of his cattle had fallen and poor Ned had wrapped himself around a fence post and begun to cry.

Now the scariest thing about quakes is that they change the way a fellow looks at the world. You may also remember my other uncle. Tobias Desmond? Owned the little sawmill up at Comox Lake? Uncle Toby drove down from his mill an hour after the quake had worn itself out and told us the entire lake had emptied in front of his eyes. Truly! Right to the muddy bottom, he said—he saw drowned trees and slime. Drained entirely down a crack which had opened up in the earth, and must have gone right out to the ocean somewhere, because it came back with tangled knots of golden-brown kelp and furious crabs and bouquets of brilliant purple anemones torn off the ocean floor and flung up onto the driftwood and shoreline trees and the sorting deck of Uncle Toby's mill.

He was uneasy about going back to his sawmill after that. Though the sound of the lake emptying all at once like water down a sucking drainpipe had been horrible enough to haunt him for the next few years, it would not have the effect upon him of those remembered moments when he stood and watched the water returning to the empty lake—leaking in at first, and spreading, then racing outwards across the mud, and swelling, deepening, rising up the nearer slopes. *He* had no reason to believe it would know when to stop. By the time the first waves slapped against the pilings under his mill, he was in his truck with the motor running, yet later confessed that he knew he would not have the will to drive out of there even if that water had kept on climbing up the posts and started out over the land. He would just have to hang around to see what happened next.

Now my Uncle Toby was a truthful man. We believed him. You only had to walk along the lakeshore yourself to see things drying in the sunlight that shouldn't be there. The problem was that this incident would trouble him far too much, he couldn't stop telling people about it. And every time he told it there seemed to be something new he'd just remembered that he hadn't told before. A whole month had gone by when he turned away from the counter of the general store one afternoon, watched a car speed past outside, and turned again to Em at the till: "My God, I just remembered! Why didn't I think of this before? There were two old men in a boat—I remember seeing them just before it started—two stiff gentlemen in coolie hats out on the lake in a punt." They weren't fishing or anything, he said. Just floating, talking, way out in the middle.

When the waves started sloshing up they rocked and bobbed but didn't start rowing for shore. They started turning, slowly turning around, turning around and around this whirlpool that had opened up, this funnel that was sucking the entire body of water down a hole somewhere. They didn't stand up, they didn't holler for help, they just turned and turned and eventually slipped into the shute and corkscrewed down out of sight. "Now what do you think of that?" said Uncle Toby. "They didn't come back, they must've gone sailing out to sea." Of course no one believed this new addition to his tale. But he continued to tell his story to anyone who would listen, adding every time a few more details that would make it just a little more exciting and improbable than it had been before. He seldom went back to the mill, or sold much lumber. He spent his time on the streets of town, or in a coffee shop, talking the ear off anyone who came along. The earthquake had given him the excuse he'd been looking for to avoid what he'd always hated doing most—an honest day's work.

So you see—that's the other thing. People will use an earthquake for their own purposes. My uncle's sawmill eventually collapsed from neglect, under a heavy fall of snow, but he hardly noticed. That's the worrying part. They're telling us now that we're just about overdue for another one. For an island situated smack on the Pacific rim of fire, as they like to call it, we've sat back for far too long and smugly watched disasters strike other parts of the world. Apparently, all those tremors we've wakened to in the night have not done anything but delay the inevitable; we will soon be facing the real thing all over again, with its aftermath of legend.

Myself, I was nearly eight at the time. My brother was five. My sister was less than a year, and still asleep in her crib in one corner of my parents' bedroom. My mother, who was kneading a batch of bread dough at the

kitchen counter, encouraged the two of us boys to hurry and finish break-fast and get outside. It appeared to be the beginning of a warm June day. My father had gone out to milk Star, the little jersey. He'd soon begin the task of sharpening the little triangular blades of his hay mower, which would be needed within the next few weeks for the field between the house and the wooden gate. Now, he had just started back towards the house with a pail of milk in order to run it through the verandah separator, when it seemed the air had begun to hum around his ears. Something smelled, an odour of unfamiliar gas. Off across the nearer pasture the line of firs began to sway, as though from a sudden burst of wind. The hayfield swelled up and moved towards him in a series of ripples. Suddenly he felt as if he were on a rocking ship, in need of sea legs, with a whole ocean beneath him trying to upset his balance. He could not proceed. He stopped and braced his legs apart to keep from falling. The milk sloshed from side to side in the pail and slopped over the rim. Before him, our old two-storey house he was still in the process of renovating, had begun to dance a jig. The chimney bent as if made of rubber bricks, then swivelled a half-turn and toppled. Red bricks spilled down the slope of the roof and dropped to the lean-to roof of the verandah, then spilled down that in a race to the eave where they could drop to the ground directly above the door I was throwing open at that precise moment in order to rush outside and join him. This was the end of the world he'd been warned about as a child himself; it was happening in exactly the way his own father had told him it would. In a moment a crack would open up somewhere and snake across his land to divide beneath his feet and swallow him, would swallow his house and his family and his farm and all his animals at once, but not until he'd been forced to stand helpless and unable to move on the bucking surface of earth while he watched his family bludgeoned to death by the spilling cascade of bricks.

My brother laughed, but wouldn't leave his chair at the kitchen table. The sight of a fried egg dancing on his plate was not an entertainment to walk away from. Cutlery chattered on the tablecloth. Milk tossed up bubbly sprays from his glass and splashed on his nose. His piece of toast hopped off his plate and landed in his lap. This was a matter for giggling. The world had decided to entertain him in a manner he'd always thought it capable of and this would make a difference to his life. From this day on, he would take it for granted that he might demand any sort of pleasant diversion he wished and need only wait for all laws of nature to be suspended for the purpose of giving him a laugh.

My mother screamed. Cupboard doors flew open and spewed dishes onto her counter. Drinking glasses and cups spilled onto the bread dough. Saucers crashed in the sink. Through the window she could see her husband swaying like a drunken man in the lane that led to the barn. When she turned—crying, "The baby!"—she saw the drying rack above the stove sway like a gentle porch swing, swishing boiled underwear and shirts back and forth over the heat. She snatched the clothing down and tossed it all in a heap on a chair. "You boys—get outside quick!" She went flying off through the French door and across the living room and into the bedroom. "I can't! I can't!" I heard her calling and ran to help. The crib had danced across the floor and was blocking the door. We pushed it open. She snatched up my sister and cried, "Grab your brother and follow." As it turned out, she was the one who would follow. The outside door of the living room was blocked by the china cabinet which had taken up the tune and gone dancing, its contents of silver and heirloom china clanging behind the glass. The baby cried at her hip. Between us we leaned against the cabinet but it would not move. "The other door!" she cried. But we had only got out as far as the verandah, saw my father hollering something at us we couldn't hear over a clatter on the roof above us, saw him waving his arms—he might have been signalling us to hurry and join him, he might have been telling us to stay where we were—when that fall of cascading bricks came crashing down off the roof less than a running step before us. Beyond it, my father rushing towards us, fell to one knee. We looked at one another, my father and I, with that thundering fall of red clay bricks between us. He might as well have been on the opposite side of an opening chasm, he might as well have been on the shore while we were going down a drain hole, he might as well have been left behind on earth while we went sailing off into eternity. That's what he was thinking. Even trapped in a house that was shaking itself into collapse around our ears I could see what he was thinking in his eyes. What sort of a father could not put a halt to a tumbling wall of bricks? I was thinking the same myself.

Now what does it feel like to be an eight-year-old boy on a Sunday morning in June with the world deciding to throw itself into convulsions and scare everyone half to death? Why, how had I got to such an age, I'd like to know, still believing that the earth would stay steady beneath your feet forever, fathers stay capable of heroic rescues forever, mothers stay calm in every sort of emergency forever, and houses you lived in stay solid and still and safe and true till the end of time?

Let me tell you this: When I was two my mother came up into the attic bedroom to tuck me in every night carrying a coal-oil lamp. One night when she had kissed me she turned to go down the stairs but tripped and fell, and fell down the length of the stairs to the landing. I ran to the head of the stairs and looked: there she was in a heap, surrounded by flames, with fire already starting up the trail of spilled oil towards me. In no time at all, my father had beat those flames out with a blanket and helped my mother away. I didn't even have the time to think he might not. Let me also tell this. When I was in my first year of school my father did not come home one day from work in the logging camp at the time he was supposed to. He did not come home that night at all: He came home the next morning from the hospital with his head wrapped up in great white bandages, nothing of him showing but two eyes, two nostrils, and a gaping mouth. He laughed. A falling limb had nearly taken off one ear, had opened up his nose. But he laughed. I could take him to school tomorrow for show-and-tell, he said, and tell that teacher and all those other kids I'd dug him up in the yard where he'd been buried by the Egyptians five or six thousand years before. He would lie stiff, he said, until everyone was through poking at him and smelling him and making notes for an assignment on the pleasures of archeology, and then he would let out a long groan and sit up and scare the teacher into immediate retirement. "This isn't funny," my mother said. "You might have been killed." But of course my father could laugh in the teeth of anything that would try to kill him in the world. The earth beneath our feet stayed firm.

Then this. What do you make of it? The bricks stopped falling. The house settled. Not a sound could be heard. It was as if the earth, worn out from its convulsion, had taken in a deep breath and held it, while it gathered up its strength to buck and heave some more and go into another fit. Still we didn't move—my father down on one knee with his spilled milk bucket not far away in the grass, my mother holding my crying sister in her arms, my brother no longer giggling but looking as though he just might get scared at last. We held our positions as if we waited for someone's permission to move. Something foul-smelling had been released into the air. The light was wrong. Far off, if you listened hard, a rumbling could be heard going away beyond the trees.

Inside, one final piece of china crashed to the kitchen floor. This was a signal. Now, could you heave a sigh and laugh to show that it was all right? Nobody laughed. My brother, like the baby, started to cry. My father stood up and whipped off his cap to slap the dirt from his knees. He picked up the pail, and stood looking into it. Was he wondering where the milk had gone? It was splashed out all around him and already drying on the leaves of grass and on the gravel along the lane. My mother made a tentative move down onto the top step, and staggered a little. "What *was* that?" she said. "What *was* that? I thought for a moment the war might have started up again, an invasion or something."

"Quake," said my dad. He took a step towards my mother, found that he could keep his balance after all, and sort of threw himself into a lope in our direction.

"You wouldn't believe what went through my head!" my mother said. "I thought something might have happened in the barn. You and that cow—" She was almost laughing now, but almost crying as well. "Blowing yourselves to kingdom come and taking the rest of us with you!"

My father took the baby in one of his arms to hush her, and used his other arm to hold my mother against him. "You okay?" he asked me. I nodded. He didn't smile. Not yet. He would make a joke of it later but for the time being he solemnly held my gaze with his to acknowledge what we both now knew what he must have known already himself but had kept secret from me too long. What was this thing we shared? That the world could no longer be trusted to stay steady beneath our feet? Perhaps, and that a father and son in such a world must expect to view each other across a space of falling debris.

Fifteen minutes later my uncle Neddie and his housekeeper Grace were upon us in their pickup truck, to see how much damage had been done. By this time we had already heard on the battery radio that we'd been at the very centre of this quake, and that it had measured seven-point-three on the Richter scale—the worst to hit the island since 1918. Grace drew fiercely on her cigarette, blew smoke down her nose, and viewed the world at a sideways glance to show she would never trust it again. She was not one to thrive on drama. Uncle Ned was white, and shaky. "I thought I'd caused it," he said. He wasn't laughing either. He looked as if he could still be convinced he'd been the one to blame.

"That sounds pretty normal," my father said. "I thought I'd caused it myself. I was just coming across from the barn and thinking how maybe we shouldn't've moved into this old house before I'd finished the renovations. Not with little kids—y'know? What a person ought to be able to do, I thought, was just pick up an old house like that and give it a shake and see what's left that's safe."

"I was making bread," my mother said. "You know how they make fun of the way I punch down the dough like I'm mad. This time I thought well *now* I've gone and done it, this dough's begun to fight back."

None of this was comfort to Uncle Ned, who was holding his hands together, then putting them into his pockets, then clenching them into fists that he pressed to his sides. "I mean I thought I'd *really* started it!" he said. "I pulled the switch on my electric fence and away she started to rip! I nearly peed my pants." So Uncle Ned told us what it was like: how he pulled the switch, and the earth heaved up, and the cows fell, and chickens exploded out of their pen, and the fence posts shook themselves free of the ground. Naturally we laughed. Naturally he had to laugh himself. Then he said, "I guess I had to come over and find out how far my damage had spread. But that don't mean I'm gonna get up on that roof and fix your chimney!"

Apparently it was all right to laugh. No one was hurt. The house was still standing. How important grownups must think they are! It had never occurred to me to think I was at fault. "Reminds me of that time we was kids," said Uncle Ned to my father. "You remember that? You and me and Toby was sleepin' up over the garage and the Old Man he comes hollering out to wake us up? This was the time that fire got loose up behind Wolf Lake and started down across the valley towards us. The sky was red and boiling black, the whole world was lit up by its flames and you could hear them roarin' across the tops of the trees. You could hear the cattle bellowin' too, scared to death. Well you know what *he* was like, he got us up on the roof with gunny sacks slappin' at sparks that flew our way. Even when that fire'd nearly surrounded us he wouldn't let us high-tail it out of there." He was talking to my mother now. "Well it wasn't until the next day when the wind had turned it away that we found out he'd been broodin' about some little root-fire he'd started that he shouldn't have, and couldn't get it out of his head that he somehow might've sent up the spark that started that whole mountain burning—and sweeping down to give him his punishment. I bet every farmer in the valley had some reason for thinking the same! What's the matter with us that we can't believe things happen just because?"

My father looked at me for a moment before he said anything to that. "I d'know, Ned. Maybe we'd really rather be the cause of these things ourselves. On the other hand, maybe we're right. Who's to say it isn't a person's thoughts that do the damage?"

Uncle Ned shook his head. Of course he wasn't satisfied. He wouldn't be satisfied until he'd made some sense of this. He bent to pick up a brick from the front step, and then another, and stacked them up on the floor of the verandah. "I know this, I'll tell you for sure. I'm gonna dismantle that fence. Barbed wire is good enough for any cow. I'll just shoot the ones that don't pay attention to it. I know this too: I ain't never gonna flick a light switch on the wall of my house without flinchin' a bit while I do it. Just in case. How's a fellow s'posed to know what to trust?"

My mother took the baby back inside. The rest of us started collecting the bricks, and stacking them on the verandah, and kept on picking up bricks until my Uncle Tobias' truck came roaring in through the gate and down the driveway. We stood up to watch him approach. Uncle Toby was out of that truck before it had even come to its usual stop against the walnut tree, and was running across the yard towards us holding his base-ball cap on his head with one of his hands. "You feel that?" he shouted. "You feel that here?" I guess he was too excited to notice our stack of bricks.

"Feel what?" my father said. "What do you mean? We didn't feel anything here." He put one hand on my shoulder. "You see anything here that's *changed?*"

----

1. RESPONDING TO THE STORY

a. Many of the adults in this selection think they started the earthquake. What was each one doing at the time that gave them this idea?

b. Who is Jack Hodgins addressing when he uses "you" in the first paragraph? Do you think this series of questions is an effective way to start the story? Why or why not?

c. How would you describe the tone of the story? Discuss how the tone of the first paragraph sets the tone for the whole story.

d. Choose a character in "Earthquake" and in your notebook describe how he or she was affected by the quake.

e. Hodgins describes many small details that, when taken together, describe experiencing an earthquake. List these details in the order they occur. Read over your list and write a paragraph of your impression of an earthquake.

2. WRITING A SHORT STORY

"The scariest thing about earthquakes is that they change the way a fellow looks at the world," writes Jack Hodgins. Use the ideas in this statement as the basis for a short story about someone who was forever changed by witnessing a powerful event, for example, a flood or a dramatic holdup.

3. RESEARCHING EARTHQUAKES

Reread the story and note how powerful the earthquake was on the Richter scale. Using the library or Internet, research the Richter scale and how, why, and where earthquakes happen. Write a brief report about earthquakes, and include at least one illustration or diagram in the report. Use labels, captions, or a legend in your diagram.

Develop a list of questions such as the following to help guide your research: What numbers on the Richter scale correspond to dangerous earthquakes? What is the *epicentre* of a quake? Why is the time after a quake often more dangerous for people than the quake itself? What are the world's major earthquake zones?

4. ORAL LANGUAGE EXPLORE PERSONAL FEELINGS

You may not have lived through an earthquake, but you may have witnessed other natural events such as thunderstorms or blizzards. Try to remember what it was like. Share your memories with others in a group. Do they have similar experiences and feelings?

5. LANGUAGE CONVENTIONS THE COMMA

The *comma* is a punctuation mark with many uses. Here are a few examples from the story.

- After a long introductory clause:

  "By the time the first waves slapped against the pilings under his mill, he was in his truck with the motor running…"

- To set off parenthetical phrases and clauses:

  "Do you remember how the post office, which was the only brick building in the entire valley, collapsed in a heap of rubble…?"

Find one or two more examples in the story for each of these uses of the comma. Then write sentences of your own to illustrate each use.

Poetry of the Seasons

"Spring Has Come"

Poem by Li Ch'ing-Chao, 12th century

(Translated by Kenneth Rexroth and Ling Chung)

Spring has come to the women's quarters.
The grass turns green.
The red buds of the plum trees have cracked
But are not yet fully open.
Blue green clouds carve jade dragons.
The jade powder becomes fine dust.
I try to hold on to my morning dream,
But I am startled by the breaking cup of Spring.

Flower shadows lie heavy on the garden gate.
A pale moon is spread on the translucent curtain
In the beautiful orange twilight.
For two years, three times, I have missed
The Lord of Spring.
Now he is coming home,
And I will thoroughly enjoy this Spring.

GOALS AT A GLANCE

- Write a descriptive poem.
- Write an essay to compare.

Low Tide at St. Andrews

Poem by E. Pauline Johnson

The long red flats stretch open to the sky,
Breathing their moisture on the August air.
The seaweeds cling with flesh-like fingers where
The rocks give shelter that the sands deny;
And wrapped in all her summer harmonies
St. Andrews sleeps beside her sleeping seas.

The far-off shores swim blue and indistinct,
Like half-lost memories of some old dream.
The listless waves that catch each sunny gleam
Are idling up the waterways land-linked,
And, yellowing along the harbour's breast,
The light is leaping shoreward from the west.

And naked-footed children, tripping down,
Light with young laughter, daily come at eve
To gather dulse and sea clams and then heave
Their loads, returning laden to the town,
Leaving a strange grey silence when they go,—
The silence of the sands when tides are low.

A January Morning

Poem by Archibald Lampman

Winter in the Country by Currier & Ives

The glittering roofs are still with frost; each worn
Black chimney builds into the quiet sky
Its curling pile to crumble silently.
Far out to westward on the edge of morn,
The slender misty city towers up-borne
Glimmer faint rose against the pallid blue;
And yonder on those northern hills, the hue
Of amethyst, hang fleeces dull as horn.
And here behind me come the woodmen's sleighs
With shouts and clamorous squeakings; might and main
Up the steep slope the horses stamp and strain,
Urged on by hoarse-tongued drivers—cheeks ablaze,
Iced beards and frozen eyelids—team by team,
With frost-fringed flanks, and nostrils jetting stream.

Nature

We have neither Summer nor Winter
Neither Autumn nor Spring.
We have instead the days
When the gold sun shines on the lush green canefields—
Magnificently.
The days when the rain beats like bullets on the roofs
And there is no sound but the swish of water in the gullies
And trees struggling in the high Jamaica winds.
Also there are the days when the leaves fade from off guango trees
And the reaped canefields lie bare and fallow to the sun.
But best of all there are the days when the mango and the logwood blossom
When the bushes are full of the sound of bees and the scent of honey,
When the tall grass sways and shivers to the slightest breath of air,
When the buttercups have paved the earth with yellow stars
And beauty comes suddenly and the rains have gone.

----

1. RESPONDING TO THE POETRY

a. Each poem describes a season. Choose one poem and in your own words, explain what the poem expresses.

b. Which two poems use rhyme schemes? How does the use of rhyme affect the way you see or understand the images of the poem? Why do you think modern poetry rarely uses rhyming words?

c. Reread "A January Morning." What time period do you think it was written in? Include examples to support your opinion.

d. Which poem is your favourite? Write a paragraph giving reasons for your choice.

e. Think of a season you like and brainstorm with a partner words and phrases that come to mind. Use some or all of these words to describe one moment during this season, for example, winter's first thaw or a sudden summer shower.

2. **WRITING** DESCRIPTIVE POEM

Weather is a cyclical process. All the particular details change from year to year, but basically each season brings similar weather. Think of another example in nature that is cyclical, for example, the change from day to night. Write a poem describing part of this cycle. Try to use images, similes, and/or metaphors in your poem.

3. **WRITING** AN ESSAY

With a small group, discuss how each of the "seasons" poems is constructed. How do the poems differ in language, rhyme, and organization of stanzas?

There are many different ways to write a poem, from a regular pattern of metre or rhythm and rhyme to a free-flowing style that sounds like everyday speech. In a poetry anthology, find one more traditional poem and one modern poem. Look at the way they have been constructed and the language they use. Write an essay describing how the style of poetry differs. As you develop your essay consider the following ideas:

- Write a brief outline that states your position on the topic. Jot down notes for three or four arguments that support your opinion.
- Use the outline to write your essay. Think about the most effective arrangement of ideas.
- For every point on your outline, write one or two paragraphs providing supporting details and examples. End your essay with a concluding statement that reflects your opening paragraph.
- Read your essay. Did you state your thesis in the first paragraph? Do the following paragraphs offer supporting evidence? Is your argument reasonable and persuasive? Revise your essay so that each paragraph supports your thesis. You could work with a group or a partner to edit and revise your first and final drafts.

SELF-ASSESSMENT: Grade your essay according to some of the points mentioned under the last bullet above. What grade do you think your essay deserves?

Persephone

A Greek Myth retold by Ann Pilling

At the beginning of time, when the gods defeated the giants, the world was divided into three by the casting of lots. Zeus won the sky, and his brother Poseidon the sea. The underworld was left to Hades. He was a brooding, lonely god, and he begged Zeus to give him a wife from the land above. He had fallen in love with Persephone, the daughter of Demeter.

Demeter was the most powerful of all the goddesses; she ruled over every living thing on earth, and without her nothing would grow. Zeus knew that she would never agree to let her daughter marry Hades, and he feared her anger if he dared ask such a question. But the king of the underworld was determined that Persephone would be his wife, and he decided to carry her off by force.

For many days, he waited and watched. Then, one morning, he heard that she was out in the meadows on the slopes of Mount Etna, picking flowers with the Daughters of Ocean. These nymphs were very beautiful, but none of them so beautiful as the radiant Persephone. She outshone them as day outshines night.

Zeus had conspired with Hades to help him trap her, and now, at her feet, she saw a most marvellous plant appear from nowhere. It was a white narcissus with a hundred flowers growing from its root, a thing so lovely and so fragrant that not only mortals but the gods themselves wondered at it.

Persephone bent down to pick the flower. But, as her fingers closed on it, the mountain split open with a terrible roaring noise, and from the depths came Hades riding on his black chariot, pulled by huge black horses. With a cry of triumph, he swept the terrified Persephone up into the chariot and galloped away, down to the underworld.

GOALS AT A GLANCE

- Research and present myths from other cultures.
- Write a myth to demonstrate understanding of a form.

Two others knew about this cruel thing. One was old Hecate, the witch goddess, who had heard how the young woman cried out in terror. The other was Helios, god of the sun, who had seen the enormous black chariot rise up from the gash in the earth, and the greedy fingers of Hades, snatching the woman away. But, he was driving his sun horses across the sky and could not cease in his labours until the day was done.

Demeter also heard the echo of her daughter's voice, from far away, on Mount Parthenia, and she set off at once to find her, wandering over the earth, not stopping to eat or drink, and taking no rest. On the ninth day, she met old Hecate, who told her she had heard Persephone cry out on Mount Etna. Then she met Helios, who confessed that he too knew what had happened, and that Zeus had plotted to help his brother Hades by setting the white flower at Persephone's feet.

When she heard this, Demeter's grief turned to rage. She left Mount Olympus, where the gods lived, disguised herself as an old woman, and went to Eleusis, where she built a temple and spent long days there, mourning and weeping for her lost daughter.

And she turned her back upon the earth, and all that she must do there to make things grow. For a whole year, the land sent up no shoots, and cattle pulled ploughs across the fields in vain. The white barley seed fell useless from the sower's hand, and rotted where it lay.

People began to starve, and in alarm Zeus sent Iris, the goddess of the rainbow, down to earth to plead for mercy from the goddess of grain. But Demeter refused to listen to her, nor would she listen to Zeus's other messengers. Day after day, she sat alone in her temple at Eleusis, vowing that she would never return to Olympus, or allow any green thing to grow upon earth until Persephone was restored to her.

At last, Zeus sent his own son, Hermes, to plead with the god of the underworld. He knew the way well, for it was his task to lead the dead from earth down to the underworld. Sad-faced, he stood before Hades's throne, having taken off his winged sandals and set aside the gold rod with which he pointed the way. And the tragic Persephone, so small on her great black throne, listened in silence as he pleaded with her husband.

"Great Hades," he said. "Upon earth people are dying because Demeter has put a curse on all her crops. Release Persephone, I beg you. If you do not, Zeus will soon have no subjects to rule over. This kingdom too will die, for the world will be empty." And the tears ran down his face.

Hades thought for a moment, then rose, and put his queen's hand into that of Hermes. "Go," he said, "since Zeus commands it. But do not forget me, Persephone. I have been kind to you. Remember too that all the souls here remain your subjects, wherever you may be." And he turned away sadly, into his dark kingdom.

So they returned joyously to earth, and Persephone was restored to her mother's arms. But then the goddess drew back, for the stain of a fruit was upon the woman's mouth. "Did you eat in the underworld?" she asked fearfully.

"Only a few seeds from a pomegranate," answered the innocent Persephone. Then Demeter knew that Hades had tricked them, for whoever eats food in the kingdom of the dead cannot ever escape from it.

So Zeus made a pact with his brother, and for six months of the year Persephone has to live with her dark king, under the earth. In those short, hard days, nothing grows upon earth. Demeter mourns for her daughter in a dress of frost and snow.

When Persephone is restored to her, Demeter's heart grows light again. Spring comes, and blossom. After this, the summer opens out in glory, and then the rich harvest appears. Only when Hades claims his queen again does the year begin to sicken and die.

Then people remember Persephone, and they remember too that the dark and cold are only for a season and that the winter woods always contain the promise of a new spring.

----

1. RESPONDING TO THE MYTH

a. This myth explains a natural event that occurs each year. What is that event?

b. What narrative elements make the story of Persephone so dramatic and moving after several thousand years?

c. The ancient Greeks believed that the goddess Demeter "ruled over every living thing on Earth." People still refer to Earth as "Mother Earth" or "Mother Nature." Why do you think Earth is often identified as female rather than male?

d. Trickery and betrayal are recurring themes in ancient myths. What examples of trickery and betrayal do you find in "Persephone"?

2. RESEARCHING ANCIENT MYTHS

All ancient cultures had myths that explained Earth's natural forces. Look for a myth similar to Persephone from another civilization, such as ancient Egyptian myths of Osiris and Isis or the creation myths of Aboriginal North Americans. Think of a creative way to present the information you research, for example: a narrative structure similar to "Persephone," a narrative poem, or a Web site with visuals and "hot-linked" text.

STRATEGIES

3. WRITING A MYTH

People still tell, read, and enjoy the ancient myths because they explain complex phenomena in terms of human emotions, actions, and values. Think about a natural phenomenon that could be explained by a myth rather than a scientific principle, for example, ocean tides. Write your own myth explaining this phenomenon. As you develop the myth, consider the following ideas:

TIPS

- With a partner, develop a list of the features of myths. Use these features as you develop your myth.
- Decide on the setting. Traditional myths are set in the past. You may choose to develop a modern myth instead.
- Develop your characters and the plot. What adventures will you involve your characters in? Think about using gods and goddesses and other fantastic characters. What conflict or problem will need to be resolved?
- Use **personification** as a technique in your myth. Which non-human characters can be personified?

Personification is a figure of speech in which non-human things (animals, objects, and ideas) are described as if they were human. For example, "the storm came marching across the lake," describes a storm as if it had legs to march on.

PEER ASSESSMENT: Ask a classmate to read your myth. Does he or she find the explanation of the phenomenon believable? Is personification effectively used? What parts of the myth can be improved?

Naming the New One

Poem by John Daniel

They came from mountains and plains
to see the new one, the smooth-skin,
who stood on shaking hind legs
and stared, his eyes struck with light.

"He'll sleep cold," Bear grunted,
and walked away. Bigfoot
was already gone, scared,
and Hummingbird had things to do.

As the others walked and crawled
and flew by, the new one pointed
and hurled a sound at each of them,
louder and louder in his harsh joy.

"Those paws are no good," said Gopher.

"Call him *Wildmouth*," said Deer.
"Does he have ears?"

"He'll learn a song, maybe," said Owl.

Long after the new one stumbled away
they heard him crashing the brush,
still trailing his strange calls.

"Doesn't see where he's going,"
Cougar said.
       "Well," said Coyote,
"we'll always know when he's *coming*."

He acted brave, but he was nervous.
"Let's watch him for a while.
There's plenty of room. When he finds
his place, then we'll name him."

GOALS AT A GLANCE

- Write a poem.
- Analyse the use of oxymoron in a poem.

1. RESPONDING TO THE POEM

a. Who is the new one? What physical qualities does he have? Why is he a "he," not a "she"?

b. Why does each of the animals find the new one so contemptible? Could you describe the poem as a *satire*?

c. Write a description or a poem about the new one as he or she exists today. Include details about how the new one has changed in relation to other species. What has happened to the animals?

d. This poem has several features of an ancient myth. What are they? What do you think the poet's message is?

2. LITERATURE STUDIES OXYMORONS

"Harsh joy" is a striking example of an **oxymoron**. This figure of speech creates a *paradox* (a statement that may be true but seems to say two opposite things). With a partner, brainstorm a list of contradictory words that when put together form a startling new image, such as "a loud stillness" or "calm anger." Discuss the effects created.

> An **oxymoron** is a figure of speech in which contradictory words or connotations are placed together for a startling effect.

3. WRITING A POEM

Write a poem as a follow-up to "Naming the New One" in which you describe an encounter between a present-day human being and an animal. What has changed? What do they think of each other?

Think about how you can create vivid pictures to make your point. See "How to Write Poetry" on pages 186–187 for more help in developing your poem.

Why We Grow Insensitive to Dangers

Essay by David Suzuki

A child's exuberant exploration of the world is a magical opportunity for a parent to relive his or her own childhood. The joy and enthusiasm of my daughters' discoveries immediately revive my own memories of catching a luna moth, noticing parasites on a beetle, or discovering a kildare's nest with eggs. When my children were very young, I usually had to call them over to show them what and how to observe. But these days my teenage daughters, Severn and Sarika, are often the first to yell, "Come over here and see what I've found," or "What do you think this is?"

Age has taken its toll on my senses of smell, sight, and sound, and the girls are in better physical condition, so they're usually in front. But there's something else that explains why I'm slower to notice things. I'm preoccupied with my work and simply not as receptive to my surroundings as I once was.

In a crowded room, it's impressive to note our ability to focus on specific signals coming into our sense organs. It's possible to engage in an intense discussion with a single person even though there is a background din of many other conversations. Somehow we can filter out extraneous noise or ambience that we're not interested in. Youngsters amaze me with their claims of being able to concentrate on homework with the TV and stereo blaring.

GOALS AT A GLANCE

- Use oral communication skills in group discussions.
- Write a letter to the editor.

An Alaskan fur trapper once visited New York City for the first time. Walking along Times Square, he remarked, "I hear a cricket." His companion scoffed at the idea that a cricket could be heard amidst the cacophony of the city. The Alaskan took out a coin and flipped it into the air. Several passersby heard the coin land and glanced down to the spot, proving that we are sensitive to what we are conditioned to detect.

There is also a desensitizing phenomenon called *habituation*. When a sense organ is stimulated, it sends an electrical signal via neurons and it registers on our consciousness. But if the stimulus persists, the intensity of signals the neurons send to our brains gradually diminishes. Thus, a loud noise or sharp odour may be quite noticeable at first, but when it persists we aren't as aware of it after a while.

Most of us are urban dwellers living in an environment awash with stimuli. Whenever I'm filming in a city, I'm shocked at how noisy our surroundings can be. We often have to wait for long intervals until a plane passes overhead, a beeping truck backs up, or people talking pass out of range of the microphone. Yet most of the time we are oblivious to the sounds. We are so habituated that we hardly notice. Perhaps that explains the way a frightening problem like ozone depletion, global warming, or toxic pollution seems to become less urgent over time even though it hasn't been dealt with.

Habituation and our ability to concentrate by screening out incoming information may protect us from being overwhelmed by the dimensions of the global *ecocrisis*. Our lives revolve around recognizing the latest hit song, TV, or movie star, seeing a puck enter the net, or paying attention to Dow Jones averages. We are sensitive to clothing styles, cars, stores, and advertisements that dominate our physical surroundings.

If we were more sensitive to the condition of the planet's physical features, like the air, climate, plants, or animals, we might be climbing the barricades to protest the fact that sunny days that were always a reason to celebrate now threaten us with cancer; Lake Ontario fish are no longer consumable; and ancient forests, wetlands, and prairies are disappearing at a horrifying rate.

Jeff Gibbs, the founder of the Environmental Youth Alliance, was a city boy who went on a kayaking trip to the Queen Charlotte Islands as a teenager. In a bay surrounded by a forest, he was suddenly overwhelmed by the vastness and power of nature. "I suddenly realized that humans had nothing to do with these incredible forests," he told me. "They have always been there and go on without any input from us." This epiphany impelled Jeff into a career of environmental activism. Many people who are leaders in the environmental movement relate similar experiences that changed their lives.

In spite of my concerns for the state of the earth, I know I've also become insensitive to my surroundings. The real reason that my daughters are able to spot things so much faster than I is that I'm not focussed the way they are. My mind may literally be thousands of kilometres away, worried about some looming deadline. It takes a deliberate effort to shut off the filtering mechanisms of the "civilized" world in order to allow the senses to inform us about the state of our surroundings.

As our lives become increasingly dominated by the artifice of shopping malls and the electronic media, we need all the more the opportunity to experience the natural world. It is vital to plan nature into our urban surroundings, where most of us live and where today's children will spend their entire lives. It's time to rediscover the "real" world.

.. RIGHT BEFORE OUR EYES...

1. RESPONDING TO THE STORY

a. Do you agree or disagree with David Suzuki that people are often not sensitive to their natural environment? Give examples to support your opinion.

b. How aware are you of the space around you? Without giving it a thought, list the sounds you can hear right now. Now listen intently for five minutes and jot down what you hear. Compare the two lists. Do your lists prove or disprove what Suzuki called *habituation*?

c. Which type of place do you prefer to be in: an urban, human-made environment or the natural world? Explain the reasons for your choice.

2. ORAL LANGUAGE DISCUSS AN ISSUE

With a small group, discuss Suzuki's suggestions of what people can do to help preserve and sustain the natural world. What other steps can you as an individual take to help preserve the wilderness and save the environment? What do you think the government should be doing? What do you think your community should be doing? How can you make these organizations aware of your concerns?

3. WRITING A LETTER TO THE EDITOR

Look through a few newspapers to find examples of effective letters to the editor. With a partner, discuss why the ones you've chosen get their points across. Do they offer concrete examples to support the point of view? Do they use irony or satire to ridicule their targets or are the arguments sincere and moving?

Choose an environmental issue or another issue that you feel strongly about, and write your own letter to the editor. If you wish, send it to your local newspaper for possible publication.

4. MEDIA MESSAGES COMIC STRIPS

With a partner, discuss the comic strip on page 332. What is its message? How does it make you feel? How does it connect with David Suzuki's message in this essay? Together, look for other comic strips, magazine articles, and newspaper articles that focus on environmental messages. Compare their messages and the way they are presented.

These Canadian birds—some now extinct—were captured on canvas by the 19th century American naturalist and artist John James Audubon.

Audubon's
Vision of Nature

PAINTINGS BY JOHN JAMES AUDUBON
ARTICLE BY CHRISTINE MCCLYMONT

In the early 1800s, John James Audubon decided to paint all the species of birds in North America. At that time, the land and seas were teeming with wildlife. But within a century and a half, humans had destroyed much of the wilderness. Fortunately for us, Audubon's paintings survive to help us travel back to a more abundant past. And happily, many of the birds he painted are still around to be enjoyed.

Audubon's goals—to paint each bird life-size, in lifelike poses, and in the correct environmental setting—were not unique. His enormous impact resulted from the fact that he was a great artist, as well as having a detailed scientific knowledge of his subjects. His paintings were wildly popular in Europe, where prints were made and sold in the thousands. Viewers were amazed by the variety of unfamiliar birds and the way in which Audubon brought them vividly to life.

Although he spent years studying birds in the wild, Audubon actually painted in his studio using dead specimens—many of which he killed himself. This seems shocking, but remember that during his time the quantity of birds was immense and the conservation movement had barely begun. Audubon did, in fact, speak out against the mass slaughter of birds for food and fashion, when he saw it happening.

Canadian wildlife historian David Lank sums up the lasting appeal of Audubon's bird paintings: "It was Audubon's unmatched understanding of Nature that gave eternal colour to his wilderness palette."

GOALS AT A GLANCE

- Write a journal entry in role.
- Analyse paintings.

Passenger Pigeon.
COLUMBA MIGRATORIA.
Male 1. Female 2.

PASSENGER PIGEON

In the 1830s, a Canadian settler recorded that during one fall migration, so many passenger pigeons passed over his cabin that, "for three days, I never saw the sun." Migrating flocks contained more than a billion birds. Yet these birds disappeared in less than one hundred years, due to hunting and the destruction of the forests. Now the passenger pigeon is a symbol of extinction, which makes Audubon's painting of a peaceful pair so poignant.

GREAT BLUE HERON

Audubon's project was to paint all North American birds life-size. The great blue heron stands 1.3 m tall, so depicting this giant in a standard-sized frame was a challenge. Audubon accomplished the feat by showing the heron bending its long neck to spear a fish. The soft plumes covering the bird's lower neck and back are part of a special display for mating season. Great blue herons can frequently be seen perched on the shores of Canadian lakes.

ARCTIC TERN

"Light as a sylph, the arctic tern dances through the air above and around you," wrote Audubon during his voyage to Labrador and eastern Canada in 1833. Diving on folded wings, the sea bird in Audubon's painting seems to fill the sky. Thankfully, terns were saved from extinction—by laws passed in England. At the time, wild-bird feathers on women' hats were all the rage.

Arctic terns migrate up to 15 000 km each way, and live up to 27 years in the wild.

1. RESPONDING TO THE ARTICLE

a. Which of the paintings did you find most appealing? Explain.

b. The article states that the extinction of the passenger pigeon was caused by people. To counter this negative act, think of something positive that humans have done in recent history. In a paragraph, explain why your example shows that there is hope for *Homo sapiens*.

c. There is a hypothesis in science that states that you cannot study something without changing it in some way. With this hypothesis in mind, compare the different ways John Audubon and Jane Goodall confronted and studied nature. What merits (if any) do either of these approaches have? Which approach do you most agree with? Explain.

2. VISUAL COMMUNICATION VIEW THE PAINTINGS

With a partner, discuss how Audubon uses elements of colour, line, shape, texture, and size to create an impact on the viewer. After your discussion, use the following questions to help you analyse the paintings:

- What parts of each painting are your eyes drawn to? Why?
- What information do the paintings give you about each bird and its habitat?
- What mood or feelings do the paintings evoke?

SELF-ASSESSMENT: Explain to your partner why you reacted in a certain way to the paintings.

3. WRITING JOURNAL ENTRY

Imagine what Canada might have been like before the great wave of European settlement—few people, land without modern towns and roads, pristine forests and grasslands, and countless wild animals. Record your thoughts in the form of a journal, as if you were either the first European to see this land, or one of the Aboriginal people already living here.

4. READING FIELD GUIDES

The modern version of what Audubon accomplished, a visual record of nature, can be found in what are called "field guides." Field guides are designed to enable observers to identify plants, birds, animals, shells, or rocks by offering pictures and useful text about individual types.

Find an example of a field guide in your library. Outline the way each entry is organized. Choose something you are familiar with, for example, dogs, popular music bands, or computer games. Create a brief field guide giving information about your topic. Be sure to include photos or drawings for each entry in your field guide.

REFLECTING ON THE UNIT

SELF-ASSESSMENT: RESEARCHING

As you worked on this unit, what did you learn about

- sources of information?
- developing questions to guide your research?
- assessing the credibility of sources?
- evaluating the relevance of information?
- assessing the bias of sources?

WRITING AN ESSAY

What view or impression do you have of nature? How do you relate and interact with it? Write a sentence that expresses your feelings about or relationship to nature. Develop your sentence into a thesis and use it as the basis for an essay about nature.

ORAL LANGUAGE PANEL DISCUSSION

With a small group, choose an environmental issue that has recently been discussed in your community or province. For example, issues such as transforming large tracts of farmland into suburban developments, logging in wilderness parks, and polluting water systems continue to be debated across Canada. Conduct a panel discussion on your chosen topic.

Abbreviation An abbreviation is a short form of a longer word. Abbreviations are frequently used in informal or technical writing.

Active Voice In the active voice the subject of a verb does the action. *The dog bit my friend.* See **Passive Voice**.

Adjective An adjective is a word that describes a noun or pronoun: *Her icy green eyes stared at the stars.* Adjectives, as well as describing, can also limit a noun: *I saw two movies on the weekend.*

Adverb An adverb is a word that modifies a verb, an adjective, or another adverb. *The rain fell steadily.*

Alliteration Alliteration involves the repetition of the same first sound in a group of words or line of poetry: *The sun sank slowly.*

Allusion An allusion is an indirect reference to a person, story, or situation in literature or history.

Anecdote An anecdote is a brief story that retells an incident or event. Like a story, it can be sad, funny, or adventurous, and often has a plot, characters, and setting.

Antagonist An antagonist is the person or thing in a story in conflict with the main character, or protagonist.

Apostrophe ['] An apostrophe has many uses. It can
- show possession: *Pierre's car*
- indicate a contraction: *I've, we're*
- replace missing letters: *How 'bout you?*
- show the plural of letters or symbols: *There are three 0's in 2000 and two o's in Ontario.*

- replace missing numbers in a date: *class of '10*

Assonance Assonance is the repetition of similar vowel sounds in neighbouring words. An example is *sweet dreams.* This technique is frequently used in poetry.

Ballad A ballad is a narrative poem that tells an exciting story in a series of vivid pictures. The stanzas are usually four lines each with a regular pattern of rhythm and rhyme.

Bias Bias involves the use of sexist and racist language. See **Racist Language** and **Sexist Language**.

Character A character is a person in a narrative (story, poem, or script). Characters are important because they're the ones that readers will like or identify with. Often, a character has what is called a *fatal flaw*—something in his or her personality that leads to a downfall.
- The main character (protagonist) should interest your audience. Readers need to feel a connection to this character.

- The antagonist is the person or thing working against the main character.

Clause A clause is a group of related words that has both a subject and a verb or verb phrase.
A **main clause** is an independent sentence: *I shut the door.*
A **subordinate clause** is not a complete sentence and doesn't stand alone as a sentence: *Although she missed the bus.*

Cliff-hanger A cliff-hanger is a story that contains a lot of suspense, especially a serial in which each episode ends with the hero in a dangerous situation. A cliff-hanger is also a technique that writers use to add suspense to the story. The reader is left hanging at a pivotal moment. See **Suspense.**

Climax   The climax is the most important, and usually the most exciting, part of a story. All the action builds up to this point. After the climax, the story winds down to its conclusion.

Colloquialism   A colloquialism is a word or phrase used in everyday speech, but not in formal language. *I've had it!* is an example of a colloquial expression.

Colon [:]   A colon is a punctuation mark that directs the reader's attention to what follows. Use colons in the following situations:
• introducing a list
• beginning a quotation in formal writing
• expressing time: *8:45, 20:00*
• separating the volume and page numbers of a magazine: *Food Lover's Digest, 4:17–19*
• addressing a business letter: *Dear Mr. Rosen:*

Comma [,]   A comma is a mark of punctuation that indicates a slight pause in a sentence. Common practice, especially in informal writing, is to use as few commas as possible without obscuring the meaning. Use commas as follows:
• between compound sentences: *Carmen thought quickly, but no solutions came to mind.*
• with nouns of address: *David, close the door.*
• with words, phrases, or clauses that interrupt a sentence: *We will, <u>however</u>, do what we can. Chuck was delighted when, <u>for the first time</u>, the baby smiled.*
• with introductory phrases, or clauses: <u>*Naturally*</u>*, I was pleased.* <u>*When we had finished dinner*</u>*, we went to a movie.*
• between items in a series: *Ravi, Jim, and Maria went to school together.*
• to set off *which* clauses: *The house,* <u>*which I own*</u>*, is on the seaside.*
• in some forms of dates: *June 18, 2000* BUT *15 June 2000.*
• in addresses: *Apt. 6, 123 Park Lane*
• between a city and a country: *Ottawa, Canada*
• after the salutation in a personal letter: *Dear Sammy,*
• to set off degrees and titles: *Lorraine Markotic, M.P., John Collins, Ph.D.*

Conflict   Conflict is a problem or struggle in a story that the main character has to solve or face. Conflict is created in four classic ways: human against self, human against human, human against nature, and human against society. Writers may choose to use more than one conflict in a story, which can create an exciting plot.

Conjunction   A conjunction is a part of speech that is used to connect and relate words or sentences. There are three main types of conjunctions:
• co-ordinating *(and, or, nor, for, but, so, yet): Carla and I are best friends.*
• subordinating *(whenever, after, if, since, because, before, unless): I break out in a sweat whenever I get on an elevator.*
• correlative *(but...and, either...or, neither ...nor, not only...but also): My watch is neither on my wrist nor by my bed.*

Connotation   The connotation of a word is an added meaning that suggests something positive or negative. *She <u>snickered</u> when I spoke* suggests "mocking." The word *snickered* has a negative connotation.

Consonance   Consonance is the repetition of similar consonants within words. An example is *wonder/wander.* Consonance is sometimes used as a technique in poetry.

Couplet   A couplet is two successive lines of verse that rhyme and have the same number of metrical feet: *Be not the first by whom the new is tried/Nor yet the last to lay the old aside.*

Dash [—] The dash is a punctuation mark used to indicate a pause or break in a sentence.

Debate A debate is a formal argument, often in a public setting, for and against an issue or question.

Denotation The denotation of a word is its exact meaning as stated in a dictionary.

Ellipsis Points [...] Ellipsis points are a series of dots used to show that something has been left out. Use ellipsis points as follows:
- to show that one or more words have been left out of a quotation. Indicate deleted words within a sentence by three dots (...).
- to indicate that a sentence or thought has been left unfinished

Explicit Meaning Explicit meaning refers to ideas and concepts that are stated clearly and openly. See Implicit Meaning.

Fable A fable is a story that was created to teach a lesson. It is not necessarily a true story.

Figurative Language Figurative language is heightened, imaginative language characterized by simile, metaphor, personification, and so on: *The wind howled like an angry giant.*

Five W's The five W's of journalism are the questions that every newspaper or magazine article should answer: *who, what, where, when, why* (and sometimes *how*). By the end of the article, the reader should know who was involved in the story or event, what happened, where it happened, when it happened, why it happened, and how it happened.

Flashback A flashback is an event or scene that took place at an earlier point in a story. Writers use flashbacks to explain something that is presently occurring in a story. Flashbacks can also explain a charac-

ter's motivation and help to clear up any unanswered questions in the plot.

Foreshadowing Foreshadowing occurs when the author hints at what will happen in the story, adding interest. The hint, however, should not be too obvious to the reader because it will give away the plot and affect the suspense. Foreshadowing is used mainly in mysteries and suspense stories, but it can be used in other genres as well.

Free Verse Free verse is poetry written without using a regular metrical pattern. It is based on natural expression and the rhythms of ordinary language rather than a specific form.

Homophones Homophones are two words that are pronounced alike but are spelled differently, such as *hear* and *here.* Homophones can be confused easily in speech and writing.

Hyperbole Hyperbole is the obvious exaggeration of facts for effect: *Waves high as mountains broke over the reef.*

Hyphen [-] A hyphen is a punctuation mark that resembles a short dash. Use hyphens in
- compound numbers between 21 and 99: *twenty-one*
- time: *the six-thirty bus*
- fractions: *one-third of the cake*
- some numerical expressions: *a five-year-old girl; a fifty-dollar bill*
- dividing a word between syllables at the end of a line: *dis-satisfied; dissat-isfied; dissatis-fied*
- some expressions with prefixes: *all-round, co-operate; de-ice, pro-Canadian*
- when a compound modifier comes before a noun, unless the first word ends in *-ly*: *rosy-fingered dawn; black-eyed Susan* BUT *carefully woven cloth*
- some compound words: since compound words are often written as one word

(*nighttime*), or as two words with or without a hyphen (*check-out, check mark*), it is best to consult a dictionary

Idiom An idiom is an expression that has a meaning that is different from the usual meaning of the individual words within it. *To be in hot water* means to be in trouble, not immersed in warm liquid.

Imagery Imagery is a technique poets and writers use to describe and appeal to the senses. There are many types of imagery, including simile, metaphor, alliteration, and personification.

Implicit Meaning Implicit meaning refers to ideas and concepts that are not stated directly, but are nevertheless present. See Explicit Meaning.

Interjection An interjection is an expression of surprise, sorrow, or delight, with no grammatical connection to what precedes or follows it. For example, *Wow! Look at that UFO!*

Irony Irony is the use of an idea, word, or phrase to elicit the opposite of its usual meaning. For example, calling a small bungalow a *mansion* is irony. Two common types of irony are dramatic and situational. **Dramatic irony** occurs when the audience knows something that a character does not. **Situational irony** takes place when circumstances turn out differently from what the reader expects or anticipates.

Jargon is the language of a particular group or profession. For example, legal jargon refers to terms commonly used by those who practise law.

Lead A lead is the opening paragraph of a newspaper or magazine article. The lead should contain as many of the answers to the five W's of journalism as possible: *who, what, when, where,* and *why.*

Logo A logo is an identifying symbol or image that is used in advertising. An example is Nike's swoosh.

Memoir A memoir is the recording of a person's own experiences, and involves the retelling of memorable experiences from that person's life. Each experience is told like a story, and is written from the first-person point of view (using the pronouns *I, me, we,* and *us*). A memoir is not necessarily told in chronological order, but in a way that appeals to the writer and has value for the reader.

Metaphor A metaphor is a comparison that likens one thing to something else, suggesting that they share a common quality: *a heart of stone, a copper sky.* As well as painting vivid pictures for the reader, metaphors help to make abstract ideas more concrete, add emotion, and show the writer's feelings.

Monologue A monologue is a long speech or part of a play in which one person speaks alone.

Mood The mood or atmosphere is the feeling that pervades a piece of writing or work of art. *The mood of* Frankenstein *is sombre and dark.* Mood is created through description, plot, and setting.

Myth A myth is a traditional story about superhuman beings, such as gods, goddesses, heroes, and monsters, and usually explains the origins of a natural event, force, or cultural practice. Some myths teach values, for example, humility.

Narration Narration is the telling of an event or series of events. Narration is used in all types of writing, including narratives, plays, and poetry.

Narrator The narrator is the person or character telling a story. See Point of View.

Noun A noun is a word that refers to people, places, qualities, things, actions, or ideas. *When <u>Joe</u> was at the <u>library</u> in <u>Guelph</u>, <u>curiosity</u> caused him to read an <u>article</u> that claimed <u>fear</u> could be cured by <u>meditation</u>.*

Object The English language has three types of objects. In the following examples, the direct object is in italics, and the indirect object is underlined.

- A **direct object** is a noun or pronoun that answers the question *what?* or *who?* about the verb: He bought a *car*.
- An **indirect object** is a noun or pronoun that answers the question *to what? for what?* or *for whom?* about the verb: He bought <u>me</u> a *car*.
- The **object of the preposition** is a noun or pronoun that comes at the end of a phrase that begins with a preposition: He bought a car for <u>me</u>.

Onomatopoeia Onomatopoeia refers to words that imitate sounds. *Hiss, thud, crash, hush,* and *twitter* are examples of onomatopoeic words.

Oxymoron An oxymoron is a figure of speech in which contradictory words or connotations are placed together for effect; for example, jumbo shrimp.

Paragraph A paragraph is a group of sentences that develops one aspect of a topic or one phase of a narrative. The sentences in a paragraph should be clearly related to each other. Sometimes, especially in essays, the point being developed is expressed in a topic sentence, and the other sentences expand on this statement.
A **descriptive paragraph** describes a person, place, thing, or idea.
A **narrative paragrap**h tells a story by sharing the details of an event or experience.
A **persuasive paragraph** expresses the writer's opinion about a topic or subject, and tries to convince the reader to agree with it. A topic sentence is often used to state the point of view. Accompanying sentences attempt to prove the topic sentence.
An **expository paragraph** gives step-by-step instructions about how to do something. It may give directions and explain ideas. Transitional expressions such as *first* and *next* are often used to show sequence and order in this type of paragraph.
A **dialogue paragraph** is used mainly in stories. These are the words spoken by the characters in a story. Every time a new character speaks, a new paragraph is used. Dialogue paragraphs are enclosed in quotation marks.

Parallel Structure In a sentence, two or more elements that are of equal importance, expressed in similar grammatical terms to emphasize their relationship, are called parallel. Sentences without parallel structure can sound both confusing and awkward. Parallel structure is especially important in lists—with expressions like *both...and, not only...but also, whether...or,* and *either...or*—and in words, phrases, and clauses.

Not Parallel:	Campers are taught hiking, swimming, and how to paddle a canoe.
Parallel:	Campers are taught hiking, swimming, and canoeing.
Not Parallel:	Raoul can't decide whether to work as a lifeguard or if he would prefer to be a teacher.
Parallel:	Raoul can't decide whether to work as a lifeguard or as a teacher.

Parentheses [( )] Parentheses are used to set off comments or asides in a sentence. They are also used within scripts to frame stage directions.

Parody A parody is a humorous imitation of a serious piece of writing. It makes fun by imitating.

Passive Voice In the passive voice, the subject of the verb receives the action. *My friend was bitten by the dog.* See **Active Voice**.

Personification Personification occurs when non-human things (animals, objects, and ideas) are described as if they were human. *The storm came marching across the lake* describes a storm as if it had legs to walk on. Personification is used most often in poetry and narrative writing, but it can also be used in other forms.

Phrase A phrase is a group of words that does *not* have both a subject and a verb.
Marcella spoke *for the first time.*
  (prepositional phrase)
Thinking fast, I covered my ears
  (participial phrase)
Catrina wants *to be a scientist.*
  (infinitive phrase)

Plot The plot refers to the events in a story that make up the action. The plot usually has five elements: exposition (set-up), rising action, climax, falling action, and resolution.
- The **exposition** sets up the story by introducing the main characters, the setting, and the problem to be solved.
- The **rising action** is the main part of the story where the problem fully develops. A number of events are involved that will lead to the climax.
- The **climax** is the highest point in the story and is where the most exciting events occur.
- The **falling action** follows the climax. It contains the events that bring the story to its conclusion.
- The **resolution** or **denouement** is the end of the story when the main problem has been solved.

Point of View Point of view refers to the position from which the events of a story are presented to us. There are two main points of view: first person and third person.
- **First-person** point of view means that the story is told from one character's point of view. Told through one's character eyes, the events are coloured by that character's experience.
- The **third-person** point of view means that the story is told by an onlooker or narrator. There are two third-person points of view: **omniscient** and **limited.** In the omniscient point of view, the narrator knows everything about all of the characters and events, and can shift from character to character. In the limited point of view, the story is told through one character's, or a group of characters', eyes.
- Many modern authors use a "multiple point of view" in which we are shown events from the positions of two or more different characters.

Prefix A prefix is a syllable or full word added to the beginning of a word that changes its meaning or forms a new word. Some common prefixes are *dis-, un-, pre-, under-,* and *co-.*

Preposition A preposition is a word that shows a relationship between a noun (called the *object of the preposition*) and some other word in the sentence. Some words that sometimes function as prepositions include *above, at, before, behind, until,* and *with.* In the following example, the prepositions are underlined, and the objects of the prepositions are in italics: The house <u>in</u> *the valley* was swept away <u>by</u> *the flood.*

Profile A profile is a concise description of a person's abilities, character, or career.

Pronoun A pronoun is a word that replaces a noun or another pronoun. Some common pronouns include *I, it, me, he, she, we,* and *them.*

Protagonist The protagonist is the main character in a story.

Quatrain A quatrain is a stanza or poem of four lines. It usually has an alternating rhyme scheme, for example, *abab* or *abcb.*

Quotation Marks [" "] Show a direct quotation by enclosing words in quotation marks.

- Separate the words that introduce the quotation (*Camila asked*) from the quotation itself by commas: *Camila asked, "Where is the notebook that you borrowed from me?"*
- A question mark or exclamation mark goes inside the quotation marks if it relates to the quoted material, and outside if it applies to the whole sentence: *Theo called out, "Where are you going?" I'm sick of hearing you say, "I'll clean it up tomorrow"!*
- A period or comma at the end of a quotation goes inside the quotation marks: *"The trouble is," he muttered, "I can't get the machine to work."*
- A semicolon at the end of a quotation goes outside the quotation marks: *Kathy announced, "I don't want any more cookies, thank you"; then she sank back down in the bed and slept until morning.*
- A quotation within a quotation should be marked by single quotation marks: *Camila wailed, "Did I hear you say, 'I lost them both'?"*
- You can use quotation marks in place of italics or underlining to indicate that a word is being defined or explained: *The term "downsizing" is a euphemism that usually means firing a lot of employees.*

Racist Language Racist language refers to particular cultural or ethnic groups in insulting terms. Racist language can also exist in more subtle forms; be sensitive to this.

- Mention a person's race only if it is relevant.
- If a person's race or ethnic origin is relevant, be as specific as possible:

Irrelevant/Vague: *Dago is African.*
Relevant/Less Vague: *Dago is proud of her Nigerian heritage.*

- Avoid making generalizations about any racial or cultural group:

Stereotype: *The Welsh are great singers.*
Better: *The Welsh have a long tradition of singing.*

- The word *ethnic* should only be used as an adjective, not as a noun.

Inappropriate: *Many ethnics live in this area.*
Better: *Many different ethnic groups live in this area.*

Rhyme Rhyme is the repetition of sound in different words, especially at the ends of words. For example, *see* rhymes with *bee*. Rhyme is one of the main techniques used in poetry.

Rhyme Scheme A rhyme scheme is the pattern of end rhymes used in a poem. It is usually indicated by letters, for example, *abba abba cde cde* and *abab cdcd efef gg* are both rhyme schemes for a type of poem called a *sonnet*.

Rhythm Rhythm is the arrangement of beats in a line of poetry. The beat is created by the accented and unaccented syllables in the words used in each line.

Run-on Sentence A run-on sentence is formed when two sentences are run into one another. To fix a run-on sentence, add the proper punctuation or change the wording to make it a single sentence or two sentences.

Run-on: *The sky is clear it is spring at last.*
Better: *The sky is clear; it is spring at last.*
                OR
The sky is clear, and it is spring at last.
                OR
The sky is clear because it is spring at last.
                OR
The sky is clear. It is spring at last.

When two sentences are separated by a

comma, it is called a comma splice. Fix the comma splice the same way you would fix a run-on sentence.

Comma Splice: *The doctor said I need rest, I am taking the week off.*

Better: *The doctor said I need rest; I am taking the week off.*

OR

The doctor said I need the rest, so I am taking the week off.

OR

Because the doctor said I need rest, I am taking the week off.

Satire A satire is a type of writing that uses humour and irony to point out the shortcomings of an organization, person, or society. "Man, You're a Great Player!" is an example of satire.

Science Fiction A science-fiction story takes readers to other worlds or times. Science-fiction writers sometimes base their stories on scientific facts or possibilities that haven't been proven yet. Plots often deal with the impact of science and technology on humans and the world. Popular science-fiction themes include space travel, time travel, advanced technology, and life in the future.

Script A script is a story written to be performed as a play, movie, or TV show. The script tells a story using setting, plot, and characters. The story is told both through dialogue between characters and narration. Characters are usually listed on the left side of a script, with their "lines" on the right. Scripts also contain stage directions for setting up the stage and instructing the actors.

Semicolon [;] A semicolon is a mark of punctuation. Use a semicolon to separate two related sentences: *I love watching TV after school; it relaxes me.*

- A semicolon may also be used along with a co-ordinating conjunction (*and, or, nor, for, but, so, yet*) to join main clauses, if one or more of the clauses already contains a comma: *I threw on my coat, picked up my wallet, and raced to the bus stop; but the bus had already left.*
- Semicolons are also used to separate items in a list when one or more of these contains a comma: *Walter has lived in Tokyo, Japan; London, England; and Estavan, Saskatchewan.*

Sentence A sentence is a group of words that expresses a complete thought. Every sentence needs a subject and a verb.

A **simple sentence** has one subject and one verb: *Yukio's house has five bedrooms.*

A **compound sentence** has two or more main clauses (that is, smaller sentences that can stand alone). The sentences are usually joined together by a semicolon, or by a comma or semicolon followed by *and, or, nor, for, but, so,* or *yet: Yukio's house has five bedrooms, and the yard is huge.*

A **complex sentence** has a main clause that can stand alone as a sentence, and one or more subordinate clauses that cannot. In the following, the main clause is underlined and the subordinate clause is in italics:

<u>Yukio's house</u>, *which he built himself,* <u>has five bedrooms</u>.

Sentence Fragment A sentence fragment is a group of words that resemble a sentence, but lack either a verb or a subject. Sentence fragments are acceptable in informal writing, dialogue, and spoken English, but not in formal writing.

Fragment: *We went to the game on Saturday. Josh and I.* (lacks a verb)

Revised: *Josh and I went to the game on Saturday.*

Fragment: *Never did understand those engines.* (lacks a subject)

Revised: *I never did understand those engines.*

Setting The setting refers to where and when a story takes place. Setting plays an important role in many types of stories—for example, science fiction, historical fiction, fantasy, and adventure.

Sexist Language Sexist language can degrade either women or men. As with racist language, it is best to avoid generalizations unless you are basing your claims on scientific fact.

• Whenever possible, replace words such as *fireman, policeman, and man-made* with non-sexist alternatives such as *firefighter, police officer*, and *fabricated*.

• Avoid using the masculine pronouns *he, him, his* (or the feminine pronouns, *she, her, hers*) to refer to both women and men. Instead, try one or more of the following methods:

• Use the plural.

Sexist: *A good teacher can always command the respect of his students.*

Better: *Good teachers can always command the respect of their students.*

• Replace the pronoun with *the, a,* or *an*.

Sexist: *Whoever holds the winning ticket has not claimed her prize.*

Better: *Whoever holds the winning ticket has not claimed the prize.*

• Substitute *one* or *you*. Use *one* in more formal writing.

Sexist: *A man never knows when his time will come.*

Better: *You never know when your time will come.*

Simile A simile is a comparison that uses the words *like* or *as: My ears buzzed like a mosquito*. Similes are used in both prose and poetry.

Slang Slang is very informal language. It might be used in dialogue between characters, but it is never used in formal writing.

Slogan A slogan is a short, catchy phrase used by a business to advertise its product or service. Slogans occur often in print, radio, and TV ads. Along with a logo, a good slogan will instantly bring to mind the product it advertises.

Sonnet A sonnet is a poem with fourteen lines and a specific rhyme scheme. An **Italian** or **Petrarchan sonnet** contains an eight-line octet of two quatrains, followed by a six-line sestet. An **English** or **Shakespearean sonnet** contains three quatrains and a final couplet.

Split Infinitive A split infinitive occurs when an adverb is placed between *to* and a verb. Try to avoid this construction, unless avoiding it will make the sentence sound awkward or confusing.

Split: *I want <u>to really try hard</u> in science this year.*

Better: *I want <u>to try really hard</u> in science this year.*

Split: *He's going <u>to fully recover</u> from the accident.*

Better: *He's going <u>to recover fully</u> from the accident.*

Split: *The girl pretended to almost drop the card.*

Confusing: *The girl pretended almost to drop the card.*

Stanza A stanza is a group of lines of poetry arranged according to a fixed plan. Stanzas usually contain the same number of lines, metre, and rhyme scheme. The term *stanza* is most often used to refer to groups of four lines or more. The four-line quatrain is the most common. In printed poems, stanzas are usually separated by spaces. Stanzas are used to organize a poem in much the same way paragraphs are used to organize prose. In free verse, a poem may be organized by stanzas, but it will not have a regular rhyme scheme.

Stereotype A stereotype is an oversimplified picture of a group of people, giving them all a set of characteristics without consideration for individual differences. Avoid stereotypes in your writing. Try to create fresh, real characters.

Storyboard A storyboard is a series of drawings used to plan a film, TV show, presentation, and so on.

Subject-Verb Agreement A verb should always agree in number with its subject. Singular subjects take singular verbs, and a plural subject takes a plural verb. When you are looking for the subject of the verb, remember the following tips:
- Prepositional phrases like *at school, under my desk, through the woods,* and *with great sadness* never contain the subject of the sentence.

Wrong: *One of the cars were stolen.* (*cars* is not the subject)
Corrected: *One of the cars was stolen.* (the subject *one* needs a singular verb)

- *There* and *here* are not usually the subject of the verb.
    There are many reasons why I like you. (subject is *reasons*)
- If a subject has two parts, joined by *or, not,* or *neither...nor,* make the verb agree with the part of the subject that is nearest to it.
    Neither my brother nor <u>my parents were</u> at my recital.
    Neither my brother nor <u>my sister was</u> at my recital.
- Some subjects look like they are plural, but they are really singular.
    <u>The Diviners *is a remarkable book.*</u>
    <u>The news *is about to come on.*</u>
    <u>Five dollars *is not enough to go to a movie.*</u>

Suffix A suffix is an ending attached to the end of a word that changes its meaning. Some common suffixes are *-less, -ish, -hood, -ous, -ness,* and *-ment.*

Suspense Suspense is a feeling of tension, anxiety, or excitement resulting from uncertainty. An author creates suspense to keep readers interested. See **cliff-hanger**.

Symbol A symbol is a person, place, thing, or event that stands for or represents something else. For example, a flag is a symbol of a nation.

Synonym Synonyms are words that mean roughly the same thing, although they may differ in the way they are used or in the shade of meaning they imply. For example, *discuss, talk,* and *chat* can all be said to mean more or less the same thing, but each has a different use, or connotation: *The council discussed the proposal at length. We need to talk to you about your report card. Eli chatted with me on the phone.* When choosing the right word for a particular context, check your dictionary or thesaurus.

Tense The tense of a verb indicates whether the action took place in the past, present, or future. It is important not to switch tenses in the middle of a piece of writing. If you have chosen to write in the present tense, for example, remember to be consistent.

Theme The theme of a story represents what the protagonist discovers about life. Common examples of theme include loneliness, betrayal, and family.

Thesis Statement The thesis statement is a sentence, or group of sentences, in an essay that states the writer's point of view and purpose. It usually appears in the first or second paragraph of an essay.

Tone Tone is the mood of a piece of writing. It can reflect the author's attitude or feeling toward a subject or a reader—for example, formal, intimate, serious, ironic, or sarcastic.

Verb A verb is a word that expresses an action or a state of being. Verbs that express a state of being are sometimes called linking verbs, because they link the subject to another word that describes it.
Action verb: *Sunil* <u>ran</u> *to school.*
Linking verb: *Mariko* <u>seemed</u> *tired.*
The verb *be* is the most common linking verb, but the verbs *seem, appear, feel, smell,* and *look* can also act as linking verbs.

INDEX OF ACTIVITIES

ACKNOWLEDGMENTS

Every reasonable effort has been made to trace owner-ship of copyrighted material. Information that would enable the publisher to correct any reference or credit in future editions would be appreciated.

10–11 "Superman's Song" written by Brad Roberts. © 1991 Polygram International Publishing, Inc.; Door Number Two Music; and Dummies Productions Inc. Used by permission. All Rights Reserved. / **12–14** "Action Hero" by Rulon Openshaw. Reprinted with permission of the author. / **16–23** 'The Michelle I Know" by Alison Lohans from *Laws of Emotion* (Thistledown Press, 1993). Reprinted with permission. / **25** "Laura Secord" by Raymond Souster is reprinted from *Collected Poems of Raymond Souster* by permission of Oberon Press. / **26** "Goliath" by Melanie Doane/Rick Neigher. © 1998 Sony/ATV Music Publishing Canada/Sylvan St. Songs. All rights o\b\o Sony ATV Music Publishing Canada, administered by Sony/ATV Music Publishing Canada, 1121 Leslie St., Toronto, ON, Canada M3C 2J9. / **28–30** "Rosa Parks's Heroism Still Inspires" by Sandy Banks, Los Angeles Times Syndicate. / **32–34** "Tom Jackson" by Brian Bergman, *Maclean's* Magazine, December 21/98. Reprinted with permission. / **38–39** "An Open Heart" by Judith MacKenzie appearing in *Coast to Coast*, edited by James Barry. © Judith MacKenzie from *The Fourth Morningside Papers*, published by McClelland & Stewart, Inc. *The Canadian Publishers.* / **53–55** "Man, You're a Great Player!" by Gary Lautens from *The Act of Writing* by Mary and Ronald Conrad. Reprinted with permission of McGraw-Hill Ryerson. / **60–65** "The Crystal Stars Have Just Begun to Shine" by Martha Brooks from *Paradise Café and Other Stories* (Thistledown Press, 1988). Reprinted with per-mission. / **70–83** "War" by Timothy Findley from *Dinner Along the Amazon* by Timothy Findley. © 1984 by Pebble Productions Inc. Reprinted by permis-sion of Penguin Books Canada Limited. / **84–89** "The Sniper" by Liam O'Flaherty from *Spring Sowing* (pub-lished by Jonathan Cape). Reprinted by permission of The Random House Group Ltd. on behalf of the Estate of Liam O'Flaherty. / **92–95** "Blue Against White" by Jeannette Armstrong. Reprinted with permission of Theytus Books Ltd. on behalf of Jeannette Armstrong. / **118–119** "The Product Is Nothing™" by Hilary Keever from *Adbusters* (Winter 1999, No. 24), The Media Foundation. / **121–125** "Market Savvy Teens" by Kathy Friedman and Lauren Krugel from *The Toronto Star* (Tuesday, October 5, 1999), pp. D1, D4. Reprinted by permission of Young People's Press. / **136** "The Forecast" by Dan Jaffe. Reprinted with permission of the author. / **138–139** "Bad Driving" from *Red Green Talks Cars: A Love Story* by Steve Smith, Rick Green, and Peter Wildman. Reprinted by

permission of CDG Books. / **141–144** "Mary, Mary Quite Contrary" by Charlotte Gray from *Chatelaine* magazine (December '95). Reprinted by permission of the author, courtesy of Chatelaine magazine © Rogers Publishing Ltd. / **154–158** "The Saga of Filming *Never Cry Wolf*" by Bruce Brown. Reprinted with permission from the February 1984 *Reader's Digest*. / **162–163** "Internet Is Hero's Window" by Maria Bellaby from *The Toronto Star* (Friday, September 17, 1999), pp. F1, F3. Reprinted by permission of Associated Press. / **164–165** ""Web Tips: The Equation." Reprinted with permission of inSites web design. / **170–176** "I've Got Gloria" by M. E. Kerr. © 1997 by M. E. Kerr from *No Easy Answers: Short Stories about Making Tough* by Donald Gallo, editor. Used by permission of Random House Children's Books, a division of Random House Inc. / **179–182** "The Adventurous Life of John Goddard" from *The Morningside World of Stuart McLean* by Stuart McLean. © 1989 by Stuart McLean. Reprinted by permission of Penguin Books Canada Limited. / **184–185** "Dry Spell" and "An Exchange of Gifts" from *The Mysterious Naked Man*. © 1969 by Alden Nowlan. Reprinted by permission of Irwin Publishing. / **193-196** "Stains" by Sharon MacFarlane. Reprinted with permission of the author. / **197** "Now I See You" from *Borrowed Beauty* by Maxine N. Tynes. Reprinted with permission of the author. / **198** "Ancestors' Graves" by Joy Kogawa was first printed in *A Choice of Dreams* published by McClelland & Stewart, 1974. Reprinted with permission of the author. / **212–214** "Putting a Colourful Life on Canvas" by Afrodite Balagh-Tyszko, paintings by Jean Chin from *The Toronto Star*. Reprinted with permis-sion of Young People's Press. / **216–219** "So, What Do You Do?" from *It Was On Fire When I Laid Down On It* by Robert Fulghum. © 1988, 1989 by Robert Fulghum. Reprinted by permission of Villard Books, a Division of Random House, Inc. / **224** "Keep Faith with Nature" by Harvey Locke. Reprinted with per-mission of the author. / **227–232** "Running Eagle— Woman Warrior of the Blackfeet" from *The Ways of My Grandmothers* by Beverly Hungry Wolf. © 1980 by Beverly Hungry Wolf. Reprinted by permission of HarperCollins Publishers, Inc. / **234–235** "I Am Maxine Tynes" by Maxine Tynes. Reprinted with permission of the author. / **236–244** "David Blackwood's Newfoundland and Labrador" paintings by David Blackwood, text by William Gough. Reprinted by permission. / **256–257** "No Room for Compromise" by Ellen Goodman. © 1989, The Boston Globe Newspaper Co./Washintgton Post Writers Group. Reprinted with permission. / **269–270** "A Little Salad with Your Night Crawlers, Sir?" from *Black in the Saddle* Again. © 1996 by Arthur Black. Reprinted by permission of Stoddart Publishing Co.

Limited. / **272-275** "Gotcha!" by Robert Fulford. Reprinted with permission of the author. / **280** "The Shark" by E. J. Pratt from *Complete Poems*, Vols. 1 and 2, edited by Sandra Djwa and R. G. Moyles. © 1989. Reprinted with permission of the University of Toronto Press Incorporated on behalf of the Estate of E. J. Pratt. / **282–287** "Attacked by a Mountain Grizzly!" by Kathy Cook. ©1996 by The Reader's Digest Association (Canada) Ltd. Reprinted by permission from the May 1996 issue of *Reader's Digest*. / **290** "Road Between Saskatoon and Edmonton" by Elizabeth Brewster reprinted from *Selected Poems of Elizabeth Brewster* by permission of Oberon Press. / **292–295** "West Coast Trail: Pacific Rim National Park Reserve" and "East Coast Trail: St. John's" from "Great Canadian Escapes" by Tom Cruickshank and Julia Asselstine. Reprinted with permission from *Equinox* magazine. / **300–306** "Jane Goodall and the Chimps" from *This Won't Hurt a Bit!* by Vicki Gabereau. Reprinted by permission of HarperCollins. / **308–317** "Earthquake" by Jack Hodgins. © Jack Hodgins. Reprinted by permission of Bella Pomer Agency Inc. / **319** "To the Tune 'A Hilly Garden'" ("Spring Has Come") by Kenneth Rexroth, from *Women Poets of China*. ©1973 by Kenneth Rexroth and Ling Chung. Reprinted with permission of New Directions Publishing Corp. / **324–326** "Persephone" from *Realms of Gold: Myths & Legends from Around the* World. Text © by Ann Pilling 1993. Reprinted by permission of Larousse Kingfisher Chambers Inc., New York. / **328** "Naming the New One" from *Common Ground* by John Daniel (Confluence Press, 1988). / **330–332** "Why We Grow Insensitive to Dangers" from *Earth Time* © 1998 by David Suzuki. Reprinted by permission of Stoddart Publishing Co. Limited. / **332** "Right Before Our Eyes" from MUTTS by Patrick McDonnell. Reprinted by special permission of King Features Syndicate. / **335** "Passenger Pigeon," **336** "Great Blue Heron," **337** "Arctic Tern" by John James Audubon from *Audubon's Wilderness Palette*. © 1998 Metro Toronto Library Board. **259-263** Reprinted by arrangement with The Heirs to the Estate of Martin Luther King, Jr., c/o Writers House, Inc. as agent for the proprietor. Copyright 1963 by Martin Luther King, Jr., copyright renewed 1991 by Coretta Scott King.

Photo Credits
8 (clockwise from top left) Corbis/Nazima Kowall; Corbis-Bettmann; First Light; CP Picture Archive/Hans Deryk; First Light; CP Picture Archive/Peter Bregg; **9** (background) First Light; **9** top Corbis/Reuters Newmedia Inc.; **9** bottom Hans Deryk/CP Photo; **13** Yoav Levy/Phototake NYC; **17** Simon Battens/Tony Stone Images; **25, 261** Ian Crysler; **27** Rudy Gold/First Light; **29** Corbis-Bettmann; **30** Corbis/Raymond Gehman; **31** Corbis-Bettmann; **32-33** Phill Snel/Maclean's; **43** Ken Straiton/First Light; **54** D. Mason/First Light; **58-59** Alistair Laidlaw/Tony Stone Images; **100** First Light; **116-117** James Cottir/Tony Stone Images; **122** David Oliver/Tony Stone Images; **127** Courtesy of Ford Motor Company Canada Ltd.; **128** Reprinted with permission of Canadian Helicopter, Nunavut; **129** Costa Rica Tourist Board; **130** Balance Bar Co.; **132** Aboriginal TV Network; **138** From *The Red Green Show*. Courtesy of S&S Productions; **141, 144** From *This Hour Has 22 Minutes*, courtesy of Salter Street Productions, Halifax, and CBC Enterprises; **155, 158** From *Never Cry Wolf*, © 1983 Walt Disney Productions/Kobal Collection (USA) Ltd.; **162** AP/Wide World Photos Inc.; **168-169** Peter Griffith/Masterfile; **180** Publiphoto/Michel Pissotte/Agence D.P.P.I; **189** David Maisel/Tony Stone Images; **191** Eric Vassal/The Image Bank; **197** Hans Neleman/The Image Bank; **212** Jean Chin; **213** Vince Talotta/The Toronto Star; **214** Jean Chin; **223** Aaron Stone/Tony Stone Images; **225** Tony Stone Images; **231** Historical Picture Archive/Corbis; **259** Corbis-Bettmann; **261** Corbis-Bettmann; **267** Brian Milne/First Light; **285** Rosane/Olson/Tony Stone Images; **289** Tim Davis/Tony Stone Images; **292-295** Equinox Magazine, June-July 1999; **300, 303** Kennan Ward/Corbis; **320** Robert Waldock; **321** Winter in the Country, A Cold Morning by Currier & Ives, Library of Congress, Washington, D.C./ Superstock; **331** CP Picture Archive/Tim Krochak.

Illustrations
Peter Cook; **8-9, 58-59, 116-117, 168-169, 222-223, 278-279**; Clarence Porter; **34, 68, 162, 166-167, 184, 298** Stephen Taylor; **64** Gary McLaughlin/3 in a Box; **71** Alex Murchison/3 in a Box; **85** Dennis Stillwell Martin; **92** Patrick Fitzgerald; **150, 154, 311** Jeremie White/3 in a Box; **171** Gordon Sauvé; **195** Brian Deines; **199, 206** Julian Mulock; **273** Francis Blake/3 in a Box.